S0-BHZ-570

Rockefeller Foundation
Innovation for the Next 100 Years

BEYOND CHARITY

A CENTURY OF PHILANTHROPIC INNOVATION

By Eric John Abrahamson, Ph.D.

Innovation for the Next 100 Years
Rockefeller Foundation Centennial Series

Twenty-second day of May, 1913, a

1409, No. 26 Broadway, in the Bor

of New York, as the place of said

waive all the requirements of the

of said meeting and the publicati

tion of such lawful business as m

authorize and empower said meetin

adopt a constitution and by-laws

and laws of the State of New York

o'clock noon, as the time, and Room

of Manhattan, City, County and State

ting; and we do hereby severally

tutes of New York as to the notice

hereof, and consent to the transac-

ome before said meeting; and we

organize the corporation and to

inconsistent with the constitution

Signed) John D. Rockefeller
         John D. Rockefeller, Jr.
         Frederick T. Gates
         Harry Pratt Judson
         Simon Flexner
         Starr J. Murphy
         Jerome D. Greene
         Wickliffe Rose
         Charles O. Heydt

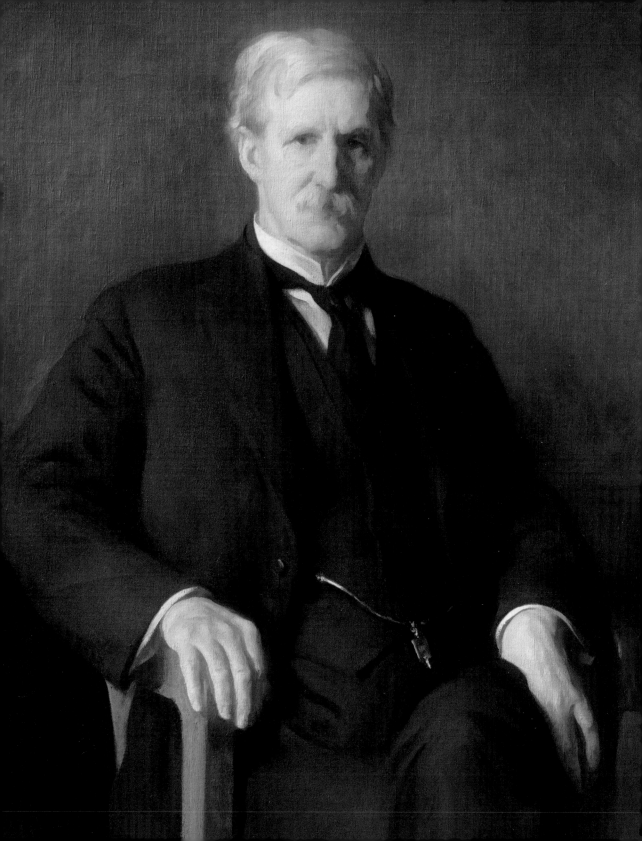

ANUAL TO
FOR

DIAG

< 5	TOTAL	
1. MALARIA	5538	1.
2. PNEUMONIA	1637	2.
3. EYES INF.	1278	3.
4. ARI	583	4.
5. DIARRHOEA	455	5.
OTHER DIAG.	395	5.

TEN DISEASES

004

OSIS

5 +

	TOTAL
ALARIA	6668
T. WORMS.	1692
R I	1551
NOR SURGERY	1021
ER DIAGNOS	99

© 2013 by
The Rockefeller Foundation
Foreword copyright William Jefferson
Clinton, 2013
All rights reserved.

Cover: John D. Rockefeller, Sr.
by Eastman Johnson.
Bottom: Getty images.

Book design by Pentagram.

Beyond Charity:
A Century of Philanthropic Innovation

Printed in the United States of America.

Published by
The Rockefeller Foundation
New York
United States of America

In association with
Vantage Point
Historical Services, Inc.
South Dakota
United States of America

ISBN-13: 978-0-9796389-2-3
ISBN-10: 0-9796389-2-5

Rockefeller Foundation
Centennial Series
Books published in the Rockefeller
Foundation Centennial Series provide
case studies for people around the
world who are working "to promote the
well-being of humankind." Three books
highlight lessons learned in the fields
of agriculture, health, and philanthropy.
Three others explore the Foundation's
work in Africa, Thailand, and the United
States. For more information about
the Rockefeller Foundation Centennial
initiatives, visit www.centennial.
rockfellerfoundation.org.

Notes & Permissions
The Foundation has taken all reasonable
steps to ensure the accuracy of the
information provided in the book; any
errors or omissions are inadvertent. This
book is published without footnotes or
endnotes. A manuscript version with
citations and references for all sources
used is available at www.centennial.
rockefellerfoundation.org.

Captions in this book provide information on the creator and the repository
from which the images in this book were
obtained. The Foundation has made its
best efforts to determine the creator
and copyright holder of all images used
in this publication. Images held by the
Rockefeller Archive Center have been
deemed to be owned by the Rockefeller
Foundation unless we were able to
determine otherwise. Specific permission has been granted by the copyright
holder to use the following works:

Jonas Bendiksen: 4-5, 8-9, 10-11, 14-15,
16-17, 49, 50 & 55, 68, 74 & 79, 151, 169,
191, 206 & 211, 215, 224-225, 226 & 231,
246 & 251, 272 & 277, 282, 296
Rockefeller University: 7, 165, 166
Russell Williams Porter, CalTech
Archives: 82
Underwood Photo Archives: 103, 138-139
Nancy Zupanc, Wagner International
Photos: 120
Suzie Fitzhugh: 123
Steve McCurry: 126 & 131, 154 & 159,
178 & 183, 264, 270
Pach Brothers: 167
TIME, Inc.: 188
Ted Spiegel: 202
Wellesley College Archives: 194
University of Chicago Archives: 200-201
Ted Spiegel, Corbis Images and
The Nobel Foundation: 204-205
Georgiana Silk: 240
AP Images: 242-243
Patrick de Noirmont: 244
George S. Zimbel: 268
Nik Kleinberg: 269
Alfred Eisenstaedt: 292
F.S. Lincoln. Colonial Williamsburg
Foundation: 295
Getty Images: 300-301

By Dr. Judith Rodin

President of the Rockefeller Foundation

I n 1913 the U.S. Congress was considering a bill to grant a federal charter to establish the Rockefeller Foundation. After three years of negotiations, the original plan had been modified substantially. To try and win passage, John D. Rockefeller's advisors had agreed to amendments that would have given high public officials the right to veto appointments to the board of trustees and limited the life of the Foundation to one hundred years. Despite these amendments, Congress failed to approve the bill. Instead, Rockefeller turned to the New York legislature to incorporate the Foundation. With Governor William Sulzer's signature on May 14, 1913, the Rockefeller Foundation was established.

The history of the Rockefeller Foundation, and much of modern philanthropy, might have been very different if the bill before Congress had been approved. It would have made the largest private foundation in the world a stepchild of the government from the outset. With this precedent, the philanthropic sector in the United States might have developed, if it had developed at all, with much less autonomy and freedom.

Instead, with its New York charter and under a system of laws that encouraged private philanthropy, the Rockefeller Foundation developed as a remarkably flexible and innovative organization. Over one hundred years, it has learned by listening to the voices of those crying out for change and supporting visionaries with new ideas and profound insights into the nature of the world. Long before the birth of computers and the Internet, the Foundation created an extraordinary global network. Using grants and fellowships, it helped bring people together whose combined knowledge, skills and resources had the power to cure disease, feed the hungry and give hope to the poor and vulnerable.

As we celebrate the centennial of the Rockefeller Foundation, we realize how much the past has to offer the future. Today's global issues are rooted in history. The lessons learned—often by trial and error—by those who came before us at the Rockefeller Foundation, help us to understand the deep patterns in our organization and, indeed, in the field of philanthropy.

In Lewis Carroll's novel *Through the Looking Glass*, he wrote that "it is a poor sort of memory that only works backwards." With that thought in mind, as we celebrate our centennial, we are determined to use memory to help us see into the future. Thus *Beyond Charity* is not a history of the Rockefeller Foundation. Instead, it uses the history of the Foundation to explore deep and abiding themes in the field of philanthropy. It looks at how the evolution of our philanthropic practice has helped to shape the pattern of innovation over a hundred years.

We hope *Beyond Charity* sheds light that will help guide us and our partners as we move into our second century. We also hope that it offers our colleagues and future colleagues, including budding philanthropists and future foundation professionals, a fascinating window into the world of philanthropy.

FOREWORD

By President Bill Clinton

L ike most people who hope to make our world a better place, I owe much to John D. Rockefeller.

The chartering of the Rockefeller Foundation in 1913 marked the dawn of modern American philanthropy. Although America's tradition of community service and generosity is older than the republic itself, Rockefeller envisioned philanthropy on a global scale unlike anyone before him. He believed that the relentless focus on innovation and efficiency, which had helped to make Standard Oil the largest company in the world, could also move giving beyond charity to address the root causes of our shared challenges.

The Foundation's trustees and staff, working with the Rockefeller family, created systems of governance and grantmaking that they hoped would achieve the founder's dream "to promote the well-being of mankind throughout the world." They also developed principles that would prioritize their efforts, and they had to refine ways of working with others—including governments—that would ensure their charitable dollars helped as many people as possible.

The Rockefeller team started with science, medicine, and health. Foundation researchers identified a vaccine for yellow fever, battled malaria and other tropical diseases, and helped bring penicillin to the wounded of World War II. They eliminated hookworm as a widespread health problem in the American South, and made similar gains in Latin America and the Caribbean.

The Foundation sought to align the actions of governments with those of schools and industry, and they backed research into nutrition and agriculture, mental illness, and health delivery systems. The academic study of public health owes its origins to Rockefeller, who financed the earliest programs at institutions like Johns Hopkins and Harvard.

The Foundation built networks, too. The Rockefeller Fellowships supported brilliant men and women in their research and linked them to others working in the same or different fields. They kept track of the activities of Rockefeller Fellows and others engaged in similar work, trying, before anyone else was doing so, to understand the levers that turn intelligence and good intentions into measurable progress.

The Rockefeller Foundation's mission was from the beginning international, working to advance Chinese medical education and universities in Ghana and Uganda, among others. All of us who work across borders today do so in the Rockefeller Foundation's footsteps.

Here at home, Rockefeller philanthropy has always aimed to support the poor and marginalized in our society and to enhance American pluralism. The Foundation made several early investments in schools and model farms in black communities in the American South. It bolstered the arts and helped to found policy organizations that guide our leaders even today.

Not many people can give what Rockefeller gave, but all of us can learn from his generosity. His extraordinary record of giving shattered the limits of what anyone thought philanthropy could accomplish, and it has inspired and guided others to give back in their own lives.

Like John D. Rockefeller, who created a remarkable second act in the "giving business" after a lifetime in the "getting business," I knew that once my career in politics was over I wanted to spend my time and energy helping others as a private citizen. I thought there were still many problems facing the world where I could continue to make a difference, and, in the tradition of Rockefeller, I wanted to go beyond charity to address the root causes of our challenges—to help build systems so that people can lift *themselves* up, and to work with governments, the private sector, and NGOs to make positive changes faster, better, and at lower cost.

That's why I started the Clinton Foundation. We work with communities and partners on six continents to improve global health, promote economic opportunities, reduce childhood obesity, and reverse climate change. Over the past eleven years, I've found that much of what we do and how we work owes a debt to John D. Rockefeller and the generations of philanthropists at the Rockefeller Foundation who showed how private wealth, scientific research, and government support can be harnessed to solve problems and save lives.

Today, we stand with farmers in Malawi and small business owners in Haiti, just as Rockefeller program officers worked with African and Caribbean communities a generation or more ago. Our work makes it possible for millions of people with HIV/AIDS to access affordable, life-saving antiretroviral medicines. Our efforts are in the tradition of the

Rockefeller Foundation's efforts to fight hookworm and yellow fever in the early twentieth century.

I've also had the privilege of working directly with the Rockefeller Foundation and its president Dr. Judith Rodin through the Clinton Global Initiative. Each September in New York around the opening of the U.N. General Assembly, we bring people together from all over the world: heads of state, business leaders, philanthropists, and non-governmental pioneers, and we ask everyone who attends to make a specific commitment to solve one of the world's most pressing problems. The Rockefeller Foundation has been an important partner of CGI, and I continue to be inspired by the commitments they've made and are keeping to empower women and girls, build sustainable capacity in the developing world, and promote entrepreneurship.

The Foundation's continuing commitment to innovation offers valuable examples to other NGOs wrestling with questions of mission, longevity, tactics, and operations, including how best to risk resources on uncertain ventures, and how to maximize leverage and partnership in philanthropic giving.

As *Beyond Charity* shows, John D. Rockefeller and his advisors embedded in the Foundation a deep commitment to processes of continuous improvement designed to ensure that its capacity to do good would not be derailed by carelessness, complacency, or inability to adapt to changing challenges.

All of us committed to advancing the promise and reducing the perils of the twenty-first century should be grateful for the long legacy, lasting lessons, and continuing activities of the Rockefeller Foundation. We can learn a lot from them.

W hen John D. Rockefeller decided to direct his vast fortune to the promotion of the well-being of humankind, he and his advisors did not intend to provide charity to ease human suffering for a day; they wanted to address the root causes of hardship. To do so, they had to invent a new kind of institution, one capable of handling the challenges of modern large-scale philanthropy.

From its earliest days, the Rockefeller Foundation was remarkably modern: global at birth, disciplined in its study of problems and formulation of strategic solutions, collaborative in its work with governments and local communities, scientific in its approach to the development of new knowledge, focused on the development of human capital to create long-term capacity, deliberate in its openness to new ideas, relentless in its efforts to disseminate new information to specialized and general audiences, and always idealistic in its belief that its initiatives, staff, and trustees could enhance the well-being of humankind.

From the beginning, the Foundation also wrestled with tensions that confront every modern philanthropic organization. The Foundation's leaders, in myriad and imperfect ways, struggled to understand how to focus the Foundation's resources to be effective, identify and address problems as they were emerging, work with grantees without making them dependent, build political support where authority was often ambiguous or contested, admit failure when noble goals seemed unreachable, and persist when problems seemed intractable.

Early on, the Foundation's leaders sought to create a culture that was decisive and opportunistic; able to collaborate with a wide range of people, communities, and organizations; willing to fight to achieve its vision; and able to adapt in response to changing circumstances and situations. They struggled to shape and maintain an organizational culture that would promote effective philanthropy. They worried constantly about becoming stale or bureaucratic. These efforts helped to sustain in the organization a habit of innovation that defies cliché.

The Rockefeller Foundation has never had sharply defined organizational boundaries. Its founding reflected the culmination of decades of philanthropy by John D. Rockefeller. During its first fifty years, the Foundation's work and management were deeply connected to the efforts of sister institutions founded by John D. Rockefeller and his family. Although pools of secretaries in New York typed correspondence, compiled reports, and assembled the extensive diaries of program officers, much of the Foundation's work took place in villages and cities around the world as staff visited scientists, policymakers, community leaders, and organizations. In their diaries, these program officers recorded their casual shipboard conversations; discussions with government officials, academic leaders, and community members; and even exchanges over the course of a simple meal, as they searched the globe for ideas and individuals capable of creating the change the world needed.

Throughout the past century, trustees, staff, fellows, grantees, governments, and philanthropic partners have contributed
to shaping the character and effectiveness of the Rockefeller
Foundation's philanthropy. During these years, the Foundation's
champions have struggled to define and understand the role
and legacy of the donor, and to establish a system of governance
and coherent and relevant programs that would earn the
public's trust. Persistently, they aimed to build and nurture
an innovative organization that partnered effectively with
grantees, governments, and other philanthropic organizations,
and to steward the founder's gifts to ensure that resources for
this work will be available for future generations.

Meeting these challenges has rarely been easy. Crisis
often became the incubator of innovation. In each case, the
institutional response reflected the personality, prejudices,
and personal histories of the individuals to whom John D.
Rockefeller, decades earlier, had confidently entrusted the
future of his Foundation and so much of his fortune.

Donations

1855			
Nov	25	To Missionary Cause	15
"	"	Mr Downey	10
"	"	Mite Society	75
"	"	Slip Rent	1 —
Dec	16	" Sabath School Contribu—	05
"	23	" present for Mr Fairen	25
"	30	" Five Point Mission	12
"	"	" Macedonian	10
"	"	" Present to Deacon Shedd	25
Jany	6	" Missionary Cause	06 —
"	"	" the poor in the church	10
Feby	3	" " " " " "	10 —
"	"	" Foreign Mission	10 —

DONORS

What motivates donors to give?

Philanthropy begins with a donor and some measure of surplus wealth—from the coins in a child's piggy bank to the shares of a great corporation. And it begins with a donor's desire to give.

Around the globe and for many reasons, people give time and money to make the world a better place. One donor hears of an earthquake or a flood and is moved by empathy to make a quick contribution by text over his mobile phone. Vision and hard work enable an entrepreneur to build a fortune, inspiring a desire to give back to the community that made that fortune possible. Another individual spends a lifetime helping a charitable organization and leaves a substantial portion of her estate to ensure that its work continues for generations.

Behavioral psychologists, cognitive scientists, economists, and a range of other researchers have tried to explain why people give. Some believe that philanthropy is about what the donor wants, not what others need. One person gives to cancer research hoping she might be saved by the development of a cure. A fan of music or dance gives to make sure that the symphony or performance group he enjoys will continue to perform. As some economists have discovered, however, the rational choice argument does not fully explain donor behavior.

A second group of researchers understands humans as moral beings: "They enjoy doing what is right. They are also emotional, empathetic and sympathetic—they enjoy gratitude and recognition, they enjoy making someone else happy, and they feel relieved from guilt when they become a giver." From this point of view, philanthropy fulfills the "expressive needs" of the donor. The "warm glow" from giving is an act of personal consumption. As economist James Andreoni points out, this motivation explains why people make contributions to people in need they do not even know.

Because most philanthropy seeks to change society, it is inherently political. To some people, philanthropy may represent a cynical gesture by the rich designed to perpetuate the position of the ruling class by dulling the edges of class conflict. A simpler, more utilitarian view is that a contribution to a foundation or nonprofit systematizes the effort to change society and relieves a wealthy donor of the burden of evaluating and responding to more direct appeals from people in need. (As we shall see, this was an important factor for John D. Rockefeller.)

Research in the United States shows that poor people are likely to be the most generous, giving more than 4 percent of their income to charity. As incomes grow, the rate of giving declines to 1.3 percent at an income of $50,000, but then increases again as additional wealth provides an extra margin for generosity. On average, the wealthy give 3 percent of their income to charity. People tend to give more as they age as they do with more education.

Levels of giving are also shaped by society. Tax incentives stimulate philanthropic giving. But if government is a major player in a certain sector, or a large philanthropy plays a dominant role, other donors and institutions can be "crowded out." They feel they do not need to give or cannot make a difference.

One typology divides donors into seven types: communitarians, devout donors, investors, socialites, altruists, repayers, and dynasts. Communitarians give out of a sense of belonging to a community, using their gifts to reinforce collective efforts to help one another and the community as a whole. Devout donors are motivated by faith, adherence to religious teachings, and loyalty to religious institutions. Investors are pragmatists who view money as a means to create social change. Socialites participate in philanthropy as a social activity. Altruists see philanthropy as a way to fulfill their life purpose. Repayers, in contrast, give out of a sense of gratitude— to a school, a community, or even the nation. Finally, dynasts are born into families with deeply embedded traditions of philanthropy.

Although these labels help us to think about types of motivation, in reality most generous people combine different aspects of all these traits, which is why, in the end, generosity remains one of the most enigmatic and marvelous of human behaviors.

Donation a/c

Mar	2	Amts for 3d page	4	33
	6	Foreign Mission		10
	21	Young M-C. Association	1	—
May	4	Foreign Mission		10
	"	Poor in Church		05
		Amts to Ledger B.	2	51

```
5.5.8
2.7.7
2.8.1
```

DONORS

AHEAD OF THE AVALANCHE

Frederick Gates was not afraid to speak his mind, even to one of the richest men in the world. As John D. Rockefeller's chief advisor on philanthropy, Gates was blunt: "Your fortune is rolling up, rolling up like an avalanche," he warned at the beginning of the twentieth century. "You must keep up with it! You must distribute it faster than it grows! If you do not, it will crush you, and your children, and your children's children!"

Gates knew what he was talking about. At the office, in church, on the road, and even at his dinner table, Rockefeller was besieged with requests for charity. Letters arrived by the hundreds in Rockefeller's offices at 26 Broadway in Manhattan. "The good people who wanted me to help them with their good work seemed to come in crowds," Rockefeller later remarked. According to Gates, "Mr. Rockefeller was constantly hunted, stalked and hounded almost like a wild animal."

Gates also reminded Rockefeller of his moral duty. Both men had been raised in devout Christian households. Gates was trained as a minister, and Rockefeller had tithed since he earned his first paycheck. Beyond a "decent provision" for his family and heirs, Gates suggested, Rockefeller's great fortune should be dedicated to "the service of mankind." Any other alternative would be "morally indefensible." According to Gates, "In the eyes of God and man" this wealth had to be "devoted to the promotion of human well-being." But how? Never before had a donor practiced philanthropy on this scale.

John D. Rockefeller Sr. With the funding he gave to found the University of Chicago, Rockefeller began a new era of major philanthropic gifts. This portrait by Eastman Johnson was commissioned for the university and presented in 1894. (Rockefeller Archive Center.)

J ohn D. Rockefeller was perhaps the most reviled as well as the most generous man in America when Gates wrote to him in 1905. As a founder of Standard Oil, the largest and most valuable company in the world, he epitomized the colossal wealth of the Gilded Age. Newspapers and magazines across the United States painted a caricature of his personality— tight-fisted, ruthless, and avaricious. Congressmen questioned his motives and worried about his long-term plans. Meanwhile, he gave millions of dollars to found and develop the University of Chicago, support Baptist missionary activities at home and abroad, finance medical research, expand educational opportunities for poor children in the American South, and further the efforts of a host of other charitable initiatives. His closest confidantes sought to form an institution that would allow him to do even more.

The son of a patent-medicine salesman and entrepreneur and a deeply devout, strong-willed mother, Rockefeller was born in 1839 in the town of Richford in the Finger Lakes region of New York. He grew up in a household that reflected the nation's Puritan origins and its westward migration, as the family drifted eventually to Strongsville, a suburb of Cleveland. According to his biographer Allan Nevins, Rockefeller inherited from his mother his "self-discipline, reticence, patience, inner equanimity and a somewhat unloving austerity." From his father he inherited a sense of "enterprise, adventurous-ness, energy and tenacity."

Launching his career at the age of sixteen, Rockefeller spent weeks searching for a job in the sweltering summer of 1855 in Cleveland. When he landed a position as a bookkeeper with a commission merchant and shipping firm, he was overjoyed. He worked at this job for more than two and a half years. Then, at the age of nineteen, he found a partner and launched his own business buying and selling produce.

After Pennsylvania entrepreneurs conceived a way to pump oil from the ground, a local chemist approached Rockefeller and his partner to invest in a new system for refining kerosene. Although he and his partner continued to operate their commission business, Rockefeller was increasingly drawn into the developing oil industry after 1863. As the industry grew through rapid cycles of boom and bust and oversupply, Rockefeller looked for a way to rationalize and stabilize the industry. In 1870, he founded Standard Oil.

Often described as the first major multinational corporation, Standard Oil grew to dominate the refining industry. Initially, the company relied on its superior refining technology to speed up production and lower unit costs. As prices fell due to increasing production throughout the industry, Rockefeller and his partners began a relentless series of acquisitions. In 1882, they consolidated these various companies to form the Standard Oil Trust, with Rockefeller as the major shareholder.

Disciplined, tough, and even ruthless, Rockefeller "colluded with railroads to gain preferential freight rates, secretly owned rivals, bribed state legislators, and engaged in industrial espionage," according to the biographer Ron Chernow. All the time, Rockefeller was a regular and devout member of a Baptist congregation.

Rockefeller's perspective on capitalism and industrialism in the late nineteenth century influenced his thinking on philanthropy. From his Puritan roots, he reacted strongly against the destructive qualities of unbridled competition. He often justified the creation of Standard Oil's monopoly as a way to rationalize the market for oil and, in the process, benefit society as well as the company's investors. A wasteful system of competition offended his desire for efficiency. After the public reacted violently against his efforts to restrain competition, he asserted: "It was right. I knew it as a matter of conscience. It was right between me and my God."

The success of Standard Oil made Rockefeller rich beyond imagination. At the beginning of the twentieth century, his net worth was $200 million. Only Andrew Carnegie was richer. To the frustration of his antagonists, when the government broke up Standard Oil in 1911, the subsequent rise

Founded in 1870, Standard Oil became the largest oil refiner in the world and provided the basis for John D. Rockefeller's vast fortune. For decades, shares of Standard Oil accounted for a significant share of the Rockefeller Foundation's endowment. (Rockefeller Archive Center.)

THE KING OF THE COMBINATIONS.

in the value of the stocks of the companies created by the breakup made him even richer. His wealth peaked in September 1916, when he became the first person in history to amass a fortune worth $1 billion. At one point, his wealth was estimated to be equal to 1.53 percent of the United States economy. In 2012, a fortune equal to this percentage share of U.S. Gross Domestic Product would be worth nearly $231 billion. To the great masses of Americans, most of whom struggled to make a living from meager farms or low factory wages, Rockefeller's wealth was something mythical.

ROCKEFELLER PHILANTHROPY

Years later, critics would charge that Rockefeller's philanthropy represented a cynical effort to buy public goodwill. The evidence suggests otherwise. His giving was rooted deep within his character and faith. From his first paychecks as a clerk in Cleveland earning $3.50 a week, Rockefeller gave to his church and church-related charities including foreign missions and the poor. "From the beginning, I was trained to work, to save and to give," he said. By 1860, the recipients of his donations included a Methodist church, a German Sunday school, an African American church, and "Catholic orphans." In a small notebook known as "Ledger A," Rockefeller even recorded an early gift to an African American man to help him "to buy his wife." His giving "freely crossed lines of creed, nationality and color," writes Allan Nevins.

Rockefeller's interest in the welfare of African Americans at an early stage in his philanthropy was no doubt strengthened by his marriage to Laura Celestia Spelman in 1864. "Cettie," as her friends called her, had grown up in a deeply religious Congregationalist household in Cleveland, where her parents were active abolitionists and supporters of the Underground Railroad. She was an early supporter of the temperance movement as well.

As his fortune grew in the 1870s and 1880s, Rockefeller's charity and philanthropy increased. By 1882, his annual giving had risen to $65,000. In May 1889, he made a single gift of $600,000 (worth more than $14.5 million in 2011) to establish the University of Chicago. His reputation for giving combined with growing public awareness of his fortune increased the number of appeals to his generosity.

Depicted as "the king of the combinations" by *Puck* magazine in 1901, Rockefeller was widely criticized for Standard Oil's monopolistic control of the petroleum industry. Ironically, the court-ordered breakup of the company in 1911 increased the value of Rockefeller's shares tremendously. (Library of Congress, Prints & Photographs.)

Rockefeller did not take these appeals lightly. Indeed, he said that the effort of investigating the capacity and quality of the organizations nearly overwhelmed him. "I investigated as I could," he said, "and worked myself almost to a nervous breakdown in groping my way, without sufficient guide or chart, through this ever-widening field of philanthropic endeavor." As one of his associates described the situation, the tasks of deciding wisely on an ever-increasing number of applications and, even more important, of providing the constructive imagination necessary for intelligent philanthropy became more and more onerous.

Ever the system builder, Rockefeller developed a set of principles to guide him in his philanthropy. Gifts should be made to organizations with a track record. Grantees had to have a plan to use the money economically and efficiently. The gifts should support good work by organizations that were clearly vital; Rockefeller did not want to contribute to dying causes. The work should never be dependent solely on Rockefeller's contributions; his gifts should always complement and stimulate contributions from others. Most important, his gift should support a path to self-reliance—for individuals,

Influenced by his Baptist faith, Rockefeller began contributing to charity at an early age. In small ledger books, including "Ledger A," he kept track of his expenses and charitable gifts. (Rockefeller Archive Center.)

organizations, and communities. But by 1905, when Frederick Gates sent his warning, principles alone were not enough to keep up with what Rockefeller called "this business of benevolence."

SCIENTIFIC PHILANTHROPY

Rockefeller was not alone in either his generosity or his effort to formulate principles for his philanthropy. A month after Rockefeller made his first major contribution to the University of Chicago, his fellow industrialist Andrew Carnegie published an article titled "Wealth" in the *North American Review*. Already worth more than $30 million in 1889, Carnegie had concluded that it was a disgrace to die rich. After achieving a certain level of income (in 1868, he figured $50,000 per year—about $833,000 in 2011 dollars), a man should give the rest to charity. The pursuit of wealth for personal benefit beyond this point would make money an idol that would debase him and others. With the great success of capitalism, and particularly mass production, Carnegie asserted, "The problem of our age is the proper administration of wealth, that the ties of brotherhood may still bind together the rich and poor in harmonious relationship."

In "Wealth," Carnegie asserted that there were three options for great fortunes: (1) bequeath everything to the rich man's heirs, (2) leave the great fortune to charity, or (3) actively spend the surplus on projects that would benefit the public. Carnegie dismissed the first option, suggesting that it represented "misguided affection ... for it is no longer questionable that great sums bequeathed often work more for the injury than for the good of the recipients." He also wrote that it was a mistake to leave great fortunes to charity to be administered by others. There was "no grace" in these gifts. In fact, they reflected an abdication of moral responsibility. The genius of the man who built the fortune should likewise see to the expenditure of that fortune for benevolent purposes. For this reason, Carnegie cheered the growing prevalence of estate taxes. "Of all forms of taxation this seems the wisest," he wrote. "By taxing estates heavily at

Andrew Carnegie sold his steel company in 1900 for $480 million. His influential essay written in 1889 and known as "The Gospel of Wealth" was praised by John D. Rockefeller. The essay emphasized the duty of the successful entrepreneur to lead by philanthropic giving. (Library of Congress, Prints & Photographs.)

death the State marks its condemnation of the selfish millionaire's unworthy life." Indeed, he believed that large inheritance taxes would remind the rich man "to attend to the administration of wealth during his life." But inheritance taxes, in Carnegie's view, were only the second-best option. It was far better for the rich man "to consider all surplus revenues which come to him simply as trust funds, which he is called upon to administer, and strictly bound as a matter of duty to administer in the manner in which, in his judgment, is best calculated to produce the most beneficial results for the community." Carnegie's advice was anchored in his sympathy for the ideas of social Darwinism articulated by his friend Herbert Spencer. Having triumphed in capitalist competition, the industrialist represented the leading edge of civilization, and it was appropriate that he should control and direct the reinvestment of this surplus for the public good.

Years after reading Carnegie's essay, John D. Rockefeller offered his support for Carnegie's position in a letter: "I would that more men of wealth were doing as you are doing with your money, but be assured, your example will bear fruits, and the time will come when men of wealth will more generally be willing to use it for the good of others."

Over the next quarter century, Carnegie and Rockefeller would endow foundations that would take lessons learned from a variety of charitable initiatives in the post–Civil War era and consolidate them into modern philanthropic practice. As donors, they were remarkably different. Carnegie played a strong personal role in the early years of the organizations he founded, receiving criticism in some quarters that his philanthropy played too much to his ego. Rockefeller, on the other hand, genuinely empowered others to direct his philanthropy. At times, he seemed distant, even indifferent, to the effect of his giving. But his demeanor did not reflect his feelings. On one occasion, he suggested that philanthropy provided the greatest and most enduring personal satisfaction that money could buy.

But giving away money also became an overwhelming chore. Increasingly, Rockefeller searched for ways to systematize and institutionalize the process. Frederick Gates became his chief advisor, but Rockefeller also gave more and more responsibility for this process to his only son.

1903

General Education Board established to promote education within the United States and especially in the American South "without distinction of race, sex, or creed." (Rockefeller Archive Center.)

Chapter One: Donors

A s the primary heir to his father's vast fortune and the devoted keeper of his father's legacy, "Mr. Junior," as he was called by his staff, often stood in for his father to articulate the vision of the founder and donor. Coming of age as his father's fortune reached its apex and public criticism became most shrill, John D. Rockefeller Jr., would spend most of his life striving to repair his family's public image and spend his father's fortune according to the dictates of his own conscience. Although his financial contributions to the Rockefeller Foundation were not substantial, he played a leading role in convincing his father to create and endow the institution and then, for nearly a half century, took an active role in shaping its program and administration.

Junior, born on January 29, 1874, shared many of his father's traits but also was profoundly influenced by his mother's homeschooling. As the only son among four children who survived infancy, Junior learned from his mother the spirit and precepts of the New Testament. The family

John D. Rockefeller Sr. and Jr. in New York. A fierce advocate for his father's legacy, Junior dedicated his career to effective philanthropy. (Rockefeller Archive Center.)

prayed, read the Bible, and recited verses on a daily basis. Every Friday night they attended prayer meeting. They respected Sunday as a day of rest and devotion. The household was not without joy and laughter. Junior would remember swimming, skating, riding, and playing blind man's bluff with his father. Yet overall, the children's upbringing reflected the Puritan and Baptist traditions of New England that aimed to curb the will of the child, instill awe and reverence for parents and elders, and cultivate an ethic of service.

Junior was modest, if not humble, in his dealings with others. He spoke in a low, easy manner and never raised his voice. His diction was careful, and he rarely used slang. He did not smoke or chew tobacco, drink alcohol, or play cards. Unlike his father, he loved to dance. From his father he learned to account for every dime, keeping elaborate records of his expenditures

Rockefeller regularly attended the Euclid Avenue Baptist Church (later renamed the Second Baptist Church) in Cleveland. Rockefeller's faith played a major role in his philanthropy. (Rockefeller Archive Center.)

from the time he was a boy. As an adult, these practices reflected his sense that he was a steward of his father's fortune.

In college at Brown University, Junior was transformed socially and intellectually. He overcame his shyness and enjoyed dancing, parties, the theater, and dating. He learned to be comfortable speaking before an audience, and was even elected junior class president. Intellectually, he was profoundly influenced by classes in political economy. He even took a course devoted to the study of Karl Marx's *Capital*. Meanwhile, Brown University's president, Elisha Benjamin Andrews, cultivated a sense of civic duty among the students and fostered a modern, sociological understanding of politics and economics. A risk taker and an idealist, Andrews inspired Junior with his passion and courage. Although Junior remained true to his Christian beliefs, and his strong support for the temperance movement reflected his Baptist origins, he graduated from Brown in 1897 more socially at ease, with his mind open to big ideas and his heart committed to social change. All of these characteristics would contribute to his remarkable success as a philanthropist, but they did not help him adjust to the world of commerce.

Soon after his graduation, Junior went to work in his father's office. Over the next decade, he helped manage his father's investments and joined the boards of a number of companies. But he soon realized that he did not like the competitive world of business and, unlike his father, he had no burning desire to make money. For Junior, according to Raymond Fosdick, "The only question with wealth is what you do with it. It can be used for evil purposes or it can be an instrumentality for constructive social living."

As a philanthropist, Junior built upon his father's principles with extraordinary commitment and creativity. As writers John Enson Haar and Peter J. Johnson point out: "He was conditioned for this not only in the constant religious indoctrination of his youth and the example set by his father, but also in his educational experience at Brown University, which almost seems to have been designed to give young men of wealth a social conscience."

Near the end of World War I, Senior began a process of transferring much of his wealth to his son. Within a few years, he had gifted nearly a half billion dollars. With these resources, Junior began a philanthropic career of his own that included the creation of national parks and the preservation of environmental resources; the promotion of historic restoration at Colonial Williamsburg and elsewhere; and support for medical research, public health and social hygiene, low-income housing and urban renewal, ecumenical religion, the arts and the humanities, civil rights, and education at all levels. At almost every turn, his philanthropy was motivated by a belief that a reasoned, scientific approach to problem solving could make the world a better place. Yet it was also deeply anchored in his religious faith.

The Role of Faith in Rockefeller Philanthropy

Senior and Junior were both moved to philanthropy by religious views derived from the Puritan traditions of New England. In the Puritan view, the faithful were bound to one another by God's love. Charity was a manifestation of that love. The Puritans of New England held tightly to the idea that their lives and their communities should be models for others. In his shipboard sermon to the Puritans bound for the New World in 1630, titled "A Model of Christian Charity," John Winthrop famously imagined the Puritan settlement in Massachusetts as "a city upon a hill" with "the eyes of all people upon us." In this sermon, Winthrop also articulated ideas about wealth and class that would be reflected in John D. Rockefeller's worldview: "In all times some must be rich, some poor, some high and eminent in power and dignity; others mean and in submission." High status or wealth, however, did not accrue to the individual, but to "the glory of his Creator and the common good of the creature, man." Thus the wealthy and the powerful were seen by the community and should be seen by themselves as God's stewards.

In the course of his life, Rockefeller frequently referred to his great wealth as something given and entrusted to him by God. Similarly, John Winthrop reminded his shipboard congregation in 1630 that every man had a duty to help others in want or distress, but that each man should provide this assistance "out of the same affection which makes him careful of his own goods." In other words, charity should not be given without bounds or conditions, but with the same kind of prudence that people should bring to all of their worldly activities. This attitude was at the heart of Rockefeller's approach to philanthropy. As writer Albert Schenkel observes, "The Rockefellers believed that the same moral principles that created wealth were also essential to managing it."

But the exercise of prudence and judgment was not an excuse to limit philanthropy. As Winthrop said, "There is a time when a Christian must sell all and give to the poor."

Junior was profoundly influenced by his parents' faith as well as the crisis of Protestantism in the late nineteenth century that was prompted by the second scientific and industrial revolution. In the context of the challenge raised by Darwin and others, believers sought to reconcile the Bible with the understandings of science. A liberal or "natural" theology saw the Bible increasingly as metaphor and rejected denominationalism because it separated Christians from one another on interpretive issues. Rather than focusing on the divine, liberal theology focused on the humanity of Christ and his good works in the world. Science in this new theology was not opposed to God or religion. It was a path to discovery of the miracles of God's creation. This was the same impulse that led English Puritans to study nature and that gave the birth to modern science.

1909
Rockefeller Sanitary Commission is created to fight hookworm disease in the American South.
(Rockefeller Archive Center.)

Like their Puritan forefathers, Senior and Junior worked assiduously to turn their high ideals into ordinary realities. Both men subscribed to the Puritan notion of two callings: one to a godly life and the other to a specific vocation. For Junior, especially, that vocation was philanthropy.

The institution that his father endowed and that Junior worked so hard to shape would struggle in its first sixty years to define its role in society independent of the influence of the founder and his family. Historians would later conclude that the tension between the role of the donor and the independence of the Foundation was, in this case, inherently creative and helped foster the Foundation's innovative approach to philanthropy. But in 1910, when the founder announced his intention to create the Rockefeller Foundation, Congress and the American people greeted this news with suspicion and hostility.

A CONTINUING CONNECTION

When David Rockefeller Jr. became chair of the Board of Trustees of the Rockefeller Foundation in 2010, he succeeded his uncle, grandfather, and great-grandfather in the role and provided new life to the vital connection between family and philanthropy that has been an important part of the Foundation's history. Like his forebearers, Rockefeller often speaks modestly about his family's role in the Foundation's work, giving major credit to the collaboration between staff, grantees, and partners over a hundred years. Historians of philanthropy, however, note that the family's continuing involvement over decades has played a significant part in the Foundation's long-run pattern of innovation and success.

David Rockefeller Jr. says that his great-grandfather's gifts to the Foundation drive his own philanthropy. He hopes they inspire new generations of philanthropists as well.

Similarly, his grandfather, John D. Rockefeller Jr., who served as chairman for more than three decades, provides a model for his own leadership on the board. According to Rockefeller, poverty, disease, the explosion of cities, and environmental degradation pose major issues for the world. His forebearers trusted future generations "to see and address the persistent and fresh challenges we face." For Rockefeller, that trust and generosity inspires his own sense of duty and faith in the future.

FOUNDATION

How do institutions
shape philanthropy?

G iving away money is not easy. Wealthy donors often create foundations to manage a process that has become personally overwhelming. They want a buffer between themselves and those seeking assistance. They want someone to perform due diligence and assess the effectiveness of their philanthropy.

Since the early twentieth century, donors in the United States alone have created more than 120,810 foundations, with assets of $582.5 billion in 2010. Most of these foundations were established by individuals or families, but some have been founded by companies or corporations. Most are primarily grantmaking institutions, although some operate their own charitable programs.

Private foundations vary in character and form with the culture, economy, and politics of each nation. In China, for example, although private philanthropy is deeply rooted in Chinese culture, foundations have only recently emerged to become a primary source of charity. In India, where the number of millionaires has increased by an average of 11 percent per year since 2000, charitable giving has risen to .6 percent of gross domestic product (compared to 1.3 percent in the U.K. or .3 percent in Brazil). Meanwhile, in Brazil, the number of private foundations increased 300 percent over two decades. In 2008, these Brazilian foundations gave away more than $5.5 billion. New donors around the world are reshaping the way that governments and nations solve problems.

The legal innovations that gave rise to broadly purposed, endowed philanthropies in the early twentieth century also continue to evolve. Many of the issues that philanthropists face are akin to those that confronted John D. Rockefeller and his advisors: How much influence will government have over the foundation? Will the assets be taxed? How will the institution be accountable to the public? Will the foundation be authorized to continue its work in perpetuity? What will happen to the assets if the foundation is dissolved?

Donors today have more options, a reflection of the continuing process of institutional innovation. With donor-advised funds at a community foundation or public charity, for example, philanthropists effectively pool their resources to hire staff to perform due diligence and administration. They can enjoy the benefits of a named fund that provides the same level of recognition that would come from the establishment of a private foundation. By collaborating, donors lower the overall costs of administration. Meanwhile, a new generation of donors is redefining the boundaries of philanthropy. Employing the tools of "philanthrocapitalism," they are looking for investment opportunities that leverage market mechanisms to create a product or service that improves the quality of life in a given community.

Some call this "venture philanthropy." Like Rockefeller and Carnegie, these new philanthropists hope the tools and strategies that fueled their success in the market-place will also change the paradigm in civil society. By investing in good ideas, they hope to strengthen manage-ment and operational skills to make charitable initiatives more effective and efficient. Meanwhile, they search for innovations—new inventions, new ways of working and new ways of delivering social services—that will unleash productivity in the philanthropic sector and enhance the well-being of communities and nations.

Though the tactics may be different, today's donors share a common purpose with the earliest leaders of the Rockefeller Foundation and other modern philanthropies —to address the root causes of social problems and make lasting changes for the well-being of humankind. They also face a common challenge—to find or create the right institution that will help them achieve their philanthropic goals.

CHAPTER II

FOUNDATION

LETTING THE WILD BEASTS FIGHT

rederick Gates was ready for a fight. For years John D. Rockefeller had taken a beating in the press and the court of public opinion. The serialized chapters of Ida Tarbell's 1904 book *The History of the Standard Oil Company* had portrayed Rockefeller as a cold-hearted monopolist. State attorneys general, officials with the U.S. Department of Justice, and politicians accused the founder and the company of illegal efforts to restrain trade. When Congregationalists received a $100,000 gift from Rockefeller, there was an uproar over accepting his "tainted money." In the middle of these attacks, Rockefeller received little credit for his philanthropy, and Gates was fiercely loyal to his boss.

Outwardly, Gates was distinctly unlike Rockefeller. In demeanor, he was outspoken and dramatic where Rockefeller was taciturn and demure. "He combined bold imagination and large horizons with shrewd business capacity and driving energy," wrote Raymond Fosdick, who would later become president of the Rockefeller Foundation.

Born in 1853, Gates was the son of a New York Baptist preacher. At age fifteen, he had become a schoolteacher to help his family pay its bills. Gates confessed to being repulsed by the repressive Puritan faith of his parents when he was a boy. Yet for Gates, like Rockefeller, this Puritan heritage would have a profound influence on his view of the world. Graduating from the Rochester Theological Seminary, a Baptist institution, Gates moved to Minneapolis to

become a pastor at the Fifth Avenue Baptist Church. Married and widowed within sixteen months, after his new bride succumbed to an undiagnosed illness, Gates remarried two years later. Through his involvement in mission activity of the state's Baptist organization, Gates met George Pillsbury, the flour magnate, and got his first taste of advising the wealthy on their philanthropy when Pillsbury came to him regarding a bequest he intended to make to support a Baptist academy in Minnesota. In 1888, Gates was picked to lead the American Baptist Education Society, with a primary goal of developing a great university in Chicago.

Ida Tarbell's book *The History of the Standard Oil Company* (1904) revealed tactics used by the company to dominate the petroleum market. Rockefeller rejected Tarbell's characterization of Standard's history, but subsequently resolved to communicate more directly with the public. (Harris & Ewing, Library of Congress, Prints & Photographs.)

Leaders of the society hoped that John D. Rockefeller, who had already given hundreds of thousands of dollars to Baptist initiatives, would make a lead gift to launch the project. Rockefeller was ambivalent about the project, which he perceived as initially grandiose. When Gates wrote to him seeking support for a more modest beginning, Rockefeller invited him to lunch. Clearly impressed with Gates, Rockefeller suggested that they travel together the next day on the train to Cleveland (with Gates heading on to Minnesota).

In March 1891 Rockefeller confessed to Gates that the appeals to his philanthropy and charity had become overwhelming. He was incapable of giving without the due diligence to reassure himself that the money would be well spent, but he didn't have the time or energy to investigate the organizations to which he was inclined to give—to say nothing of the hundreds of appeals to which he was not interested in contributing. He needed to either shift the burden of giving to someone else or "cease giving entirely." Rockefeller asked Gates if he would be willing to move to New York to help.

"I did my best to soothe ruffled feelings, to listen fully to every plea, and to weigh fairly the merits of every cause," Gates wrote in later years, but as he began to direct the enormous flow of Rockefeller's benevolence, he confirmed Rockefeller's frustrations at not being able to exercise sufficient due diligence with all of his beneficiaries. Gates discovered "not a few of Mr. Rockefeller's habitual charities to be worthless and practically fraudulent."

Working with Gates, Rockefeller transitioned to a practice of "wholesale" philanthropy. For example, rather than give directly to local appeals from Baptist congregations or pastors, he increased his giving to state and national organizations and let them do the due diligence on local projects. Internationally, Rockefeller had been giving to a host of foreign missionary projects, each one seeking his assistance individually. Working with Gates, Rockefeller "cut off every one of these private missionary appeals" and referred them back to the Baptist Foreign Mission Society, which Rockefeller strengthened with larger contributions.

IL FAUT VAINCRE LA TUBERCULOSE COMME LE PLUS MALFAISANT DES _ REPTILES _

"Comité National de Défense contre la Tuberculose".66ᵉ Rue Notre-Dame-des-Champs.Paris.
Avec le Concours de la "Fondation Rockefeller".3.Rue de Berri.Paris.

1918
With tuberculosis raging in post-World War I France, the Rockefeller Foundation sponsors a prevention campaign. (Rockefeller Archive Center.)

TIMELINE

Gates was astonished to discover how many individuals wrote to Rockefeller seeking money for themselves. "These appeals came in multitudes from every part of the United States and, after Mr. Rockefeller became widely known, from nearly all foreign lands and the islands of the sea." They came "in a flood" each time the newspapers reported on a Rockefeller donation or gift. At one time, Gates counted 50,000 such requests within the space of a month. "Few were answered, but every one was opened for a glance as to its character. Our office force was swamped with them."

Rockefeller increasingly recognized that even with Gates he could not keep pace with the need to give money away. As Rockefeller biographer Ron Chernow points out, he was often vilified in public for hoarding his money. Newspapers noted that his giving did not keep pace with that of Andrew Carnegie.

Nevertheless, Rockefeller was focused on the problem. In 1899, speaking on the ten-year anniversary of the founding of the University of Chicago, he called on men of great wealth: "Let us erect a foundation, a trust, and engage directors who will make it a life work to manage, with our personal cooperation, the business of benevolence properly and effectively."

"Those appeals came in multitudes from every part of the United States and ... from nearly all foreign lands and the islands of the sea."
Frederick T. Gates, 1927

Until the late 1890s, and during the early years of his association with Gates, most of Rockefeller's giving was devoted to religious missions and traditional charity. The University of Chicago benefited substantially from Rockefeller's philanthropy in these years. In the summer of 1897, however, while on vacation with his family at Lake Liberty in the Catskills, Gates immersed himself in an unlikely book for beach reading—William Osler's *Principles and Practice of Medicine*, a 1,000-page textbook used by the College of Physicians and Surgeons in New York. By this time in his life, Gates was as skeptical of physicians' curative abilities as he was of the miracles described in the Bible. Osler confirmed Gates' skepticism by asserting that of all the diseases known to man, medicine at best knew how to cure only four or five. Although Pasteur had developed his germ theory, Osler pointed out that only a few germs had actually been isolated and identified. Using Osler's work, Gates made a list "of the germs that we might reasonably hope to discover." Reading Osler also prompted the realization that the commercialization of medical education had divorced it from the academic process of scientific research. "It became clear to me that medicine could hardly hope to become a science until medicine was endowed, and qualified men were enabled to give

Attorney Starr J. Murphy played a key role in helping to establish several Rockefeller philanthopies. Murphy joined Rockefeller's staff in 1904 and drafted the charter for the Rockefeller Foundation. (Library of Congress, Prints & Photographs.)

themselves to uninterrupted study and investigation, on ample salary, entirely independent of practice." Gates recognized that "here was an opportunity for Mr. Rockefeller to do an immense service to his country and perhaps the world."

Upon returning to New York from his summer respite, Gates dictated a memo for Rockefeller making the case for an American institution devoted to research in medical science. In one sense Gates aligned himself and Rockefeller with a growing movement in the United States to give new emphasis to research as opposed to teaching or practice. At the same time, he was inherently a pragmatist, resisting what some were calling "pure science," a movement toward the pursuit of knowledge without the burden of practical application. Gates wanted research that would make a difference in the world.

Gates recruited attorney Starr J. Murphy to visit leading physicians and medical researchers to promote the idea, but found little support. Most preferred small subventions for their own work. Despite this lack of imagination in the field, Murphy and Gates pushed ahead. As Murphy wrote to John D. Rockefeller Jr., a separate institute was needed to "take up the problems where the medical schools leave them, and treat them in their broadest aspect." He envisioned a dynamic and cooperative relationship between research and teaching reflected in the institute's relationship with medical education. "[H]ospitals and the medical schools, so far as they carry on research work, will lead up to and be feeders for the Institute, which will be the crown of the whole system."

In 1901, the Rockefeller Institute was launched in a loft building on Lexington Avenue in New York. Rockefeller promised $20,000 a year for ten years to pay for salaries, lab equipment, and rent. Several men who would play a leading role in the overall development of Rockefeller's philanthropy became leaders in the new institution, including Dr. William H. Welch of Johns

Chapter Two: Foundation

Hopkins, the first president of the Institute, and Dr. Simon Flexner, a professor of pathology at the University of Pennsylvania, the first director.

The creation of the Rockefeller Institute marked the beginning of a new pattern of Rockefeller philanthropy. In 1903, the General Education Board received a federal charter and was incorporated to enhance education in the South "without distinction of sex, race or creed." With a series of gifts, Rockefeller endowed the GEB with $43 million by 1907. After the work of the GEB revealed that widespread infections with hookworm impaired the ability of many southern students to learn, and the parents to earn a living, Rockefeller endowed the Rockefeller Sanitary Commission in 1909 to wage a public health campaign in the South to cure the infected and prevent further infections. To support this effort, Rockefeller pledged $1 million.

Despite these initiatives, Gates realized that Rockefeller's philanthropy was not keeping pace with his income. Although all of these institutions worked to practice wholesale philanthropy, the scale needed to be greater still given the continued growth of Rockefeller's fortune. In 1905, he had advocated a broader approach, a series of organizations that would go beyond science to address cultural issues including ethics and citizenship. Gates suggested that Rockefeller create a series of "great, corporate philanthropies" to deal with the promotion of scientific agriculture, the enrichment of rural life in the United States, the development of fine arts and refinement of taste, the promotion of Christian ethics and civilization around the world, and the development of intelligent citizenship and civic virtue in the United States. But Rockefeller had begun to think about creating a single foundation with a very broad mission.

Gates wanted a federal charter. Although Rockefeller's attorney, Starr Murphy, had concluded there was very little consequential difference between a New York and a federal charter, Gates believed a federal charter was more

Physician and scientist Simon Flexner served as the first director of the Rockefeller Institute for Medical Research. As a trustee for the Rockefeller Foundation, he was a strong supporter of medical science. (Rockefeller Archive Center.)

appropriate given Rockefeller's desire to give to national and international projects. Gates recognized that some representatives in Congress would be hostile to anything that Rockefeller proposed, but he announced: "I would not hesitate to throw this charter right into the arena and let the wild beasts fight over it if they like."

Gates thought the issues were on Rockefeller's side. "Will Mr. Rockefeller's enemies make a bitter fight against his right to give away his own money as he deems fit? If they do, will they win or will Mr. Rockefeller win?" He thought that if Rockefeller's enemies sought "to prevent his doing good to his fellow men," it would backfire against them. "Mr. Rockefeller has given away vast sums of money; he is using the great fortune which he has acquired for the promotion of human welfare. That is a feature of his character and life which is never mentioned by his enemies." He hoped the charter fight would get reporters to pay attention to Rockefeller's generosity. "Even if the bill suffers defeat," he wrote, "it cannot but raise up friends to Mr. Rockefeller."

John D. Rockefeller Jr. thought the timing was right. By 1907, the impulse to create an institution with a very broad mission had begun to build momentum. A panic on Wall Street that year was reversed by the actions of several New York capitalists, including Rockefeller, earning them some measure of goodwill in Washington. The following year, a chance encounter between John D. Rockefeller and Senator "Pitchfork Ben" Tillman of South Carolina gave Rockefeller an opportunity to charm a potential critic in Congress.

The Rockefeller Sanitary Commission was created to cure and prevent the spread of hookworm disease in the American South. The Commission's county dispensaries provided medicine and sought to educate the population about the disease. The organization was absorbed by the Rockefeller Foundation's International Health Board in 1914. (Rockefeller Archive Center.)

A powerful U.S. Senator from Rhode Island, Nelson W. Aldrich was also John D. Rockefeller Jr.'s father-in-law. Junior hoped that Aldrich would help steer the Rockefeller Foundation's charter through Congress. (Library of Congress, Prints & Photographs.)

On the strength of these events, Junior turned to his father-in-law. Junior had met the charming and self-confident Abby Aldrich when they were both students at Brown University. They were married in October, 1901. Abby was the daughter of Nelson Aldrich, the senior U.S. Senator from Rhode Island. Described by *McClure's Magazine* as "the political boss of the United States, the power behind the throne, the general manager of the U.S," Aldrich knew how to move legislation through Congress.

Junior talked to his father-in-law about a bill to create a foundation to promote the development of Christian civilization. He suggested that he and Abby might travel to Washington to visit with members of Congress. Junior also talked to Albert Shaw, the editor of *The Review of Reviews* and a member of the GEB, who offered to talk to President Theodore Roosevelt about support for a Congressional charter.

But the bill, crafted by Starr Murphy, was not submitted. A year later, in January 1908, Junior sent a draft to John Spooner, a former U.S. Senator from Wisconsin who had recently left politics to practice law in New York City. Junior wanted Spooner's advice on "the wisdom of undertaking to secure a Federal charter." Spooner advised Junior to avoid references to religion because they might spark "covert" opposition. He also suggested some other minor changes and offered to quietly test the waters. Junior continued to press his father-in-law, but no bill was introduced. Meanwhile, the campaign to pick Roosevelt's successor heated up, and William Howard Taft was elected in November 1908.

With these discussions in the background and the election over, there was some optimism that eventually a bill would be introduced and passed. John D. Rockefeller signed a deed of trust to turn over 72,569 shares of Standard Oil of New Jersey, stocks worth more than $50 million, to a newly created entity to be known as the Rockefeller Foundation. He named three trustees: his son, his son-in-law Harold McCormick, and Frederick Gates. Before the end of the year, Junior and Gates were appointed as a committee of two "to prepare and present to the Congress of the United States a bill for the incorporation of The Rockefeller Foundation." With a draft of the Act already written, Junior sent it to Aldrich with the understanding "that you think it will not

Chapter Two: Foundation

be difficult to have it acted upon at an early date." Weeks more passed. Since the bill proposed to create the Rockefeller Foundation as a corporate entity in Washington, D.C., Rockefeller's advisors pressed New Hampshire Senator Jacob H. Gallinger, the Republican chairman of the District of Columbia Committee, to sponsor the legislation. After Junior wrote to Gallinger, Starr Murphy went to visit the senator in Washington. Gallinger promised that he would introduce the bill and call Murphy as a witness. He introduced the bill as S. 6888 on March 2, 1910.

According to the *Washington Post*, there would be no limit to the "sphere of usefulness" of the new foundation. In the world of philanthropy, the Rockefeller Foundation would "become what the Standard Oil Company has long been among corporations," and the Rockefellers planned to gradually merge all of their other philanthropic endeavors under the umbrella of the new foundation. The day after the bill was submitted, John D. Rockefeller Jr. announced that he had retired from the board of Standard Oil so that he could run the Foundation and take charge of his father's philanthropy.

Charles W. Eliot served as president of Harvard University for nearly 40 years, retiring in 1909. He was the first trustee to be added to the original board. (Library of Congress, Prints and Photographs.)

Gates and Rockefeller Jr. believed they were creating a new kind of philanthropic institution "that made earlier philanthropic ventures seem somewhat amateurish," historian Robert Bremner writes. "Most earlier charitable trusts had been established for some narrowly defined purpose." By contrast, the new Rockefeller Foundation took as its mission "the well-being of mankind," and it proposed to carry out this mission through the disciplined process of research and study. Indeed, Frederick Gates emphasized this point to reporters after the Rockefeller Foundation bill was first submitted to Congress in 1910: "Every other eleemosynary institution has been organized for some specific object," he said, "and thus limited its sphere of usefulness." In the face of disaster or some new social problem, these institutions didn't have the authority in their charters to allow them to respond. With a broad charter, the Rockefeller Foundation would have much greater flexibility.

To the dismay of those who worked in the Rockefeller offices at 26 Broadway, the proposal to create the Rockefeller Foundation did not meet with broad approval. Harvard President Emeritus Charles W. Eliot, who would later serve on the board of the Foundation, expressed skepticism. "It is just as possible to throw money away in this manner as in any other," he said, "and many undeserving charities may impose on Mr. Rockefeller's agents." He declared that he was not in favor of "applying the principles of incorporation to such an undertaking, for in my mind that is to commercialize the matter too much." He also feared that the overwhelming scale of Rockefeller's philanthropy might discourage others from giving, although he did suggest that the Rockefeller Foundation would ultimately "be a great benefit to all humanity."

The Roots of Change

The foundation that the Rockefellers proposed to establish reflected a confluence of ideas that were dramatically changing western, and especially American, society at the beginning of the twentieth century. The rise of large industrial companies, especially Standard Oil, depended on the development of efficient systems of management that coordinated production and distribution across the globe. This new managerial capitalism was buoyed by a growing faith that breakthroughs in science and engineering would unleash a new era in history guided by reason and logic.

Frederick Winslow Taylor became the leading voice behind this movement towards the rationalization of human activity. Influenced by his training as an engineer to look for efficiencies in mechanical systems, the author of *The Principles of Scientific Management* abhorred the idea of waste. Indeed, in Taylor's view, systems trumped leadership. "In the past the man has been first;

in the future the system must be first." Scientific management, in Taylor's view, was not about "invention," but innovation, developing new ways of organizing work or practice. To Taylor, and many of the business leaders of his generation, every human activity needed a "system," including "our philanthropic institutions."

Industrial assembly lines, like the one developed by the Ford Motor Company, reflected a widespread effort to organize work and society according to the principles of scientific management. Efficiency expert Frederick Winslow Taylor suggested that even philanthropy needed a "system" to be effective. (Library of Congress, Prints & Photographs.)

As Taylor suggested, the idea of systems and organization was applicable to more than engineering and manufacturing. In fact, with the dramatic growth in the scale of industrial production, the rise of great cities with increasingly complex systems for transportation and sanitation, and the need for sophisticated approaches to management, the United States experienced what historian Louis Galambos has described as an organizational revolution that affected almost every walk of life, including philanthropy. Another historian, Robert Wiebe, called it a national "search for order." In some sense, it also reflected the triumph of modern bureaucracy in the private, public and nonprofit sectors.

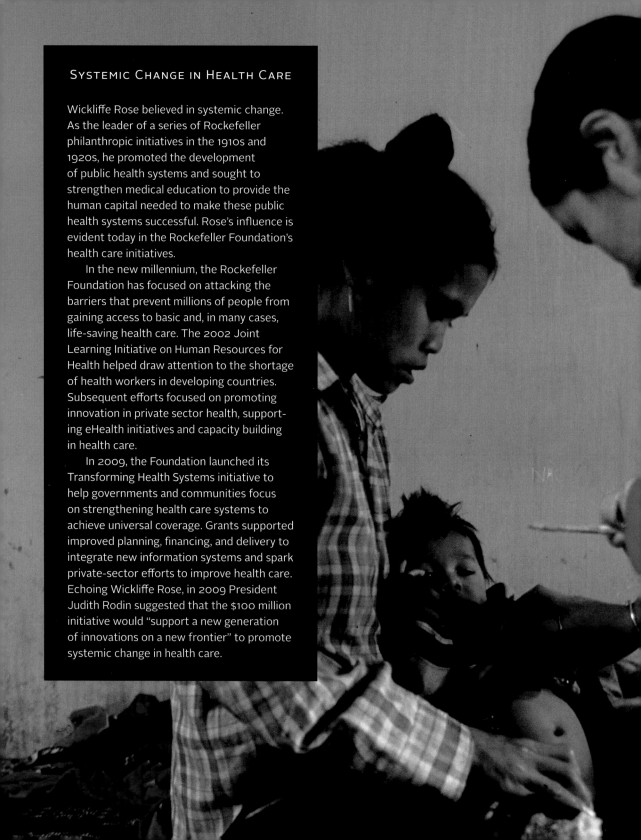

SYSTEMIC CHANGE IN HEALTH CARE

Wickliffe Rose believed in systemic change. As the leader of a series of Rockefeller philanthropic initiatives in the 1910s and 1920s, he promoted the development of public health systems and sought to strengthen medical education to provide the human capital needed to make these public health systems successful. Rose's influence is evident today in the Rockefeller Foundation's health care initiatives.

In the new millennium, the Rockefeller Foundation has focused on attacking the barriers that prevent millions of people from gaining access to basic and, in many cases, life-saving health care. The 2002 Joint Learning Initiative on Human Resources for Health helped draw attention to the shortage of health workers in developing countries. Subsequent efforts focused on promoting innovation in private sector health, support- ing eHealth initiatives and capacity building in health care.

In 2009, the Foundation launched its Transforming Health Systems initiative to help governments and communities focus on strengthening health care systems to achieve universal coverage. Grants supported improved planning, financing, and delivery to integrate new information systems and spark private-sector efforts to improve health care. Echoing Wickliffe Rose, in 2009 President Judith Rodin suggested that the $100 million initiative would "support a new generation of innovations on a new frontier" to promote systemic change in health care.

The effort to rationalize and organize American society by engineers and social reformers was closely aligned with a movement known as Progressivism, which included a faith in the wisdom of experts and professionals. In many ways, the leaders of the Rockefeller Foundation embraced the ethos of the Progressive era, but they were also sensitive to the fact that Progressive journalists, dubbed "muckrakers," were among the greatest critics of the founder and his commercial empire. Coming of age as the Progressive movement was in full force, John D. Rockefeller Jr. became an enthusiastic proponent and participant. Invited to serve as the foreman of a special grand jury investigating forced prostitution or "white slavery," Junior threw himself into the work and emerged as a committed social reformer.

In the context of all of these broad changes in society, leaders in the philanthropic community hailed the development of "a more scientific spirit and method in philanthropy." This movement was anchored in two parallel developments: the first a series of innovations in law that gave shape to the modern foundation; and the second, closely related, developments in administration and methods that addressed the operations of the new institutions.

Legally, the modern private foundation evolved from a series of key court decisions in the nineteenth century. In 1819, in a case involving Dartmouth College, the U.S. Supreme Court ruled that the contract clause in the Constitution protected chartered institutions from unreasonable interference by the government. The Court also held that although Dartmouth College was established for the purposes of general charity, it was not a public corporation susceptible to the control of the state. The ruling helped to ensure the autonomy of charitable institutions. A second Supreme Court decision, regarding the estate of Stephen Girard, a Philadelphia merchant and banker who bequeathed his $7 million estate to the city of Philadelphia to establish a school for poor, white orphan boys, confirmed the right of donors to give to charitable corporations and of those corporations to carry out the donor's wishes. These court decisions provided the foundation for the establishment of new institutions after the Civil War in the United States. An important precursor for the Rockefellers was the Peabody Education Fund, established by the wealthy Baltimore merchant George Peabody, who provided a $1 million gift to improve education in the South.

In some sense, there was nothing new in these institutions. The leaders of the new era, according to historian Robert Bremner, "took the 'do's and don'ts'—especially the latter—handed down from generations of charity reformers, organized them into a comprehensive system of rules, and applied them more rigorously than ever before in American history." In the late nineteenth century the science in this new philanthropy focused primarily on systematizing the institutions of charity. In many northeastern cities new organizations like the New York Charity Organization Society were founded to document and authenticate the conditions of the poor and to prevent the undeserving from taking advantage of the generosity of charity organizations. These new entities also focused on services—employment, childcare, education—that would help the poor escape from poverty. As they gathered a growing amount of information and data on the conditions of poverty, many philanthropic leaders increasingly realized that social systems affecting education, health, and employment contributed substantially to poverty. They began to search for programs that would address the root causes of society's ills.

This effort to address the root causes of problems and to create large endowments for general-purpose foundations with broad charters marked the primary innovation that inaugurated the age of modern philanthropy. The scale of the effort made some in Congress nervous.

The Fight Begins

The political environment for the Rockefeller Foundation charter in 1910 also turned out to be inauspicious. When a copy was given to President Taft, he consulted with the Attorney General, who objected to the idea that Congress would approve the charter while the government was seeking to break up Standard Oil for violating the Sherman Antitrust Act of 1890. Congressmen hostile to Standard Oil raised similar questions, especially when Standard Oil attorneys filed briefs with the U.S. Supreme Court only a week after the Rockefeller Foundation bill was introduced in the Senate.

Many officials who were suspicious of the Rockefeller proposal focused on the aspects of the concept that were most innovative: the proposed broad charter "to promote the well-being of mankind throughout the world;" the idea that the foundation might continue in perpetuity with unimaginable resources; and, above all, the lack of public oversight. "Many newspapers saw the vagueness," says biographer Ron Chernow, "as a gauzy curtain behind which the evil wizard of Standard Oil could work his mischief." They accused Rockefeller of creating the foundation to buy back the public's good will.

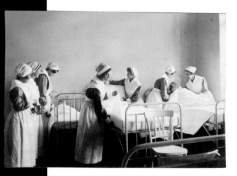

1924
Rockefeller Foundation launches its nursing education program as part of a larger effort to promote medical education and public health. (Rockefeller Archive Center.)

Chapter Two: Foundation

There were other criticisms that left little middle ground. Proponents of business felt that if Rockefeller's fortune were pulled out of the market, according to the *New York Times*, capital would be constrained for industrial investment, "thereby appreciably diminishing the prosperity and business progress of the country." To dispel these concerns, Frederick Gates provided a report to the Secretary of the Interior detailing the investments of the General Education Board, to show that they were broadly distributed among a host of corporate stocks and bonds. But this evidence failed to enlist the government's support.

For three years the proposal languished in Congress. Finally, in January 1913, Jerome Greene believed the Rockefellers were on the cusp of victory. By this time Congress had extracted numerous concessions from Rockefeller. He had agreed to limit the total assets of the corporation to $100 million and committed to spending the income rather than letting it accumulate with the corpus of the fund. The size of the board had been increased, and election of trustees would be subject to disapproval by a host of public representatives. After fifty years, the corporation would be allowed to distribute its principal as well as income. After a hundred years, Congress could force the Foundation to spend itself out of existence. Meanwhile, Congress would have the complete power to amend or repeal the Foundation's charter. In the mind of Rockefeller's advisor Jerome Greene, Rockefeller's acceptance of these amendments made it clear that the charter was sought "solely because the gift is to the people of the United States, and is to be controlled by them rather than in the interest, however beneficent, of any one section." Greene also thought that, with these concessions, Congress would finally give its blessing to the endeavor.

On January 20, 1913, the House of Representatives approved the Rockefeller Foundation charter by a vote of 152 to 65 and sent it to the Senate. Anticipating success at last, Rockefeller gave $3.2 million in bonds to four trustees to be given to the Rockefeller Foundation immediately upon passage of the bill. On February 19, the Senate Judiciary Committee favorably reported the measure to the full Senate. But there it died, as a small group of opponents prevented the Senate from passing the measure before Congress adjourned.

Undeterred, Rockefeller and his advisors turned to the New York Legislature. Scrapping the concessions that Rockefeller had given Congress, Starr Murphy provided a much simpler charter. On April 24, 1913, the New York Legislature unanimously approved the bill. On May 14, with Governor William Sulzer's signature, the Rockefeller Foundation was born and empowered with a remarkably broad mission.

Unable to win Congressional approval for a federal charter, John D. Rockefeller turned to the New York Legislature to incorporate the Rockefeller Foundation in 1913. (Rockefeller Archive Center.)

Form 60-418. 1-3-16-400 (2-13085)

UNITED STATES OF AMERICA

STATE OF NEW YORK

BY

FRANCIS M. HUGO

Secretary of State and Custodian of the Great Seal Thereof

It is Hereby Certified, That CHARLES W. TAFT was, on the da date of the annexed Certificate and Attestation, Second Deputy Secretary o of the State of New York, and duly authorized by the laws of said State t such Attestation and Certificate and to perform the duties belonging to the tary of State in making such Attestation and Certificate, in like manner Secretary of State; that the said Certificate and Attestation are in due for executed by the proper officer; that the seal affixed to said Certificate and tion is the seal of office of the Secretary of State of the State of New York the signature thereto of the said Second Deputy Secretary of State is in le proper handwriting and is genuine; and that full faith and credit ma ought to be given to his official acts; and, further, that the Secretary of S the Custodian of the *Original Law* so ce and attested and Custodian of the Great Seal of said State, hereunto affixed

In Testimony Whereof, The Seal of the State is hereunto affixe

Witness my hand at the City of Albany, the *twenty-fourth* day of *January* in the year of our Lord one thou nine hundred and *seventeen*

Secretary of St

CHAP. 488
AN ACT

To incorporate the Rockefeller foundation.

Became a law May 14, 1913 with the approval of the
ernor.   Passed, three-fifths being present.

The People of the State of New York, represented in
ate and assembly, do enact as follows:

Section 1.   John D. Rockefeller, John D. Rockefeller,
ior, Frederick T. Gates, Harry Pratt Judson, Simon Flexner,
rr J. Murphy, Jerome D. Greene, Wickliffe Rose and Charles
Heydt, together with such persons as they may associate with
mselves, and their successors, are hereby constituted a
y corporate by the name of The Rockefeller Foundation,
the purpose of receiving and maintaining a fund or funds
applying the income and principal thereof to promote the
l-being of mankind throughout the world.   It shall be
hin the purposes of said corporation to use as means to
t end research, publication, the establishment and mainte-
ice of charitable, benevolent, religious, missionary, and
lic educational activities, agencies and institutions, and
e aid of any such activities, agencies and institutions
ready established, and any other means and agencies which
m time to time shall seem expedient to its members or
stees.

§ 2.   The corporation hereby formed shall have power to
te and hold by bequest, devise, gift, purchase or lease,
her absolutely or in trust for any of its purposes, any
perty, real or personal, without limitation as to amount
value, except such limitation, if any, as the legislature
ll hereafter specifically impose; to convey such property,

st and reinvest any principal,
income and principal or the cor
n the judgment of the trustees
.   It shall have all the power
restrictions which now pertain
ations created by special law s
ble thereto and are not inconsi
of this act.   The persons name
this act, or a majority of ther
ganize the corporation and adopt
s not inconsistent with the cons
ate.   Ths constitution shall p
on of members, the number of men
e a quorum for the transaction o
e corporation, the number of tr
nd affairs of the corporation s
fications, powers, and the manne
stees and officers of the corpo
ng the constitution and by-laws
ther provisions for the manageme
operty and regulation of the aff
h may be deemed expedient.

No officer, member or employee

f New York   } ss:
SECRETARY OF STATE)

B 1

I have compared the
in this office, and do he
transcript therefrom, ar
Given under my ha
of State, at the City of
day of
nine hundred and

MISSION

What is
the mission?

Organizations are formed for a purpose. Mission statements articulate that purpose. In the context of private foundations, they embody the donor's intent. Shaped by the donor's personality, philosophy, values, religious background, and experience, they serve as a guidepost for the board, the staff, and the public. The mission statement provides the standard by which the foundation and its programs will be measured and judged. A successful mission statement also inspires trustees, staff, and other stakeholders.

Before the founding of the Rockefeller and Carnegie foundations, narrow missions were embodied within the trusts and wills of donors who were often said to be exercising a "dead hand" from the grave. If the mission of the trust became out of date (teaching boys to make buggy whips, for example), it was very difficult to put these funds to work for a new purpose. Donors framed these narrow missions then, as they do today, to ensure that they will honor the donor's intent over the life of the foundation.

Others believe that broad mission statements are better. They remove the "dead hand" of the donor and provide latitude for future generations to adapt to the changing needs of society. By adopting broad mission statements, the Rockefeller Foundation ("to promote the well-being of mankind"), Carnegie Corporation ("promote the advancement and diffusion of knowledge and understanding"), and Russell Sage Foundation ("the improvement of social and living conditions in the United States") inaugurated a fundamental innovation in the practice of philanthropy in the early twentieth century.

This freedom to change to address the needs of a new generation comes with its own challenges. For busy, results-oriented trustees, these broad missions can be frustrating in the apparent lack of direction they provide. Some observers suggest they lead to a lack of organizational focus. Each generation is forced to reinterpret the mission in light of the needs of its era. And each generation is challenged to set benchmarks or measures that will define progress in the context of such broad missions. None of this is easy work, but it is exactly what founders like Rockefeller intended.

Margaret Olivia Slocum Sage was a pioneer of modern philanthropy. After her husband's death, she established the Russell Sage Foundation in 1907 "for the improvement of social and living conditions in the United States." (Library of Congress, Prints & Photographs.)

BEYOND CHARITY

CHAPTER III

MISSION

A MORAL FRAMEWORK

I n 1712, a young Irish Protestant took to the pulpit at Trinity College in Dublin to offer a sermon. Twenty-seven years old and already on his way to becoming one of Britain's three great empirical philosophers (along with John Locke and David Hume), George Berkeley was trying to understand the essence of virtue, morality, and law. In his interpretation, they were all rooted in the will of the Divine. God, being of infinite goodness, could only seek "the general well-being of all men." Thus, "the great end to which God requires the concurrence of human actions must ...[be] to promote the well-being of the sum of mankind, taking in all nations and ages, from the beginning to the end of the world."

John D. Rockefeller was not a bookish man, so it is unlikely that he read Berkeley's sermon. Frederick Gates may have read it while he was studying at the Rochester Theological Union. Regardless, neither man could have avoided Berkeley's influence. As one of the great empiricists of the Enlightenment, Berkeley helped to frame the ways of thinking that would lead to the Scientific Revolution. He suggested that there was order in nature and that this order reflected God's purpose. Our human instinct is to try to understand this order and by doing so draw closer to the mind of God. Ideas like these helped shape the mission of the Rockefeller Foundation.

Rooted in the Baptist traditions of Rockefeller and his family, the mission idealized the notion of service to humanity. It also reflected the fundamentally

rationalizing forces of the era. To these men, as Ron Chernow has written, "Science seemed to beckon as a new secular religion." Gates articulated this idea in 1911, on the tenth anniversary of the founding of the Rockefeller Institute, when he suggested that the work of the researchers at the Institute would affect every man, woman, and child on the planet. "So your work in the scope of its values is as universal as the love of God."

The confluence of all of these ideas led to the Rockefeller Foundation's broad mission: "To promote the well-being of mankind throughout the world." As many historians of philanthropy have noted, it represented a major break from the historic pattern of charitable giving. The breadth of this mission, combined with a very large endowment, marked the Rockefeller

Foundation, along with organizations established by Andrew Carnegie and Margaret Olivia Slocum Sage, as fundamentally new players in the field of philanthropy in the early twentieth century.

The broad purpose of the Foundation was designed to give future leaders flexibility and a chance to be opportunistic, and to address problems or solutions as they emerged. Though not specific in the language, it was clearly the intent of the founder and his advisors to turn away from the centuries-old idea of charity as a momentary relief for the symptoms of social problems. Instead, the Rockefeller Foundation would address the roots of social problems. "Instead of giving alms to beggars," Rockefeller said, "if anything can be done to remove the causes which lead to the existence of beggars, then something deeper and broader and more worthwhile will have been accomplished."

THE · TWO · HVNDRED · INCH ~
TELESCOPE · LOOKING · NORTHWEST

1928

A 200-inch telescope to be built on Palomar Mountain in Southern California receives an initial $6 million appropriation from the International Education Board, whose work in the natural sciences was taken over by the Rockefeller Foundation the following year. (Rockefeller Archive Center.)

The Rockefeller Foundation's mission was also novel because it was distinctly international. Intellectually, the Foundation's leaders aspired to create a scientific community that transcended political borders and extended around the world. They subscribed to the idea that unrestricted scientific exchange was critical to the progress of science and human civilization, and they worked to create networks for transmitting these ideas. Indeed, according to historian Mary Brown Bullock, the Foundation became "the most important American organization to promote and finance transnational scientific communities."

Like many scientific internationalists, Rockefeller and Gates believed that the practice and promotion of science in society would also shape patterns of social behavior and support values like reason, restraint, moderation, idealism, tolerance, compassion, devotion, and discipline. Indeed, Gates hoped that medical research would eventually unlock the secrets of human behavior as part of an effort to mitigate and even control humans' impulse to destruction.

Because the Rockefeller Foundation was international in a colonial era, the mission

has also been described as culturally imperialistic. "The foundation used the ideologies of American science and medicine as a template for its engagement with countries as different as the United Kingdom and Ceylon," writes historian Mary Brown Bullock. Labeling this as cultural imperialism does not really do justice to either the work or the motivations of Rockefeller Foundation trustees and employees even in the earliest years, Bullock says. Instead, she suggests we have to understand that as the Rockefeller Foundation sought to act upon its mission, it was in turn profoundly shaped by the peoples and cultures it encountered. It also evolved in response to the ideas, knowledge and worldviews developed by grantees.

Besieged by requests for money, John D. Rockefeller Sr. went out with pockets bulging with dimes and nickels which he gave to adults and children. Along with the money, he offered children advice to work hard and to save what they earned. But this charity was no substitute for philanthropy. (Rockefeller Archive Center.)

At times, the breadth of the Foundation's mission statement has been criticized. It can seem to leave the staff and leadership in the middle of an ocean with no land horizon to aim for. It can undermine the popular notion in strategic philanthropy today that focus is the key to success.

Occasionally, leaders at the Rockefeller Foundation have revisited the mission statement. In the late 1920s, Wickliffe Rose suggested that, in the end, all of the Rockefeller philanthropies were working toward the progress of civilization through the advancement of human knowledge. Anson Phelps

Stokes agreed, but wanted to add "diffusion" of knowledge as well. Education and teaching paved the path to the future.

With the end of World War II, the institutional landscape for international work changed dramatically. New governmental and quasi-governmental entities appeared—including the United Nations, the World Bank, and the World Health Organization—whose resources far exceeded those of the Foundation. In this new environment, the board of the Foundation struggled to define its working relationship with these new entities and to redefine the Foundation's program. In doing so, the trustees returned to the mission statement.

"Yellow fever vaccine carries no flag and is not the property of any nation."
Raymond Fosdick, 1946

As the end of the war suggested an end to the prewar colonial regime, the board began to see the language of the mission statement in a new light. The board asked if the mandate to promote the well-being of mankind "throughout the world" meant the Foundation should be making grants or operating in every country. Raymond Fosdick, who had become president of the Foundation in 1936, was quick to respond that the Foundation had in the past seen this phrase to mean that the Foundation chased problems without regard for "flags and frontiers." He believed that, given the growing ideological conflict of the postwar era, this kind of internationalism was needed more than ever. "Our aim must be the healing of mankind—the search for unity—regardless of race or color or political or social creed," he wrote to Chester Barnard. "Yellow fever vaccine carries no flag and is not the property of any nation. Penicillin cannot be slanted in favor of Marxism or capitalism. There is not a Russian sulfadiazine as distinguished from an American sulfadiazine. We must work in the laying of cornerstones like these—humble as our contribution may be—trying to find the common factors, the common interests, that will serve men everywhere." Fosdick went on to emphasize the vision of the founders: "The Foundation can always afford to take the broad view, the long view, and if we fail to do this, we fail those who in 1913 described the purpose of the Foundation in liberal and prophetic words."

John D. Rockefeller III, who became chairman of the board of the Rockefeller Foundation in 1952, agreed with Fosdick. In April 1965, when representatives of the newly created Volkswagen Foundation came to New York to learn more about the practice of philanthropy, they asked him about the founding of the Rockefeller Foundation. If he could go back in time, would the grandson change the mission? No, Rockefeller responded. His grandfather had articulated a remarkably broad purpose, empowering each generation of trustees to reshape the program to meet the needs of the day. As a result, the Foundation was remarkably flexible.

Nevertheless, trustees, presidents and Foundation staff in subsequent generations often yearned for more definition. In the summer of 1973, staff searched for a unifying theme that would encompass the Foundation's past and sharpen its focus on the future. The group embraced John D. Rockefeller's mandate to search for and address the root causes of the problems that troubled humanity, but they noted that over sixty years the Foundation's work had been and should continue to be focused primarily on the poor and disadvantaged around the world.

The global implications of the mission statement became increasingly important as the Rockefeller Foundation approached the end of the twentieth century, and grantees and development partners realized the implications of an increasingly interdependent world. In 1999, when British agricultural scientist and environmental champion Gordon Conway stepped into his role as the new president of the Rockefeller Foundation, the organization once again revisited the mission statement. Again staff and trustees recommitted to John D. Rockefeller's basic purpose, as well as the insight of the 1970s that the Foundation should be a champion for the poor and excluded peoples of the world. Echoing Wickliffe Rose, they also reaffirmed the conviction that it was in the development and dissemination of knowledge that the Foundation could "enrich and sustain the lives and livelihoods of the poor and excluded throughout the world."

> "to enrich and sustain the lives and livelihoods of the poor and excluded throughout the world."
> *Rockefeller Foundation, 1999*

Conway suggested that the Foundation's strategic planning initiatives in 1999 should focus on "the redefined Rockefeller Foundation and the work that we will be doing starting with the new millennium." In some sense this was only half true. In the new millennium, the mission was reframed to remove the semantic gender bias of an earlier age, but the message remained as relevant as it was encompassing—to promote the well-being of humanity.

The challenge for a new generation of board members was to interpret this mission, just as John D. Rockefeller had intended, within the light of their own era, and to do so in a way that would inspire the collaboration of grantees and partners as well as the confidence of the public.

BOARD

Who should sit on the board?

Private foundation boards operate with extraordinary autonomy, especially in the United States. Without shareholders or members, foundations have governing boards that are self-perpetuating, with board members selecting their own successors. Except to comply with government regulations, foundation boards are rarely accountable for their decisions, except in the public eye. Thus the composition of the board is extremely important.

A foundation's initial board often reflects historical, personal and institutional factors rooted in the founder's personal and business relationships. It is the donor's money, after all. As they choose new members, boards look for individuals who will share a passion for the foundation's mission and an interest in the fields in which it operates. They look for people who will bring vision and perspective to the board's decision-making. Sometimes they seek specific expertise—in the law, accounting, investment management or disciplines related to the foundation's program. Fundamentally, they want people willing to commit time and energy to the board's work.

The danger in a self-perpetuating board is that members will tend to pick successors who are like themselves. When board members have too much in common, the foundation runs the risk of being limited in its vision. Or, worse, conflicts of interest can develop that undermine the integrity of the organization. Over the past several decades, many boards have diversified their membership to avoid these problems.

Early in the life of a foundation, the board works to develop a shared vision for the mission and program of the organization. It is not easy. Many factors can undermine the coherence of the board: competing ideas of the mission, inattention or apathy, or a lack of capacity to understand the challenges faced by the organization. The board chair plays a critical role in keeping the members focused and attentive to the needs of the institution.

The board does not run the foundation on a day-to-day basis. Although the board sets the strategic direction and formulates policy, it must empower and trust its president. This is easier said than done. Powerful personalities and visionary trustees may exert a strong influence on the staff or intrude on the day-to-day management. In these cases, the president may struggle to maintain clear lines of managerial authority. At other times, boards may be too deferential or passive, neglecting their duty to provide oversight or failing to provide the support the president needs to move forward.

The evolution of the Rockefeller Foundation's board reflects many of these patterns, as well as lessons learned along the way. For John D. Rockefeller Jr., the quest to build the right board began with a confrontation on the witness stand.

John D. Rockefeller Jr. testified before the federal Commission on Industrial Relations in New York in January 1915. (Library of Congress, Prints & Photographs.)

BEYOND CHARITY

CHAPTER IV

BOARD

A CRISIS OF PUBLIC TRUST

The chairman gaveled the room to silence. Wearing a three-piece suit with a starched, rounded collar and a stickpin for his tie, John D. Rockefeller Jr. sat quietly in the witness box in New York's City Hall. His hands on the witness table were unadorned, without even a wedding ring, despite fifteen years of marriage. His hair was parted on the side and neatly combed over. His broad, open face with its strong chin was composed and ready for his third day of interrogation.

Before him, a panel of eight men and one woman took their seats. Empowered by Congress to investigate the roots of violent conflict between labor and business, the Commission on Industrial Relations had been created after a wave of deadly clashes between labor and business sparked alarm throughout the United States. Chairman Frank Walsh, a crusading fifty-one-year-old lawyer from Kansas City, had turned the investigation into a full-fledged inquiry into what he described as threats posed by industrialists to American democracy. Morning and afternoon for two days Walsh had grilled Rockefeller Junior, hoping to hold him responsible for an incident that had shocked the nation.

Mr. Junior, as his staff called him, had expected this treatment. Months earlier he had testified before a Congressional committee about a strike at the Colorado Fuel and Iron Company. At the time, the Rockefellers owned nearly 40 percent of the stock in this company. They were strong supporters of the management's anti-union policies. Rockefeller's testimony then had been unimpressive, even embarrassing. Frequently he was unable to answer the committee's questions, evidencing the worst of what some called "absentee capitalism."

Two weeks later, the company's private guards, working with the Colorado National Guard, engaged in a pitched battle with the striking workers, wielding machine guns and torching the workers' encampment. The dead included two women and eleven children who were asphyxiated in an underground shelter as fire consumed the striking workers' camp. The "Ludlow Massacre" turned the nation against the Rockefellers.

In the months that followed, Junior was vilified in the press. "Never before had the younger Rockefeller been so keenly and painfully aware of his isolation from the American public," wrote Raymond Fosdick. Through the Rockefeller Foundation, Junior recruited Mackenzie King, a well-known Canadian authority on labor. With King's help, the strike was settled in December 1914. Junior gradually embraced a more progressive attitude toward labor relations that was often ahead of his father's or that of Frederick Gates and the older generation of capitalists that surrounded him. To pursue that vision, the Rockefeller Foundation asked King to undertake a broad study of industrial relations.

When the Foundation announced this study, Chairman Walsh became suspicious. He feared that the Rockefellers were planning a major anti-labor campaign to be conducted under the aegis of the Foundation. He scheduled hearings in New York City, with Junior expected to be a star witness.

The atmosphere had been tense when Junior began his testimony. With threats against the Rockefellers in mind, the mayor had assigned his personal bodyguard to escort Junior to City Hall.

Intent on avoiding a repetition of his embarrassing testimony before Congress, Rockefeller and his staff had spent more than a month preparing for the hearings. They had compiled a 103-page booklet with answers to fifty-five questions submitted ahead of time by the Commission.

The first day, Walsh grilled Junior for five hours. Self-possessed and courteous, Junior won over many in the crowd, including the famous labor organizer Mother Jones. He even got the audience to laugh, prompting Walsh to chastise the public. On the afternoon of the second day, Walsh shifted his focus to the Rockefellers' philanthropy.

In a series of questions, he highlighted ways in which the boundaries between the Foundation and the Rockefellers' business interests in Colorado had been blurred. Mackenzie King, who had brokered the resolution of the strike, had been hired by the Foundation. A public relations agent, Ivy Lee, hired by the Rockefellers to handle the Colorado situation, sat in on Rockefeller Foundation meetings even though he was not a trustee or staff member.

Junior stumbled over this line of questioning. He explained that the staff in the Rockefeller offices was "a sort of family affair. We talk over all sorts of things of common interest." On the issue of Ivy Lee, for example, Junior reported, "He can exert just such an influence over the Foundation as any competent disinterested individual with whom we might confer."

Walsh understood that not just any "competent disinterested individual" could sit down with the Rockefellers. He also pointed out that two members of Rockefeller's paid personal staff had served as directors of Colorado Fuel and Iron *and* as trustees of the Foundation during the period of the strike. A third member of the staff was also a Foundation trustee. Junior, himself, served on both boards.

Walsh wanted to know what qualified someone to serve on the board of the Rockefeller Foundation. He quoted Starr Murphy's testimony before Congress: "men of wide vision, men of wide experience, and of sound wisdom, and men of enthusiasm in the work which is before them, and

Tension between striking workers and management at the Colorado Fuel and Iron Company erupted into violence on April 20, 1914. After the workers camp was torched, two women and eleven children were asphyxiated in an underground shelter. (Library of Congress, Prints & Photographs.)

who are willing to give freely of their time." Junior affirmed that sentiment. Walsh asked whether trustees should be compensated and, if so, how much. Should the Foundation pay their expenses? What about the expenses of family members? Should Congress or the legislature have a voice in the selection of trustees? These questions came thick and fast, and Junior seemed to backpedal as if he had never thought about them before.

Now Junior sat waiting for the third day of interrogation to begin. As the room quieted, Walsh pressed Junior to define the proper limits of a foundation's activities. Could it engage in for-profit business? No. Could it hire publicity agents? Yes. Could it become an advocate in labor policy issues? "I don't see why any foundation should not have the same right to legitimate means of publicity as any such organization as you have spoken of," Junior responded.

Chairman Frank Walsh questioned the ties between the Rockefellers' business interests and their philanthropy. (Library of Congress, Prints & Photographs.)

Then Walsh sought to deliver the coup de grâce. Noting Rockefeller's role and duties as a director of Colorado Fuel and Iron, a trustee of the Rockefeller Foundation, and a personal advisor to his father on investments, he asked how Junior could possibly separate these various conflicting interests. Junior was disturbed. He responded by saying:

> Mr. Chairman, the question is apparently based upon the assumption that if a man has one interest he can not be conscientious in the performance of his duty in relation to any other interest. That is not the basis on which the foundation has proceeded. If that basis were accepted, no man could do but one thing. I am assuming that there are men in this country, and hundreds of thousands of them, who can be trusted to try to do what they think is right in various circumstances, and if there can not be found men who can be so trusted, then there should be no funds, and there should be no responsibility of any kind given to men.

In the weeks that followed his testimony, Junior began to rethink his perspective on the governance of the Rockefeller Foundation and the concerns raised by Walsh and others that were amplified in the press. Of the eleven members of the Rockefeller Foundation's board of trustees, six received salaries or some compensation from either John D. Rockefeller Sr. or one of his endowed foundations, including Simon Flexner, Wickliffe Rose, Starr Murphy, Charles Heydt, Jerome Greene, and Frederick Gates. Among the other five trustees, two—Dr. Judson and Dr. Charles W. Eliot—were presidents of universities (Chicago and Harvard) that had received substantial contributions from Rockefeller.

Junior realized that it was not enough for honorable men with good intentions to work to do the right thing. According to writers John Enson Haar and Peter Johnson, "The lesson for Junior was that never again would he ask the Foundation to become involved in an activity that had anything to do with a personal or family problem." Governance of the Foundation must be distanced from the Rockefeller family offices. The board of the Rockefeller Foundation would need to be shaped in a way that would inspire the public's trust. But what did that mean? Over the course of the next century, Junior and his successors on the board would seek to answer this question in ways that reflected the issues, concerns, and priorities of their respective eras.

The First Board

Congress might have changed the course of philanthropic history in 1913. While the charter for the Rockefeller Foundation was being debated, some members pushed for amendments that would have given public officials a strong voice in the selection of new trustees and set a precedent for foundations in the future. Under one of these amendments, any nomination to the Rockefeller Foundation board could have been vetoed by a majority of the following: the president of the United States, the chief justice of the Supreme Court, the president of the Senate, the Speaker of the House of Representatives, and the presidents of Harvard, Yale, Columbia, Johns Hopkins, and the University of Chicago. Surprisingly, Rockefeller agreed to this condition. But when Congress failed to pass the bill, he went to the New York Legislature, which did not ask for a similar amendment. As a result, the board of trustees of the new Rockefeller Foundation included eight members of the Rockefeller inner circle, but governance remained a big question.

Unlike Andrew Carnegie, the founder of the Rockefeller Foundation never took an active role in its governance. Although he was a member of the board for years, he never attended a meeting. The board elected him "Honorary President of the Foundation" for life, but as biographer Ron Chernow notes, "[Rockefeller] was receding to a more distant supervisory role with his philanthropies and yielding more power to his son, although he never surrendered his veto power." After the Walsh Commission hearings in 1915, Rockefeller Sr. was convinced that he should delegate all of the management of the Foundation to others.

Senior's reticence hardly reflected a lack of interest in the board or the Foundation. Indeed, he was keenly aware that boards play a key role in the fate of an institution. In 1889, as he was considering whether to support the development of the University of Chicago, he had peppered Frederick Gates with questions about members of the proposed board. He stressed that the board should be "disinterested" or, rather, have no vested interest in the fate of the institution. "He warned me against cabals with axes to

For three years, Congress considered a bill to grant the proposed Rockefeller Foundation a federal charter. Despite major concessions on governance and finances by the Rockefellers, the bill was not approved. (Library of Congress, Prints & Photographs.)

Chapter Four: Board

grind," Gates wrote, "and he intimated that we might have to sift for years before we could get the right kind of Board."

Gates too believed that getting the right board would make all the difference for the future of the Foundation. Trustees, he wrote to Rockefeller in 1905, served the public as much as any agency of government. Their decisions should "attract the attention of the entire civilized world, their administration become the subject of the most intelligent criticism of the world." Jerome Greene, the secretary of the Foundation, wrote that the selection of future trustees "must be the very first concern of the original trustees and of all their successors until the best method of selection shall be determined." Greene noted that history seemed to show that over time charitable trusts tended to be controlled by a few men of high station who were often too busy to devote their attention to the institution, and therefore the institution tended to lose its innovative qualities. Greene hoped that the adoption of a set of principles, along with a flexible attitude toward the future, would help to preserve the freedom that would energize future boards.

But the question of the public's role in governance remained. Greene proposed the creation of a public council to advise the board and the Foundation. He had in mind Frederick Gates's admonition that without the influence of the people in a democratic society, a private foundation would tend toward paternalism and rigidity. Greene thought this public council should be geographically diverse, representing all of the major sections of the country as well as foreign countries where the Foundation was working. He proposed that this council would meet annually to review the Foundation's work and make recommendations. Junior did not dismiss Greene's proposal, but, in the years before Ludlow and the Walsh Commission hearings, his instinct was guarded. "I should rather keep the foundation as free and as flexible as possible during the early years of its existence while its founder and his representative are on hand to guide and mould it."

Even before the Walsh Commission hearings, however, the Rockefeller insiders on the board sought to expand membership by inviting well-known public men who were also familiar to the Rockefellers to serve. The first was Charles W. Eliot, the eighty-year-old president emeritus of Harvard University. Still a commanding presence, Eliot was a member of the board of the Carnegie Endowment for International Peace and had been a trustee of the GEB since 1908. He was also a founding member of the Rockefeller Foundation's International Health Commission and a leading advisor on the China program.

Eliot urged the Foundation to expand the board further "to secure the confidence of the public." In March 1914, the board elected A. Barton Hepburn, the president of Chase National Bank. But after testifying before the Walsh Commission the following January, Eliot urged further action. "It [the board] ought to be doubled at once," he wrote to Jerome Greene on March 3, 1915. "All the new members should be successful professional or business men known to the public as men of public spirit and good will." Eliot felt that expanding the board was critical if the Foundation wanted to address the criticisms leveled by socialists and labor leaders. Eliot was also cognizant of the Rockefellers' desire to keep a close rein on the management of all of the foundations. Although Rockefeller insiders were often appointed to multiple Rockefeller boards, Eliot recommended that "outsiders" be appointed to only one board as a way to broaden the number of men "interested in the wise discharge of the Rockefeller trusts in general."

Junior agreed. In May 1915, the board elected former president of the United States William Howard Taft. He wanted to be free to speak his mind in the political realm, however. Taft was concerned critics would say that, as a member of the Rockefeller Foundation board, his opinions were affected "by my association with the Foundation." So he resigned from the board in August 1915.

Taft's concerns raised an issue that would reappear throughout the history of the Foundation—whether to name prominent politicians to the board, particularly while they were still active in public affairs. In 1948, for example, Lewis Douglas was a member of the board. A former congressman from Arizona, Douglas had served as head of the Budget during Franklin Roosevelt's first term, but resigned to protest Roosevelt's deficit spending. Still active in politics in the 1940s, he was named ambassador to the United Kingdom in 1947. In a letter to John D. Rockefeller 3rd, Junior noted that it was generally his preference that men who accepted national appointments resign from the board "lest they, or the board, be embarrassed by the relationship." In Douglas's case, Junior hoped that if Douglas resigned it would be with the understanding that, when he returned to private life, he might return to the board. And under this informal rule, Douglas did return to the board in the 1950s, as did a number of other trustees who served in public office over the years.

Disappointed with Taft's decision, Junior continued to recruit new trustees. In January 1916, the board welcomed Harry Emerson Fosdick, a popular Baptist minister from Montclair, New Jersey, and brother to Rockefeller advisor Raymond B. Fosdick. The board also recruited Martin

Former U.S. President William Howard Taft was an attractive potential board member in 1915. Taft worried that if he was on the Rockefeller Foundation board, the public would believe his views were influenced by the Rockefellers. Ultimately, he turned down the board's request. (Library of Congress, Prints & Photographs.)

A. Ryerson, a Harvard-educated lawyer from Chicago whose father had been a lumber magnate, and who was a patron of a number of cultural institutions, including the University of Chicago. The board then elected Frederick Strauss, the first Jewish member. A graduate of the College of the City of New York, Strauss and his brother Albert were partners in the investment banking firm of J. & W. Seligman & Co. In 1917, after the aging Eliot left the board, several new trustees were added: Wallace Buttrick, the head of the General Education Board; Charles Evans Hughes, the Republican candidate who ran against Woodrow Wilson for president in the 1916 election; and Julius Rosenwald, the man who built Sears, Roebuck into a commercial giant and founded the Rosenwald Fund. In this way, Junior refashioned the Rockefeller Foundation's board so that it would win the public's respect and trust.

George Vincent became president of the Rockefeller Foundation in 1917. Well-regarded as a public speaker, Vincent was recruited from his position as president of the University of Minnesota to help build public support for the Rockefeller Foundation's work. (Rockefeller Archive Center.)

THE ROLE OF THE BOARD, THE DONOR, AND THE CHIEF EXECUTIVE

As the Rockefeller Foundation and the Carnegie Corporation developed the practices of modern philanthropy in the early twentieth century, the role of a board and its relationship to the everyday work of a foundation was far from clear. In part this reflected differences in the character of the founder. "Carnegie regarded the trustees as working executives," observes historian Robert Kohler. He paid them a salary, and he dominated board discussions the way an executive might oversee his staff. As a result, in the early years, the Carnegie Corporation "was more like an old-fashioned family charity than a modern foundation." Although some board members felt the institution would do better with professional management, these voices were not able to shape the institution until after Carnegie's death in August 1919.

At the Rockefeller Foundation, the relationship of the founder and his family to the board was quite different. Senior refused to take an active role. Junior, who acted in the

1933
China's National Agricultural Research Bureau established. The Rockefeller Foundation provides grants to support scientific research and farm demonstration programs in Nanking related to insect control. (Rockefeller Archive Center.)

TIMELINE

© UNDERWOOD & UNDERWOOD
STUDIOS, N. Y.

role of the founder, was elected president and chairman of the board. But he was far more deferential to the expertise of his fellow board members and to the proper role of the staff. Jerome Greene as secretary (effectively chief executive) ran the Foundation's day-to-day business. At Carnegie, according to Robert Kohler, "there was no one comparable to Jerome Greene; the executive committee [of the board] made policy and ruled on applications."

To further distance the Foundation's day-to-day management from the family after the Walsh Commission hearings, the Foundation's offices were moved from 26 Broadway to 61 Broadway, where the General Education Board was headquartered. Junior relinquished the role of president, but remained as chairman. Jerome Greene saw this as a natural evolution. He believed that individuals long associated with the Rockefellers' personal philanthropy would gradually give way to new trustees who would understand "the changing conditions and needs of future generations."

Unfortunately for Greene, these moves resulted in the appointment of a president who replaced him as the administrative head of the Rockefeller Foundation. Seeking someone with a national reputation as a public speaker who could defend the Foundation to a suspicious electorate and politicians, Junior and the other trustees chose George Vincent, the president of the University of Minnesota, to lead the Foundation. Greene resigned as secretary and from the board.

The multiple charitable institutions created by John D. Rockefeller (General Education Board, Rockefeller Institute, etc.) created board problems that Vincent soon recognized. In an effort to coordinate the work of their various charities, Senior and Junior had often asked board members to serve on multiple boards. Charles Eliot had felt this was a mistake because it limited the number of people with good ideas participating in the governance of these institutions. In an era still concerned with the idea of secret trusts, Vincent echoed Eliot's concerns and also suggested that the Foundation should be careful to avoid arousing public criticism of a "combine" in the philanthropic sector. Vincent would find other challenges in working with the board.

The Capacity of the Board

In common with the directors of most philanthropic organizations, presidents of the Rockefeller Foundation struggled early on to gain the attention of busy board members, to get them to focus on critical decisions, and to balance the need to inform with the duty to avoid overwhelming them. George Vincent noted in 1925 that "It is difficult to interest the trustees in somewhat complicated technical proposals presented in voluminous agenda which must be acted upon within a few hours." Often, he felt the board's decisions were perfunctory. "There is little time for discussion, almost no opportunity for individual trustees to make suggestions, etc." Vincent worried the board was too dependent on the staff for an evaluation of the effectiveness of the Foundation's programs. He suggested that the board might consider occasional independent audits, but conceded that each of these methods had strengths and weaknesses.

Raymond B. Fosdick played an enormous part in shaping the Rockefeller Foundation. After becoming a close advisor to John D. Rockefeller Jr. in the 1910s, he joined the Foundation's board of trustees in 1921 and orchestrated the reorganization of 1928. He became president in 1936 and served until his retirement in 1948. In retirement, Fosdick wrote and published a history of the Foundation and a biography of John D. Rockefeller Jr. (Rockefeller Archives Center.)

Raymond Fosdick, one of Junior's closest advisors, solicited opinions in the following year on the structure of the Foundation and the administrative operations. Some board members expressed frustration with their role. David L. Edsall, dean of the Harvard University Medical School, who served as a member of the International Health Board, felt that the staff over-prepared for meetings and usually framed their recommendations very specifically. Moreover, in an effort to keep the board materials from becoming unwieldy, arguments were "very succinctly stated." As a result, "The members of the Board come unprepared to reach judgments about most of the things and they therefore avoid giving judgments or opinions." Edsall suggested that certain members could be designated as experts in certain subject areas and deferred to for comment when these issues came up. He acknowledged that if the board took more responsibility it would mean more work, and he recognized that some board members might resist being asked to do this additional work. But in his view, with board membership came responsibility.

Edsall's comments were echoed by the colorful William Allen White, editor and owner of the *Emporia Gazette* in Kansas. "I have felt uneasy and a bit unhappy now and then about my connection with the Rockefeller Board," White confessed to Raymond Fosdick, "chiefly because I feel so ignorant about many matters." He sometimes felt that the board seemed "to be a group of 'yes yes' men." White conceded that he did not know how to fix the situation. "I try to read the documents that come to me, but in the end I have a rather sketchy knowledge of things." He wondered if board meetings could be held more frequently and for longer periods of time so that, instead of an "advisory relation," the board would have more of a "legislative relation" to the work of the Foundation.

Jerome Greene's brother Roger, who was head of the Rockefeller Foundation's China Medical Board, probably did not have Edsall or White in mind when he complained to Fosdick that board members seemed "impatient to get on with the business and get away." Yet he too conceded that it was difficult "to imagine how any board of trustees can have great interest in such a mass of detail as is submitted to the Foundation meetings." Greene proposed strengthening the executive committee of the board to empower it to make most of the financial decisions, "leaving the trustees free to discuss general policies in a leisurely way and to take action on a few matters of great importance, especially those involving new principles." This was a proposal that would recur many times in the history of the board. Unfortunately, it risked marginalizing trustees who were not on the

The offices of John D. Rockefeller Jr. on the 14th floor at 26 Broadway were frequently used for meetings of the Rockefeller Foundation's executive committee. (Rockefeller Archive Center.)

Chapter Four: Board

executive committee. Greene felt board members could not have it both ways. If they were not willing to delegate these powers to the executive committee, then they should be willing to meet at least every month (except in the summer) "in order to keep in closer touch with the work and to dispose of business in a less hurried manner as it comes up during the year."

Rockefeller Foundation President George Vincent felt that the question focused inevitably on the kind of people who served on the board. On one hand, board members who were well known to the public and could "command confidence" were generally "too busy to give more than very general and largely uncritical consideration to business." As a result, "the officers are likely to have very much their own way." On the other hand, if the organization chose "younger men or persons with leisure," they might "offer little assurance to the public." Vincent also noted that experts were very useful at times, "but too many of them might easily make for professional bias and inflexibility."

For many years, the Rockefeller Foundation board did rely heavily on the executive committee, which was dominated by Rockefeller office insiders. This reliance raised a continuing issue about the relationship of the donor and his family to the policies of the Foundation.

Autonomy and Family

Nearly two decades after the founding of the Rockefeller Foundation, the board still struggled with its relationship to the founder and his family. In reality, governance and financial management (see chapter XI on Perpetuity) were closely tied to John D. Rockefeller Jr. and the family offices. Junior continued to serve as chairman of the board. In December 1931, his eldest son, John D. Rockefeller 3rd, joined the board as well. Meanwhile, two of the most influential members of the inner circle—attorneys Raymond B. Fosdick and Thomas Debevoise—exerted enormous influence because of their close association to Junior.

Roger and Jerome Greene (who had rejoined the Rockefeller Foundation board in 1928) felt that the influence of Junior and his staff was stifling the Foundation and the work of other Rockefeller philanthropies, including the China Medical Board. Roger complained when John D. Rockefeller 3rd was appointed to the CMB and became its secretary as well as a member of its finance committee. Roger felt that the younger Rockefeller (who was twenty-five at the time) sought to have a voice on the board that was not commensurate with his experience. Tensions between the two of them, and the support that the younger Rockefeller received from Fosdick and other members of the Rockefeller office, led Greene to criticize the governance of the CMB and all of the Rockefeller philanthropies, which he believed were not truly independent of the family. In a letter to Jerome, Roger suggested that it was inappropriate "to have on the Board men whose incomes are largely dependent on the Rockefeller family such as [Raymond] Fosdick and [Arthur] Woods." Escalating tensions led Junior to decide, in collaboration with Fosdick, that it was time for Greene to go.

In the aftermath of his brother's dismissal, Jerome Greene expressed his concerns to Junior. He noted that despite the supposed authority of the board, "vital matters tended to gravitate to a small group accessible to the office of the Foundation, chiefly Mr. Rockefeller, Mr. Fosdick, Mr. Debevoise, and perhaps the President of the Foundation." According to Fosdick's biographer Daryl Revoldt, this group could exercise what Greene called "in effect a Rockefeller edict." This practice undermined the autonomy of the institution. Never shy, Jerome Greene presented these arguments to Junior in a meeting on November 16, 1934. He also offered the same argument to Debevoise. But Greene was unable to persuade Junior, Fosdick, or Debevoise that things should change.

Through the Depression years, Greene continued to press his concerns. In October 1935, following the resignation of Max

Chapter Four: Board

7249

Trustees of the Peking Union Medical College (PUMC) at the time of the dedication in October 1921, including William H. Welch, Richard M. Pearce, George Vincent, John D. Rockefeller Jr., and Roger Greene. As head of the PUMC in the late 1920s, Roger Greene increasingly clashed with the Foundation's leadership in New York. (Rockefeller Archive Center.)

Mason as president, Greene wrote a "strictly confidential" memorandum articulating his continuing concerns regarding the role of the trustees. Greene noted that "Mr. Rockefeller has divested himself and his family from the ownership and control of large funds and entrusted them to the ownership and control of corporations created by the State and responsible in a real sense, therefore, to the public. Only on this ground do the funds of the Rockefeller Boards enjoy exemption from taxation—an exemption that needs no defense in principle because the funds are under a quasi-public control, are applied exclusively to public uses and are free from any element of private profit." Greene noted that it was "natural and proper" that, in the beginning, the boards of these new corporations were made up of people chosen and trusted by the founder. "He was but perfecting the organization of a work that had won well-nigh universal admiration and approval." But twenty-two years later, Greene wondered whether the trustees were "sufficiently alive to their responsibility to the public" to exercise independent control of the Foundation.

Greene believed the answer was "no." "A trusteeship in the Rockefeller Foundation," he wrote, "ought to be recognized as one of the gravest responsibilities to be found in civic life." Trustees should be willing to accept the sacrifices demanded of the position, even if that meant more frequent meetings of the board. Unfortunately, trustees too often left real decision-making to "a few members of the Board and to an office organization still closely identified with the Founder's family."

Greene was quick to say that he was not suggesting that Junior or his son, John D. Rockefeller 3rd, were trying to hold on to control. Indeed, it had been their vision from the beginning to devolve this responsibility. However, "in the absence of a more lively demonstration by trustees of a vital and responsible concern for the welfare of the Foundation, the influence and control naturally gravitate to those who feel most strongly." As a result, the trustees and the institution had not only failed to move towards greater independence, but were actually moving in the opposite direction. "The fact is that it [the staff of the Foundation] is really under the control, direct or indirect, of Mr. Rockefeller—direct, and quite properly so, through his chairmanship of the Board, for which his competence is beyond question; indirect through his son and through the influence of Trustees in his employ whose contact with the staff is closer than is that of other Trustees, or even Mr. Rockefeller, Jr. himself."

Greene was also concerned about the fact that the Foundation had moved from 61 Broadway back to the floor below Junior at 26 Broadway. He was equally disconcerted by the planned move to Rockefeller Center made "without a real decision of the Trustees." In leveling this criticism, Greene noted that the executive committee, often chosen according to which trustees were readily available in New York, tended to be made up of "persons identified with Mr. Rockefeller's office or salaried officers of one or more of the Boards." These participants were joined by officers of the corporations, many of whom were members of the Rockefeller office staff, including the treasurer, comptroller, counsel, assistant counsel, directors of divisions, and some of their assistants. "More than once," Greene said, he "had the experience of sitting in meetings of one of the Executive Committees as the only 'outside' Trustee." Greene warned that if the family and the trustees continued in this way, they did so at their own peril.

Greene offered a series of recommendations: relocate the offices away from the family; disallow anyone who received a salary from any of the Rockefeller boards or the Rockefeller office from serving as a member of the executive committee of the Foundation; disallow anyone who served as counsel to the Rockefellers from also serving as counsel to the Foundation; avoid having Rockefeller intermediaries interact with Foundation staff on behalf of the chairman (Junior); and make the finance committee "entirely independent of Mr. Rockefeller's office." He also suggested that the committee should have the services of a competent and independent treasurer.

Junior appeared to take Greene's criticisms to heart. As chairman he empowered a committee of three—John W. Davis, a lawyer and the Democratic candidate for president in 1924; E.M. Hopkins, president of Dartmouth College; and medical scientist George H. Whipple—to review the situation. Several weeks later, Junior reported to his father that the Davis Committee helped diffuse Greene's frustrations and generally affirmed the benefits of the Foundation's close relationship with the Rockefeller family offices.

But the committee was not as light-handed as Junior seemed to suggest to his father. Although they were reluctant to intervene in the day-to-day involvement of Fosdick, Debevoise, and other Rockefeller insiders, the committee expressed strong support for Greene's idea that the board needed to step up to its responsibilities. The committee seemed to believe this should begin with a stronger board and a more vigorous selection of trustees. The current system, they said, was "inadequate to elicit the full consideration of the Board." The committee recommended that the full board act as a nominating committee, that names be provided to all board members at least fifteen days in advance of the board meeting, and that board members provide a written ballot indicating their preferences. The committee proposed that in nominating new members the board seek geographical diversity, looking for representatives from all the major sections of the country. Board members should also reflect a diversity of expertise that mirrored the various lines of activity represented by the divisions of the Foundation. The committee further recommended that the board increase from two to three the number of meetings per year, to allow more time for discussion, and that this third meeting should be devoted entirely to policy and program. The committee asked that the board receive a list of grant applications rejected by the staff, as well as those recommended for approval.

The board's assertion of authority took time and was resolved over several years. A major step forward came in 1936, when Fosdick became president of the Rockefeller Foundation, clarifying his role and making him responsible for communications between the board and the staff. The power of the outside members of the board was also enhanced as Junior approached his sixty-fifth birthday in 1940, which meant retirement under the board's existing rules.

Junior's retirement from the board marked an important transition. No one else had served as chairman. Walter Stewart, a prominent economist who had become the director of the Institute of Advanced Study at Princeton University, succeeded him with Junior's blessing. "No trustee has taken greater interest in the Foundation than Mr. Stewart," Junior wrote. "No trustee has given more generously of his time, thought and effort to its work."

For a moment, however, the Rockefellers had hesitated. John D. Rockefeller 3rd had asked Debevoise whether the board should think about making an exception to the mandatory retirement age for the son of the founder. Debevoise did not think this was a good idea. Some members of the public remained concerned that donors like the Rockefellers continued to manipulate corporate control through the agency of the

1937
To enable fundamental research in physics, new grants from the Division of Natural Sciences support the construction of accelerators or "atom-smashers."
(Rockefeller Archive Center.)

Chapter Four: Board

philanthropic institutions they created. In 1937, Debevoise had suggested that "This talk has increased very much in the past year or so and it may sooner or later result in an investigation." If such an investigation was launched, "the Rockefeller Funds will be among the first questioned." Debevoise was confident that neither John D. Rockefeller nor his son had used any of the philanthropies as a way to exert corporate control. However, as he pointed out to John D. Rockefeller 3rd, "your father's connections with the Funds, the offices he has held, the services that have been gratuitously furnished by his office for the benefit of the Funds and every other little thing that a public investigator appealing to popular prejudice can find will be emphasized and exaggerated without any regard to the fundamental facts." Changing the retirement rules to allow Junior to remain on the board would be a negative in the public eye. Applying the same rule to the son of the founder that had been used to retire Justice Charles Evans Hughes, Frederick Strauss, Yale President James Angell, and Dr. Simon Flexner would send a powerful message about the autonomy of the Foundation.

The Rockefellers saw the wisdom in Debevoise's perspective. The lawyer, however, suggested a compromise. The board invited Junior to continue to attend board meetings as chairman emeritus and to join in the discussion, recognizing that he would not be able to vote. This courtesy was then extended to subsequent chairmen emeriti. Junior continued to sit with the board through most of the rest of the decade.

Some sign of Junior's ambivalence over letting go is also evident in a letter he wrote to Raymond Fosdick in 1943. Since the beginning of the Foundation, he noted, two members of the Rockefeller family had always served on the board: Senior and Junior in the earliest days (though Senior never attended a meeting), and then Junior and his son John D. Rockefeller 3rd. With Junior's departure, he wondered if the board might consider nominating Nelson Rockefeller. "He would, of course, regard John as the ranking family representative and would work with him if elected," Junior offered. Fosdick embraced the suggestion and Nelson welcomed the idea, but it did not happen.

The presence of one or more Rockefellers on the board clearly made a difference. Fosdick offered more than flattery or personal affection in 1948 when he wrote to Junior that "for me something went out of the life of the Foundation when you left as Chairman of the Board. It has never been quite the same; somehow or other the job has not been quite so satisfying or rewarding." Years later, Waldemar Nielsen would suggest that John D. Rockefeller 3rd's chairmanship of the Foundation in the 1950s and 1960s had played a key role in sustaining the Foundation's vitality.

A Representative Board

T he interrogations of the Walsh Commission in 1915 had led Junior, Charles Eliot, Jerome Greene and others to recognize the importance of the board in earning the public's trust and confidence. Over the years, the trustees increasingly saw that keeping that trust depended on having a board that was representative of the nation, at first, and then of the global community.

In the early days, building a representative board meant geographic and religious diversity as well as recruiting a balanced set of skills and expertise. Through the first two decades, most trustees came from either the Northeast or the Chicago area. When Ray Lyman Wilbur, the president of Stanford University, was elected in 1922, the board gained a West Coast member, but a multi-day transcontinental train trip made it difficult for Wilbur to attend the board's quarterly meetings. When James Angell retired from the board in 1936, he reminded Junior of the importance of geographic diversity, suggesting the board should look for "outstanding individuals who represent the greatest diversity of outlook on the basic problems of humanity." But the issue remained a challenge. In 1940, the board had one member from the Midwest, two from the Far West and one from the South, while fourteen others came from Middle Atlantic states and two were from New England. Fosdick wrote to William Allen White of Kansas, who was retiring from the board, that he hoped White would be able to suggest a replacement. "Here in the East," he said, "I get the impression that we are rather out of touch with the country as a whole, and we need some elements on our Board of Trustees who will help to interpret to us the United States that lies west of the Allegheny Mountains." This issue of geographic diversity within the United States would continue for decades, until the board began to see the need for broad international representation.

Given the strong Baptist and Puritan origins of the Rockefellers and many of their associates, it is interesting to note that two of the earliest board members, Frederick Strauss and Julius Rosenwald, were Jewish. And when it came time to nominate two new trustees in 1938, John D. Rockefeller 3rd noted that *New York Times* publisher Arthur Sulzberger "would make a real contribution to the Board" because of the quality of his intellect and his Jewish faith. It took longer for Catholics to join the board, although by the late 1940s, according to Junior, several Catholics had been "splendid" members. The board welcomed Father Theodore Hesburgh to the board in 1961, the president of the University of Notre

Dame. Hesburgh would become the board's chair in 1977, serving until 1982.

Professionally, the board over many decades reflected the Foundation's emphasis on science and research, particularly in the context of higher education. In 1934, for example, board member George H. Whipple, a medical researcher, won the Nobel Prize for his work on anemia. By 1946, the board included two doctors, two newspapermen, three college presidents, one representative of agriculture, one of the humanities, with the rest of the nineteen members coming from business and the law.

Ray Lyman Wilbur was president of Stanford University when he was elected to the board in 1922. Wilbur's presence provided some geographic diversity to a group that came primarily from New York and the Northeast. (Library of Congress, Prints & Photographs.)

Diplomat and political scientist Ralph Bunche joined
the Rockefeller Foundation board in 1955. Pictured
at this 1963 board meeting, Bunche (seated at end
of table) was the first person of color to serve on
the board and helped sharpen the organization's
interest in Africa as well as equal opportunity in
the United States. (Rockefeller Archive Center.)

Chapter Four: Board

The board also tended to balance itself between academics and men of affairs. In 1940, when four seats came open because of retirements, the split was about even. Warren Weaver, the head of the Natural Science program, urged Raymond Fosdick to ensure that scientists were on the board, though he was quick to write that they should not be seen as "special representatives of and special pleaders for the NS [Natural Sciences] division."

Given its strong international approach, it is surprising that the Foundation did not recruit a non-U.S. citizen in the early years. Remembering the challenges of the Charter fight and the Walsh hearings, however, the Foundation's leaders were extremely sensitive to the idea that the Foundation was legally an American institution. In 1941, Fosdick seems to have been interested in having a board member who understood South America. And the following year, when names were suggested for board candidates, a prominent Canadian came to the fore, but board member John Foster Dulles said he doubted that the board would be interested in someone who was not a citizen of the United States. These doubts were apparently removed by 1960. That year, Foundation president Dean Rusk put forward the name of Sir Oliver S. Franks, the former British ambassador to the United States and the chairman of Lloyds Bank Limited of London. "It is my thought that his name might be considered solely as an individual," Rusk wrote, "and that we would not thereby say to ourselves that we would try to have any foreign country represented as such or that his election would force us to take other foreign nationals. It is my impression that his qualities are such that it would be fully understood that we had elected him as an individual." Franks's election to the Rockefeller Foundation board was followed in 1967 by the selection of Alberto Lleras Camargo, the former president of Colombia. Lleras Camargo was a distinguished journalist and the first former head of state to serve as a trustee. He was also the first Hispanic.

Given the importance of labor issues at the time the Foundation was created, it is not surprising that from time to time the board wondered whether it should elect someone who could speak to labor's issues. Board members were quick to say that they did not want someone who would have to "speak for Labor" on the board; they wanted someone who understood "Labor's point of view." This desire would lead to the election of Lane Kirkland, the Secretary-Treasurer of the AFL-CIO as a trustee. The board also felt that it needed a representative from the media. William Allen White, a famous author and editor from Kansas, was the first. In the 1940s and early 1950s, Douglas Freeman (Richmond, VA) and Arthur Hays Sulzberger, publisher of the *New York Times*, filled that role. In later years, board members from the press included Frank Stanton, Bill Moyers and Frances Fitzgerald.

In the 1950s, the growing influence of the civil rights movement in the United States compelled trustees to think again about what constituted a representative board. Several times the name of Ralph Bunche appeared on the list. Bunche had been awarded the Nobel Peace Prize in 1950 for brokering the 1949 Armistice Agreements between the Arabs and the Israelis. In December 1954, the board unanimously voted to nominate Bunche. When he accepted and became a trustee, he was the first person of color to serve on the board. Perhaps just as importantly, he was the first trustee to have grown up in poverty.

Bunche's election was not without controversy. In 1954, he had also received the Theodore Roosevelt Medal for Distinguished Service. Archibald Roosevelt, the fifth child of President Theodore Roosevelt, protested the award. Well-known as a militant conservative and anti-communist, Roosevelt wrote and published a 44-page treatise attacking Bunche for his communist sympathies. Roosevelt sent the treatise to all of the members of the Foundation's board. Sulzberger forwarded his copy to John D. Rockefeller 3rd with a note: "In view of our action in electing Dr. Bunche a trustee—an action, incidentally, of which I'm very proud—I thought it nonetheless advisable to pass the attached on to you which I received from Archie Roosevelt." It took more than a decade for the Foundation to nominate another African American trustee. In 1967, Whitney M. Young Jr., the executive director of the National Urban League since 1961, joined the board and became the second African American member.

In 1982, Clifton R. Wharton Jr. was elected chairman of the Foundation. The son of the first African American to pass the Foreign Service examination, Wharton had received a Ph.D. in economics from the University of Chicago. As a staffer with the Agriculture Development Council, he worked with the Rockefeller Foundation in Southeast Asia early in his career. At the time he joined the Rockefeller board in 1970, he was the newly appointed president of Michigan State University. During his tenure, he became Chancellor of the State University of New York.

For years trustees had discussed the possibility of appointing a woman to the board. From time to time the names of presidents of some of the nation's leading women's colleges—Bryn Mawr, Vassar—surfaced, but no woman was appointed. Following World War II, John D. Rockefeller 3rd asked Raymond Fosdick whether the issue should be considered, noting that "it would not appear that the matter has ever been officially discussed." It is unclear whether any discussion of this proposal took place, but no woman joined the board in the next quarter century. Rockefeller, however, did not forget the issue. As chairman in 1959, for example, when he was developing lists of possible nominees to the board, he suggested Aline B. Saarinen, the associate editor and art critic for the *New York Times*. The same year, Mary L. Bunting, the president of Radcliffe College, and Mrs. John G. Lee, the former president of the League of Women Voters, also appeared on a list of potential nominees. Bunting's name was suggested following

> "Clearly there are outstanding women who could add substantially to the deliberations of the board."
> *J. George Harrar, 1969*

a discussion in which several trustees recommended that a woman should be considered for the board. In the late 1960s, the board nearly elected Howard University law professor Patricia Roberts Harris, but chose broadcaster Bill Moyers instead. By 1969, however, both John D. Rockefeller 3rd and Foundation President J. George Harrar recognized that the time had come. "Clearly there are outstanding women who could add substantially to the deliberations of the Board," Harrar wrote to John D. Rockefeller 3rd. Rockefeller agreed. On the eve of his retirement from the board in 1970, he raised the issue again. This time, Harrar passed the recommendation on to the board's nominating committee.

Dr. Mathilde Krim was a geneticist specializing in cytogenetics and tumor-inducing viruses at the Sloan-Kettering Institute for Cancer Research. Born in Italy, she earned her Ph.D. at the University of Geneva, was on the staff of the Weizmann Institute of Science, then joined the Division of Virus Research at Cornell Medical College in 1959. She had moved to Sloan-Kettering in 1962. In addition to her leading research in the fields of cytogenetics and tumor-inducing viruses, Krim was active in the Urban League and the African American Institute. Krim joined the board in 1971 with enthusiasm. She was followed by several other women, and, in 1981, Eleanor Holmes Norton, a senior fellow at the Urban Institute and former chair of the Federal Equal Employment Opportunity Commission, joined the board as the first woman of color.

Mathilde Krim was the first woman elected to the Rockefeller Foundation Board of Trustees. With a Ph.D. from the University of Geneva, Krim was a geneticist at the Sloan-Kettering Institute for Cancer Research when she joined the board in 1971. (Rockefeller Archive Center.)

The Foundation's move to diversify by race and ethnicity was well ahead of the majority of foundations in the United States, but about on par with its peers among the largest foundations. A 1980 study by the Council on Foundations, for example, found that of 294 foundations surveyed, 96 percent of trustees were white and 79 percent were male. Most of the women who served as trustees served on the boards of smaller foundations. Among the largest foundations (over $100 million in assets), only 12 percent of the trustees were women. At the Rockefeller Foundation, there were three women among twenty-three trustees.

Alice Ilchman's election as chair of the Rockefeller Foundation in 1995 marked several milestones in the Foundation's history. She was not only the first woman to serve as chair, but the first chair who had trained professionally in the field of development, having received her Ph.D. from the London School of Economics in 1960 with a dissertation focused on agricultural planning in India. Her resume reflected both scholarship and administrative experience in academia, as well as service in the U.S. Information Agency (USIA) and the Department of State before becoming president of Sarah Lawrence College in 1981.

Diversity took on new meaning in the 1980s as the Foundation sought to internationalize the board. Despite the fact that five previous members of the Board had been non-Americans, the board struggled with the concept. In the early 1990s, however, a significant transition began. Alvaro Umaña, an environmental scientist and former minister for Energy and Environment in Costa Rica, brought a Central American perspective. Ela R. Bhatt, the general secretary of the Self Employed Women's Association, brought an intimate knowledge of the women, microfinance and entrepreneurship in India. By 1993, Foundation president Peter Goldmark declared that "We have at last breached the international barrier and ... we have good diversity in ethnic, gender, geographic dimensions, and a terrific sense of collegiality and involvement." The trend continued over the next decade. In 1999, Mamphela Ramphele, the vice chancellor of the University of Cape Town, became the first African to join the board. Vo Tong Xuan, the rector of An Giang University in Vietnam, was elected in 2002. By 2003, members from the developing world accounted for 28 percent of the board's makeup.

From Advisors to Professional Trustees

As it evolved over a century, the culture of the Rockefeller Foundation board of trustees was not only shaped by the relationship with the Rockefeller family, the staff, and the public at large, it was also heavily influenced by the evolution of its own standards of practice. An informal process of identifying and nominating prospective trustees, and then the terms of trustees and the chair, became increasingly formal. These innovations sometimes led and sometimes followed the development of the field of philanthropy, but they played a critical role in shaping the governance of the Foundation.

During the early years, the board developed a number of rules that would be handed down to their successors. The Foundation paid for travel expenses related to meetings, but the trustees were not paid for their service. When conflicts of interest arose—a potential grant to a university whose president served on the Foundation's board, for example—the custom developed that the trustee would step out of the meeting during the discussion.

As self-perpetuating entities, boards face a major challenge in deciding how long a member should serve. In 1929, trustee Ray Lyman Wilbur suggested and the board adopted a mandatory retirement age of sixty-five. Until the 1970s, age was the only limit on trustee tenure. Many trustees served for more than a decade. Junior and his son were each on the board for more than three decades. In 1969, however, George Harrar recommended some changes. Board members would be elected for three-year terms, with a virtually automatic renewal for a second three-year term. Board members could continue for a third three-year term, but the nominating committee was charged with making this re-nomination contingent on attendance and board service. "The contribution of Trustees who cannot undertake any activities beyond attendance at full board meetings may largely be fulfilled during the first two terms." The board adopted these rules in 1970, then revised them in 1982 to limit membership to two five-year terms. At that time, only one other foundation among the largest thirty-five had both a mandatory retirement age and a limit on the number of terms that a trustee could serve.

Throughout the history of the Foundation, the board has also tried different approaches to its overall size and the frequency of its meetings. After he became president of the Foundation, John Knowles expanded the role of the board in the mid-1970s. The number of board meetings was increased from two to four [cut back to three in 1978]. To deepen the board's understanding of the Foundation's work, trustee-staff review committees were created to stimulate dialogue between the officers and the trustees. Knowles also revised the ways in which information was presented to the board, and revived the practice of encouraging board members to visit project and field stations abroad.

By the early 1980s, however, there was a sense that things weren't working. With twenty-four members in 1982, the board was too big, according to some. [It may have been the largest board among private foundations with assets over $10 million]. With more than twenty members, discussions were too formal. After extended debate, the board set a target of not fewer than fifteen members, but fewer than twenty-five.

One board member in particular played a key role in pushing for reforms that would formalize expectations and procedures. Scion of the founder of the Dayton-Hudson department store in Minneapolis, Kenneth Dayton was CEO of the firm when he joined the Rockefeller Foundation board in 1977. A powerful advocate for ethical board reform within the corporate and nonprofit worlds, Dayton pushed for a number of changes at the Rockefeller Foundation, including a definite limit on the chairman's tenure. "No public institution with a public purpose should be too closely tied to one individual, no matter how good he/she may be," Dayton suggested in a paper on the governance of philanthropic institutions. He also advocated strengthening conflict-of-interest rules, including the board's established custom for members to recuse themselves from discussions of grants for institutions they had an interest in. He recommended that board members rotate between committees so that they had the opportunity to serve on more than one committee during their tenure on the board.

Eleanor Holmes Norton, as the former chair of the U.S. Equal Opportunity Commission, increased awareness of issues related to women and poverty after she became a member of the Rockefeller Foundation board in 1981. (Rockefeller Archive Center.)

Eleanor Holmes Norton and Dayton both pushed for a trustee search process that relied less on board members' personal knowledge of potential candidates. Dayton and fellow board member Victor Palmieri suggested engaging a professional search firm. At the time, most private foundations engaged in a relatively ad hoc approach to trustee recruitment. Board members exchanged lists of personal recommendations. Staff researched these individuals and shared their research with the board. The president or board members vetted candidates that were high on the board's list to determine whether they would "fit" and whether they were willing to serve. This was true at the Ford Foundation, the Carnegie Corporation, the W.K. Kellogg Foundation, and the Andrew W. Mellon Foundation. Some institutions rejected the idea of using an outside search firm. Several people suggested the idea was gauche, if not "kooky." At least one board member said that if a board of the caliber of the Rockefeller Foundation was not able to identify prospective trustees, something was wrong. But Dayton's point was that the board needed to open its search process to candidates who might not fall within the networks of the existing board. That was the only way it could avoid shutting out other perspectives.

All of these reforms in the 1980s and 1990s helped to professionalize board practices. Many of these initiatives were at the forefront of changes taking place throughout the philanthropic sector. Though they had not been introduced by John D. Rockefeller Jr. and his associates in the 1910s, they built upon years of effort by the Foundation's leaders to fashion a board that would be broadly representative first of the United States, and eventually of the world in which the Foundation practiced. Over the course of these years, cultural prejudices that discriminated by race and gender had to be overcome. The long, slow process of balancing the influence of the donor and his family with that of outside board members had to be negotiated. And professional expectations for board service had to be developed and accepted by all the trustees. By the end of its first century, the Rockefeller Foundation board undoubtedly continued to struggle with many of the issues confronted by earlier trustees, but it was also the beneficiary of past crises and inspired reforms.

FINANCIAL STATEMENT

The statement of expenditures presented on the following page shows that the Commission expended a total of $157,731.08 during the eighteen months from July 1, 1913, to December 31, 1914. Of this amount $34,038.79 was devoted to administrative work; $3,108.15 being for property in the form of furniture and equipment, and $30,930.64 for current expenses. O[n] an annual basis this would represent approximately $20,000 for current expenses, of whic[h] about $5,000 represents expenditures for trave[l]ing purposes.

The $14,113.14 used for educational and i[n]formational work was devoted to the collecti[on] of material, and the preparation and display [of] exhibits by the Department of Surveys a[nd] Exhibits; the development of the library a[nd] the printing and distribution of publication[s].

The $109,579.15 used for the hookworm ca[m]paign in the field was expended partly ou[t of] special budgets adopted for work in for[eign] countries and partly directly out of the C[om]mission's central office budget. The latter [in]cluded items for the purchase of thymol, equipment, travel expenses of directors in g[?] to and in returning from the field, and salar[ies of] directors of field work up to the time these [were] charged to special budgets.

127

Fig. 17. Group of cases of uncinariasis, Church Mission Hospital, Cairo. About 300 such photographs were made

THE ROCKEFELLER FOUNDATION 1995 ANNUAL REPORT

CANDID WITH THE PUBLIC

To many people philanthropy is a private act. Tax deductions for charitable contributions, however, suggest that the public has a right to know how philanthropic dollars are used. As late as the 1960s, very few private foundations published annual reports. Fewer still shared their financial information.

The Rockefeller Foundation's first annual report, published in 1915, marked an important step in the evolution of modern philanthropy. The extensive document provided details on the Foundation's grantmaking as well as photographs from its programs around the world. It listed the names of all the trustees as well as the staff so that the public would know who was involved with the organization. The financial statement listed every security owned by the Foundation along with its book value.

To be sure, controversies surrounding the breakup of Standard Oil and the violent conflict between labor and management at the Rockefeller-owned Colorado Fuel and Iron Company played a role in the decision to publish all of this data. John D. Rockefeller Jr.'s experiences before Congress and the Commission on Industrial Relations in 1915 further convinced him that candor was important.

Over decades the Foundation's annual reports have evolved to keep pace with the culture and operations of the organization. Today, readers are more likely to access them online rather than read them in print. But they still serve as an important tool for engaging the public in the shared work of promoting the well-being of humankind.

PROGRAM

How should the program be organized?

B road missions empower boards to establish boundaries through programming, but also provide latitude to future generations to adapt to the changing needs of society. At any given time, however, foundations must focus their resources to be effective. Inevitably they have to ask, which problems are solvable and at what scale? Given the resources we have available, can we make a difference?

With its creation in 1913, the Rockefeller Foundation was at the forefront of "scientific" philanthropy. Focused on addressing the root causes of society's ills, scientific philanthropy embraced the systems approach to organization and the use of the scientific method to study a problem before developing possible solutions. Researchers launched field surveys to compile information on the scope of a problem—the incidence of hookworm in a community, numbers of patients in mental wards, or the prevalence of laboratories in medical schools. Programs were anchored in this research. Many foundations still take a systems approach when establishing their programs.

Relative to the size of the private and public sectors of the economy, foundations and philanthropy are small. To make change, most look for ways to leverage their investments by either catalyzing contributions from others (financial leverage) or igniting larger processes of social change (social leverage). This can be a delicate art. Finding points of leverage demands a sophisticated knowledge of the social systems that surround a given problem. Success or failure is often determined by the timing and quantity of resources employed. Too much investment can become a disincentive to others. Too little may mean a project or idea never gets off the ground.

Leverage is also possible when a concept or project is scalable, meaning it can easily grow without huge additional capital investments. In some cases, other organizations are able to replicate a new way of doing things—tracking disease, introducing new seeds, or offering vaccinations. In other situations, a project or program that proves successful in one community can be adopted by government to benefit a nation.

At its core, the idea of leverage depends on a theory of change. For the Rockefeller Foundation and many other philanthropic initiatives, the theory of change has been rooted in the transformative power of knowledge and education. Investing in the development of new knowledge, whether it is in basic science or human behavior, opens the door to innovation. New insights can lead to new ways of living or doing that solve problems. But knowledge alone is rarely transformative. Ideas need to spread. Figuring out how to develop and disseminate information and ideas isn't easy. Philanthropic organizations struggle with this critical issue every day. Fundamentally, it shapes their decisions about what they will and what they won't do with the limited resources they have available, just as it did in New York in 1913.

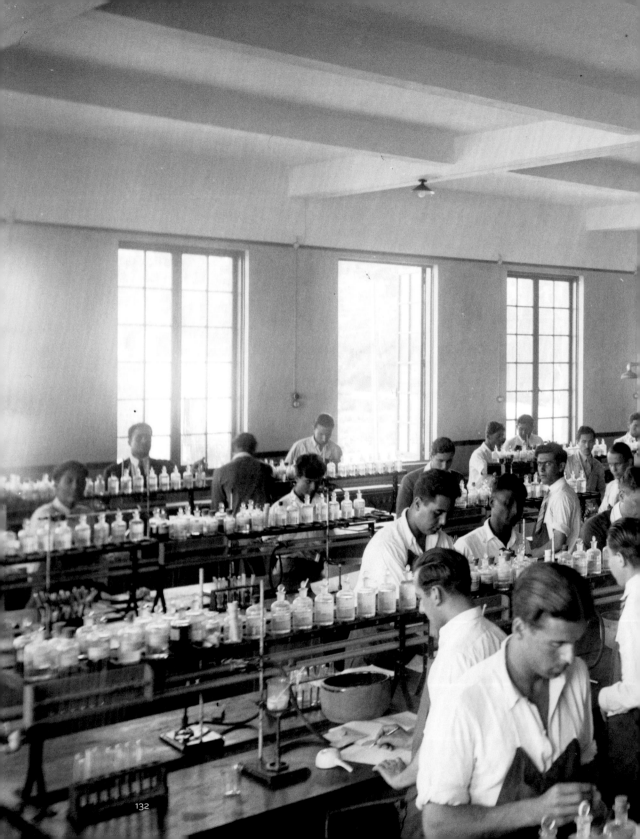

At the American University in Beirut, students studied chemistry in a new classroom building funded by the Rockefeller Foundation in the late 1920s. In its early years, the Foundation's program focused heavily on improving medical education, scientific research and public health. (Library of Congress, Prints & Photographs.)

In the early days of the
Rockefeller Foundation, trustees
often met in the Whitehall Club
on the thirtieth floor overlooking
New York harbor. (Library of
Congress, Prints & Photographs.)

PROGRAM

FLOOD WATERS RISE IN OHIO

On Easter Sunday, March 23, 1913, it began to rain across Ohio. Through the night and the next day it poured, water saturating fields, flowing into creeks, rushing downstream to swell the four rivers that converge at the city of Dayton. At midnight on Tuesday, March 25, the police activated warning sirens and alarms. By 5:30 in the morning, the water was streaming over the tops of levees and flooding downtown streets. Then the levees on the south side failed and a rush of water poured through the city. As residents fled for high ground, carting whatever valuables they could carry, buildings collapsed and houses were carried off. Meanwhile, gas mains broke. Explosions and fires filled the morning sky with an eerie light. By the time the floodwaters had receded, more than 360 people were dead and 65,000 displaced. Property damage was assessed at more than $100 million (more than $2 billion in 2012 dollars). Dayton bore the brunt of the flood, but all along the Ohio River and its tributaries, other communities suffered devastation. Appeals for help and relief went out across the nation. Charitable New Yorkers raised more than $400,000 within a matter of days to help feed and shelter families and begin the process of reconstruction. But the rebuilding would take years and millions of dollars in capital. The Young Men's Christian Association (YMCA) turned to the newly established Rockefeller Foundation for help.

COPYRIGHT 1900 BY DETROIT PHOTOGRAPHIC CO.

017552 WHITEHALL BUILDING, NEW YORK.

Barely six weeks had elapsed since the governor of New York had signed the Act creating the Foundation. In their first two meetings, the trustees had focused primarily on establishing the administrative structure of the organization. On July 1, 1913, the trustees gathered at the Whitehall Club on the thirtieth floor of the Whitehall Building, overlooking New York Harbor, and considered grant requests for the first time—including an appeal from the YMCA in Ohio to help rebuild and rehabilitate damaged YMCA buildings in Dayton and other communities in the Ohio River Valley.

Students and staff at the Peking Union Medical College. Medical science, medical education, and public health emerged as the primary fields of focus for the Rockefeller Foundation and its sister organizations in the 1910s and 1920s. (Rockefeller Archive Center.)

Rockefeller attorney and board member Starr Murphy didn't need to explain why the devastated communities in Ohio needed help, but he took the time to remark that, given the disaster, the YMCA could not tap local resources to pay for this work. As waiters in white coats served plates of food and a cool breeze blew in through the windows on a mild summer day, the request from Ohio undoubtedly made the men around the table uncomfortable. The devastation was enormous, one of the worst natural disasters in

American history. It was difficult to imagine the hardship in the Midwest, and tougher still to decide if this was the kind of work the Rockefeller Foundation should do.

The petitions from Ohio forced the trustees to wrestle with fundamental issues. How would they decide among many requests for funding? How would they prioritize? What would be their attitude in the face of crisis and grave human suffering? How would they balance the needs of the present against the good they might do over the long run?

As the discussion continued, Gates made the point that the Foundation could not afford to consider these kinds of requests for relief. Instead, "the Rockefeller Foundation should in general confine itself to projects of an important character, too large to be undertaken, or otherwise unlikely to be undertaken, by other agencies." With this determination, the board declined to provide money to the YMCAs of Ohio.

To give the board some kind of structure for giving, over the next several months Jerome Greene, the secretary and chief administrative officer, prepared a memorandum on principles and policies as a kind of distillation of the lessons learned by Rockefeller and his advisors over the course of many years of philanthropic practices:

- individual charity and relief was excluded;
- institutions and enterprises that were purely local were excluded, except those that might serve as models for other places and communities;
- grants should not be made without significant local matching contributions;
- grants should never be seen to be permanent and ongoing and should never exceed more than half of the organization's current budget;
- gifts should not be made in perpetuity (avoid restrictive endowments);
- grants should address root problems rather than ameliorate immediate suffering because the effects of these grants are more long lasting.

Greene's principles, as Fosdick later observed, formed a program only in the negative. They outlined what the Foundation would not do, but not what it would do. Over the next several years, the trustees worked to establish the basic framework for a program that would last in broad strokes for decades. But the staff and trustees were rarely comfortable with its contours. Over the next century, they would constantly revise it at the margins and occasionally make dramatic and sweeping changes as each generation learned from the past to innovate for the future.

Rockefeller Foundation relief efforts during World War I were designed to catalyze contributions from others. John D. Rockefeller Jr. personally helped promote community giving. (Rockefeller Archive Center.)

Rockefeller and his advisors were committed to a scientific approach to philanthropy. Their strategy was shaped by the pattern of Rockefeller's past giving, the exigencies of the moment, and their collective goals for the future. In 1913, that pattern suggested a certain framework—church missions, health and sanitation, and education. In this framework, the Rockefeller Foundation would establish quasi-independent operating entities that would focus on delivering services within specific communities.

Gates was clear about his program preferences. "Disease is the supreme ill of human life," he told the board, "and it is the main source of almost all other human ills—poverty, crime, ignorance, vice, inefficiency, hereditary taint, and many other evils." During the charter fight, Jerome Greene had made it clear to Congress that the Rockefeller Foundation would expand the hookworm campaign internationally, "not for altruistic motives merely but because no one country can be safe until all have been cleared of this pest." Thus, one of the board's first acts was to ask Wickliffe Rose, the director of the Rockefeller Sanitary Commission, to plan for the internationalization of the hookworm campaign. The board established the International Health Board to carry forward this work.

With the support of several other board members, Gates also pushed through a major initiative in China to create the Peking Union Medical College (PUMC). With its investments, the Foundation hoped the PUMC, modeled after Johns Hopkins University School of Medicine, would introduce science-based medicine to China. Over the next three decades, the Foundation would invest nearly $45 million in PUMC and other China projects. In constant dollars, this was the largest investment the Foundation made in any one project in its history.

While Gates focused on medicine and health, the trustees also considered establishing an Institute for Economic Research and explored major initiatives focusing on industrial relations and mental hygiene. In the aftermath of the Ludlow massacre in Colorado and the highly publicized hearings by the Commission on Industrial Relations, however, the board shied away from controversial subjects and followed Gates and Rose into the fields of medical education, public health, and medical science. In these arenas, the Foundation operated directly. In other programmatic areas, the Foundation favored grant-making to outside agencies that were not under the Foundation's control.

World War I brought human misery beyond imagination. John D. Rockefeller had challenged the Foundation's leaders to address the root causes of human misery rather than provide relief for current problems. Confronted

with the devastation of the war, and despite their resolution in the face of the Ohio floods, the trustees agreed to provide more than $22 million ($285 million in 2011 dollars) in aid to avoid mass starvation in Belgium and fight disease in France and other war-ravaged European nations. For five years, the war and its aftermath consumed much of the focus of the Foundation's activities.

In Brazil and other countries, nurses were critical to the Rockefeller Foundation's efforts to increase the capacity of health systems in various nations around the world. (Rockefeller Archive Center.)

Through the 1920s, the Foundation worked alongside sister Rockefeller philanthropies including the Rockefeller Institute for Medical Research, the General Education Board (GEB), the International Education Board (IEB), the China Medical Board (CMB) and the Laura Spelman Rockefeller Memorial (LSRM). Each of these organizations was separately incorporated with its own funds and trustees, but some trustees sat on multiple boards, and John D. Rockefeller Jr. served on all of them. The Rockefeller Institute studied disease in its New York laboratories. The GEB continued its support for the nation's leading universities and for education in the South, primarily for African Americans. The IEB worked to advance research and develop higher education abroad, particularly in Europe. The CMB oversaw the development of the Peking Union Medical College. Meanwhile, the LSRM, under the direction of Beardsley Ruml, worked in the fields of social science, the humanities and race relations. Within the Foundation, the International Health Board operated as a semi-autonomous entity. Sometimes it was hard for outsiders to distinguish the differences among these organizations. Internally, competing programs and ambiguous lines of authority created confusion.

In 1928, trustee Raymond Fosdick, with the advice and support of Rockefeller Senior and Junior and the cooperation of president George Vincent, facilitated a reorganization of some of the Rockefeller philanthropies. The LSRM became a part of the Rockefeller Foundation, and its assets and obligations were added to the Foundation's books. The China Medical Board was organized as an independent, self-perpetuating organization with its own board of trustees and ownership of the project's assets, including land and buildings in Peking, as well as endowment funds and annual appropriations to be given by the Rockefeller Foundation. In the new structure, the public health program would be under an International Health Division supervised by a group of seven scientific directors. Meanwhile, the natural science and humanities programs of the GEB and the IEB were moved to the Rockefeller Foundation. With this reorganization, the Foundation also made a fundamental shift in program.

With the creation of the World Health Organization and the establishment of the United Nations after World War II, the Rockefeller Foundation shifted its primary focus to food, nutrition, and development.

Advancement of Knowledge

With the consolidation, the program of the Foundation was reoriented around a key goal: advancing human knowledge. The International Health Division (IHD) continued its fight against hookworm, yellow fever, malaria, and other diseases in its laboratories in New York and in the field from Thailand to Nigeria. Meanwhile, under the new structure, the Foundation focused primarily on grantmaking in four broad arenas: medical sciences, natural sciences, social sciences, and the humanities. With these grantmaking activities, the Foundation worked closely with research institutions in the United States and Europe. Its grantees made spectacular contributions to the development of basic knowledge in physics and molecular biology. They also created treatments for disease, including penicillin. Some grantees received Nobel Prizes for their work.

Through the 1930s, the Foundation placed new emphasis on laboratory work while the world struggled with a global economic depression and the Foundation's officers nervously watched the rise of totalitarianism in Germany, Italy, Spain, the Soviet Union, and Japan. The IHD worked on malaria, influenza, typhus, syphilis, yaws, streptococcal infections, and other diseases. Among its many breakthroughs, the development of a vaccine for yellow fever, led by Max Theiler, would be recognized with the Nobel Prize in 1951.

The Foundation's other programs also focused heavily on research. Under director Warren Weaver, the Natural Sciences Division played a leading role in the emerging field of molecular biology. Rockefeller Foundation funding helped scientists build and use critical new tools including the ultra-centrifuge, the cyclotron, and powerful new telescopes to see into space. Meanwhile, in the social sciences, the Foundation invested in increasingly quantitative efforts to study business cycles and address the root causes of the economic depression.

The rise of totalitarianism and the onset of World War II, however, were profoundly disruptive to the Foundation's work. Many scholars and scientists working in Europe were forced to flee totalitarian regimes. Through its refugee scholars program, the Foundation helped a significant number of these researchers find new intellectual homes in the safety of Britain and the United States. National governments, focused on research and development that would help them win the war, recruited many of these scientists into war-related research. Under these changed circumstances, the Foundation re-evaluated its program. Raymond Fosdick even asked the officers whether the Foundation ought to suspend its major activities. Beyond the immediate question, Fosdick recognized that once the war was over, the world would be profoundly different. Though he and others at the Foundation could not foresee the details, they were already beginning to recognize the contours of the new landscape.

Agriculture, Education and Development

The program of the Rockefeller Foundation shifted dramatically after World War II to respond to major changes in the political and institutional environment in which the Foundation operated. On the one hand, the demise of the colonial system brought opportunities to engage directly with newly independent governments and peoples in what became known as the developing or Third world. The rise of the Cold War, however, sharply limited these opportunities to countries not aligned with the Soviet Union and China and cast geopolitical overtones on nearly all international initiatives. The establishment of the United Nations and the World Health Organization obviated the traditional role of the International Health Division. Increases in government spending in the United States for basic research in science—under the auspices of the National Science Foundation, the National Institutes of Health, and other government entities—forced the Rockefeller Foundation to rethink its role in basic research. A dramatic expansion of the philanthropic sector that included the emergence of the Ford Foundation as the world's richest private

Josephus Daniels (pictured above), the U.S. ambassador to Mexico, and John Ferrell of the Rockefeller Foundation talked several times in the 1930s about an effort to promote agricultural development in Mexico. These conversations came to fruition in 1943 when the Rockefeller Foundation launched an effort to help increase agricultural yields. (Library of Congress, Prints & Photographs.)

foundation forced the Rockefeller Foundation to shift from its prewar traditions of solo initiatives to focus more on collaboration and cooperation with other foundations and international agencies. Most of these changes played out over many years. The Foundation's ability to adjust, however painfully at times, would provide lessons to future generations of philanthropic leaders.

In 1946, the trustees sought to cope with this changing world. They appointed a special committee (Chester Barnard, William Myers, John D. Rockefeller 3rd, and Walter Stewart) to review the program and plans of the foundation. As the committee pointed out, this was the first complete review of the program undertaken in eleven years.

As the trustees struggled to reinterpret the mission in light of postwar concerns and the Foundation's resources, they defined three primary objectives: 1) to understand human behavior; 2) to promote a better American national life, and 3) to facilitate international understanding and cooperation. The committee acknowledged that the objectives were broad. Providing continuity with the past, they reaffirmed that the core principle of these three programs should be "the extension and application of knowledge." They noted that people in many parts of the world were not yet benefiting from existing knowledge, so they stressed application. "World conditions stress the need not only for the continuation of important basic research but also for concentrated and intense effort upon the application of existing knowledge to man's well-being." To achieve these goals, the committee recommended programs that would focus on health, agriculture (including nutrition), and education "since these are basic and fundamental to the well-being of man and not controversial, and since the Foundation and its sister organization, the General Education Board, have had considerable experience in these fields."

While the officers and trustees focused on understanding the postwar world, the future of the Foundation was largely being shaped in the field. A new initiative had already been launched during World War II that reflected the Foundation's historic opportunism and pragmatism and would play a profound part in the Foundation's postwar history.

With Europe and Asia in chaos during the war, the Foundation looked again to Latin America. For many years the International Health Division had worked with Latin American governments on public health campaigns. In the 1930s, however, Foundation staff, encouraged by the U.S. Ambassador to Mexico Josephus Daniels, had been urging the Foundation's leaders to consider a program in Mexico to increase food production. After U.S. Vice President and former Secretary of Agriculture Henry A. Wallace joined this chorus early in 1941, president Raymond Fosdick agreed to see what could be done. These conversations would open a whole new era in the Rockefeller Foundation's efforts to promote the well-being of humankind and lead to a significant shift in focus from health to agriculture.

What came to be known as the Green Revolution started in Mexico in 1943 with a simple focus: to dramatically increase agricultural production by developing higher-yielding varieties of basic food grains like wheat and corn, improving irrigation, and enhancing fertilizing techniques. Along the way, working closely with the national government, the Foundation supported the training of a generation of Mexican agronomists and scientists to lead and sustain a permanent increase in food production. The program was enormously successful. By preventing widespread famine, the increase in food production alone is estimated to have saved over one billion lives. In 1970, Rockefeller Foundation scientist Norman Borlaug was awarded the Nobel Peace Prize for his work on this initiative.

As chairman of the Foundation, John D. Rockefeller 3rd (left) strongly supported efforts by presidents Dean Rusk (middle) and George Harrar (right) to fight hunger in the developing world. (Rockefeller Archive Center.)

The simplicity of the model in Mexico made it easily exportable to other countries. Similar programs were launched in Colombia, Chile, and then India. In each country, the program was changed to fit the circumstances of local government and the environment. The ascent of the agriculture program was accompanied in 1951 by the historic end of the International Health Division, which had been criticized by a board review committee for having lost touch with the socioeconomic factors affecting public health. The IHD's remaining programs were merged with the Foundation's Division of Medical Sciences.

After Dean Rusk became president in 1952, the Foundation's work in economic and social development took on new meaning. Having seen the world for many years from the perspective of U.S. State Department, Rusk believed that the success and stability of the newly independent nations of Africa, Asia, and the Middle East was critical to the well-being of their citizens and to world peace.

Rusk's support for the agriculture program was evident in 1959, when he promoted J. George Harrar, who had joined the Rockefeller Foundation as a field scientist in Mexico, to become vice president of the Foundation with broad administrative responsibility. Harrar also enjoyed the support of the board and the chairman, John D. Rockefeller 3rd. In 1961, after President John Kennedy tapped Dean Rusk to be Secretary of State, the board promoted Harrar to be president of the Foundation.

1942
Millions of doses of yellow fever vaccine produced by the International Health Division in New York were provided to Allied soldiers and civilians during World War II. (Rockefeller Archive Center.)

Agriculture dominated the Foundation's programs in the 1960s. From country-specific programs, however, the Foundation increasingly shifted to the creation and stabilization of specialized international research institutes in agriculture. Funded collaboratively with the Ford Foundation, the W.K. Kellogg Foundation, and various international agencies, these institutes eventually became independent. Foundation support focused on funding research.

Harrar oversaw a fundamental realignment of the Foundation's program in 1963, a realignment that confirmed the new direction of the postwar era. In September of that year, the board articulated five major goals for the Foundation, three of them focused on the developing world: 1) overcome hunger and malnutrition, 2) stimulate the development of

strong universities; 3) stabilize the growth of populations. The other two goals were aimed primarily
at the United States: focus on issues affecting equal
opportunity and enhance the development of the
nation's cultural resources.

Through the 1960s and early 70s, the
Rockefeller Foundation worked to strengthen
health, agriculture, and social science programs
at universities in Asia, Africa, and Latin America.
Foundation staff worked as faculty members in
these universities. They were supplemented by
visiting professors from schools in the United
States, United Kingdom, and Canada. Meanwhile,
promising indigenous scholars were given opportunities to complete pre- and post-doctoral work
abroad with the expectation that they would return
to their home countries and join the faculties of
national universities.

Faced with rampant inflation and a
weak stock market, President John
Knowles, a physician and former
hospital administrator, launched
a fundamental review of the
Rockefeller Foundation's programs
in the 1970s. (Daniel Bernstein.
Rockefeller Archive Center.)

A dramatic drop in the stock market coupled
with rapid inflation in the 1970s forced the Rockefeller
Foundation to reevaluate its programs. Under a new
president in 1972, the board began a fundamental review,
soliciting input from other foundation leaders as well as
the Foundation's staff. As part of this review, President John
Knowles raised existential questions. With diminished
resources, should the foundation continue the expensive
operating programs—like the university development and the agriculture
programs—that had been so successful? Could it afford such staff-intensive
initiatives? Or should the foundation pivot and focus more on grantmaking? Should it become a think tank or a non-profit consulting firm? Or
should it find a way to balance or fuse these various options?

Knowles published the results of these deliberations in *The Course
Ahead* in 1974. In general, the report supported the work of the existing
programs, but added two more: a renewed emphasis on the arts and
humanities and the creation of a program to focus on international relations. But as financial pressures increased in the latter part of the decade,
Knowles pulled back. In 1977, he announced that the Foundation would
begin winding down the Education for Development Program.

During the first half of the 1980s, the Foundation took stock. The
staff-intensive field operations that had characterized the eras of the

International Health Division, the Green Revolution, and
the University Development Program no longer seemed
viable given the Foundation's assets and income. Moreover,
as Rockefeller Foundation officer Joyce Moock pointed out,
developing countries were no longer tolerant of highly vis-
ible expatriate staff in key positions within their national
institutions. Neither were they willing to allow foreigners to bypass normal
administrative channels or cut through bureaucratic red tape to launch
new initiatives. In addition, with an increasing emphasis on collaboration
with other foundations and non-government organizations, the strategic
options for the Foundation seemed to revolve around a more centralized
grantmaking program.

When Richard Lyman became
president in the 1980s, he cut
staff dramatically and shifted the
focus of the Foundation from
field operations to grantmaking.
(Rockefeller Archive Center.)

Building on its long-term strengths, the Rockefeller Foundation announced a major new program in 1986 to promote science-based development. Richard Lyman, who had become president in 1980, pointed out that
national independence and development were increasingly reliant on the
presence of a cadre of scientists in every nation. Investing in this human
capital was critical to the future of developing nations. Arguably, the program
continued many of the traditions of health, agriculture and education initiatives created earlier in the Foundation's history. But Lyman and his senior vice
president Kenneth Prewitt, as well as other leaders, imagined a radical break
from the past.

Having learned from prior experience, the Foundation sought to ensure
that techniques and strategies were introduced in ways they could be adapted

to fit local conditions and communities. They imagined a profoundly inter-disciplinary initiative that would look at problems from multiple points of view. In many ways, they were taking a significant risk. As one of the Foundation's consultants pointed out, despite enormous attention to the problem there was very little agreement in the field of development theory and even less understanding of the role of science. If successful, the Rockefeller initiative "may induce first-rate minds to address this formidable challenge."

Under the aegis of the Science-Based Development Program, the Foundation continued to emphasize many traditional themes, but with a fresh approach. The investment in human capital continued as the Foundation sponsored Leadership for Environment and Development (LEAD) to broaden the conversation among mid-career professionals working in these fields in the developing world. Between 1985 and 2000, half of the Foundation's staff in Agricultural Sciences was dedicated to rice biotechnology for Asia. The Foundation invested nearly $110 million in this effort. The argument for this investment was straightforward: over 70 percent of the world's poor lived in Asia, and rice provided anywhere from a third to half of the food calories consumed in the region. In health, the Foundation also looked for ways to take relatively simple steps that would make large-scale differences. In 1980, the Foundation launched the International Clinical Epidemiology Network (INCLEN) to strengthen health policymaking in developing countries and focus care in areas that could make the biggest impact for the most people. With the leadership of the Rockefeller Foundation, the organization soon attracted support from a wide variety of international organizations. INCLEN also hoped to serve as an early warning system when new pandemics like HIV/AIDS struck.

HIV/AIDS was a critical target of the Foundation's philanthropy in the late 1980s as Rockefeller played a leading role in urging American founda-tions to focus on the disease in the developing world. At a time when U.S. foundations were spending $150 million for treatment and research, only $8.6 million was reaching the developing world, and the Rockefeller Foundation provided half of this total.

By 1990, when the Foundation awarded nearly $95 million in grants and fellowships, its science-based development programs in agriculture, health, and population received about 43 percent of the total. Newer science-related initiatives tied to the global environment accounted for another $6.5 million or 7 percent. Long-standing domestic programs fo-cused on arts and humanities and equal opportunity accounted for another 32 percent. Newer initiatives focusing on school reform and international security made up 7 percent of the awards. The remaining 11 percent went for a variety of special projects and initiatives.

Collaboration had become a driving component of program strategy. In 1990, for example, the Foundation joined with the John D. and Catherine T. MacArthur Foundation and the Pew Charitable Trusts to create the Energy Foundation. The goal: to help the United States on the road to a policy of high energy efficiency and energy renewables. This effort was matched in the developing world with support for alternative energy initiatives to help triple the production of electricity and other energy services for the poor. Meanwhile, in Africa, the Foundation convened the Working Group on Female Participation in Education, a collaboration organized under the auspices of the World Bank, which led to the establishment of the Forum for African Women Educationalists (FAWE). By encouraging the education of girls in Africa—where only ten percent of females attended secondary schools—the project hoped to reap long-term benefits in terms of economic self-sufficiency, improved health management, and family planning at the household level. In the United States, the Foundation also joined the Ford Foundation-led National Community Development Initiative to help promote grassroots efforts to renew inner city neighborhood infrastructure.

New initiatives often grabbed the attention of the Foundation's leaders, but initiatives like the Foundation's Population Sciences Program, first developed in the immediate postwar years, evidenced the value of a sustained commitment. In 1991, the *New York Times* noted "a remarkable success story in international development." Since the mid-1960s, population growth rates in the third world had been cut in half. The *Times* called this "a Contraceptive Revolution that is every bit as impressive as agriculture's Green Revolution."

Despite the success of the population program, the Rockefeller Foundation had begun to move away from its internationalist perspective. In the 1980s, under Richard Lyman, although nearly 70 percent of annual spending went overseas, offices abroad were closed and international staffing was reduced.

Under Peter Goldmark, who became president in 1988, the Foundation's traditional emphasis on science also declined. Goldmark was more focused on the environment, equal opportunity, community development, school reform, and other domestic issues in the United States. When it came time to look for his successor, the Foundation wanted an internationalist, according to trustee Alice Ilchman, "someone with strong on-the-ground experience in developing countries and proven expertise in the science and technology of hunger and disease"—someone who would, in effect, return the Foundation to its traditional emphasis on scientific internationalism.

As the 12th president of the Rockefeller Foundation, Gordon Conway reaffirmed that focus on scientific internationalism. An agricultural ecologist born in the United Kingdom, Conway had trained at the universities of Bangor, Cambridge, and West Indies, and had received a Ph.D. from the University of California (Davis) in systems ecology. He became a pioneer in the field of sustainable agriculture in the 1960s. Over the next two decades, he worked on projects sponsored by the Ford Foundation, the World Bank, and USAID in Asia and the Middle East. Remarkably, he was a leading critic of some of the methods of the Green Revolution.

Conway moved to make the Rockefeller Foundation "more explicitly global." Even before he officially stepped into his role, he encouraged the staff to think of ways in which the Foundation could "make a real and significant difference to the well-being of the poor" that would result in people being "better fed, in better health, better educated and skilled." "We should be aiming at sustainable livelihoods," he wrote. As president, he revitalized two of the Foundation's signature areas—agriculture and health—under the themes of Food Security and Health Equity. He also initiated an interdisciplinary or "cross-theme" initiative called Global Inclusion to focus on biotechnology, intellectual property, and world trade. He strengthened the Foundation's international field offices.

In 2005, Judith Rodin replaced Gordon Conway as president of the Rockefeller Foundation. The former president of the University of Pennsylvania, and the first woman to lead an Ivy League university, Rodin recognized that the Foundation needed to adjust to changing dynamics.

1943
Mexican agriculture program becomes the forerunner to the Green Revolution.
(Rockefeller Archive Center.)

With an awareness of the complexity, dynamism, volatility and uncertainty of globalization in mind, Rodin led the Foundation through a strategic review of its programs. A new plan emerged that continued the Foundation's efforts to promote the well-being of humankind by focusing especially on the poor and vulnerable, but under Rodin the Rockefeller Foundation assessed the opportunities and challenges raised by globalization. Rather than return to the concept of "program areas," the Foundation positioned itself to itself to address five major issues related to "smart globalization." It organized much of its work around time-limited initiatives in which the Foundation would address a specific problem – such as transforming

health systems – and then target programmatic investments to enable systemic change. By 2012, the Foundation
continued to face an evolving global context, one which
it described as "more people, more connected and distributed in new ways." To better meet the demands of this
changing environment, Rodin sharpened the focus of
the Foundation's work on four primary goals that aimed
to secure livelihoods, transform cities, advance health
and revalue ecosystems. Within each of these issue areas,
the Foundation developed goals that fit within John D.
Rockefeller's broad mission—to promote the well-being
of humanity. These goals aimed to build resilience to
enable people, communities and nations to bounce back
after shocks and respond to stresses. They also worked to
promote equitable growth so that the benefits of economic
improvement were more widely shared. Among other
priorities, Rodin also stressed the important role of private
capital in addressing the problems of the future.
(see Chapter IX – Social Investing.)

Chosen to become the first woman
to lead the Rockefeller Foundation,
Judith Rodin became president in
2005. Rodin led a strategic effort
to focus the Foundation's programs
on promoting systemic change in
a number of critical issue areas.
(Rockefeller Foundation.)

As the Foundation entered its second century, the
remarkable story about its program was its basic consistency
across generations of leaders and staff. The emphasis on
education and training as a way to create the capacity for
people in a given community to fight disease, malnutrition,
and poverty was manifested in the earliest days of the International Health
Commission in 1913, and it was apparent in the Foundation's efforts to
empower communities to tackle the challenges and opportunities of globalization in 2013. The belief that science and technology could mitigate the rav-
ages of disease, increase food supplies, and ease the overwhelming pressures
of overpopulation has carried through the Foundation's work for decades.

As the relationships between technology and culture became increasingly
apparent over the course of the century, the Foundation adjusted its strategies
to give local leaders and communities the ability to adapt technology to their
own needs. These efforts have not always been successful. Frequently, larger
historical forces including political instability, global capitalism, and environmental change have overwhelmed the modest contributions that philanthropy is able to make to the well-being of humankind. Persistence in the face
of long odds and an increasing tendency to organize all programs around the
idea of collaboration, however, have resulted in remarkable improvements in
the human condition.

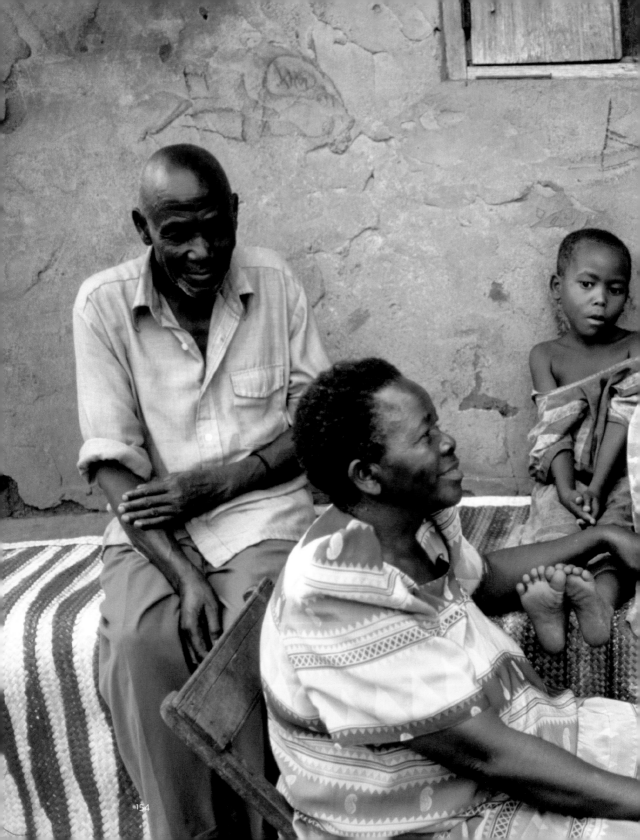

KNOWLEDGE

Who should control knowledge that can benefit humankind?

With the rise of the knowledge economy, we face a profound paradox. At no time in history has it been easier for people to access the accumulated wisdom of humankind. And yet, in a world where ideas create enormous wealth, the legal control of information through patents and copyright has never been more fiercely contested. In this brave new world, products that derive their value from this intellectual property—including pharmaceuticals, medical technologies, bioengineered crops, computers, and more—are often too expensive for poor and vulnerable communities to afford.

A new brand of philanthropy has emerged that makes patents available to the public for the greater good. Some call it "patent philanthropy." Inventors and corporations contribute their intellectual property rights to charitable organizations and foundations to lower the costs of making these technologies or ideas available to poorer peoples around the world. Under this kind of regime, pharmaceutical companies have established drug-pricing systems that offer highly reduced rates for low- and middle-income regions. Companies have also contributed intellectual property to patent pools designed to promote research to fight neglected diseases.

Patent pools can also help to spark economic development. According to some estimates, less than five percent of the patents that have been filed by innovators around the world are actually being developed for commercial use. When companies donate their unused patents to patent pools, they provide opportunities for consortia in developing regions to find new products and processes that will create jobs for local residents.

All of these approaches to disseminating knowledge derive from fundamental issues that confronted the Rockefeller Foundation and other early philanthropies in the twentieth century. If philanthropic dollars enabled the creation of new vaccines or hybrid seeds, who should control this new knowledge? Should the inventors, even if their work was subsidized by philanthropy, reap a financial return? Would society be better off and would the search for innovation be promoted by rewarding these inventors? The Rockefeller Foundation dealt with these issues as it sought to rid the world of the scourge of yellow fever and other diseases.

KNOWLEDGE

PRINCIPLES, PROFITS, AND PHILANTHROPY

R aymond Fosdick was not happy. As he sat in the office of the
Acting Surgeon General of the United States, the president of the
Rockefeller Foundation listened to one side of a telephone conversation about vaccines. In Washington, D.C., for a meeting with
the vice president of the United States to talk about Mexico, Fosdick
had not anticipated getting caught in the crossfire of a bureaucratic feud
between scientists.

In January 1941, the United States was preparing for war while much
of the rest of the world was already engulfed in the fighting. Germany had
suffered its first defeat when it lost the air Battle of Britain. Now Congress was
debating President Roosevelt's proposed "Lend-Lease" program to provide aid
to the Allied nations. In Asia, fighting continued as the Chinese struggled to
resist the Japanese invasion. Meanwhile, in North Africa, Britain had launched
two major offensives—one in Egypt and the other in East Africa—to liberate
Ethiopia and end Italy's plans for conquest. British troops, however, faced an
unseen enemy as an epidemic of yellow fever raged in the Sudan.

Brilliant and dangerous work by Rockefeller Foundation scientists had
led to the development of a vaccine for yellow fever in 1937. The Foundation
had produced tens of thousands of doses for people in Brazil and other
tropical countries. But now the British government wanted 50,000 doses a
week. And the U.S. War Department, fearing that the Japanese were planning

biological warfare, including the release of clouds of mosquitoes carrying the yellow fever virus, had decided that if the U.S. was drawn into the war, military personnel destined for the tropics should all be vaccinated.

Raymond Fosdick met with the acting surgeon general of the United States at the office of the U.S. Public Health Service in January 1941. The government wanted to privatize the manufacturing of yellow fever vaccine, which had been developed by Rockefeller Foundation scientists. (National Library of Medicine.)

The unseen man on the other end of the telephone conversation, Dr. Milton Veldee, wanted private drug companies to begin making the Rockefeller Foundation's yellow fever vaccine. A bacteriologist and Harvard-trained physician, Veldee had been a faculty member at Johns Hopkins before he joined the U.S. Public Health Service as chief of the Laboratory of Biologics Control in 1931. Under the authority of Congress, his division regulated the production of vaccines in the United States.

Fosdick, with the active support of scientists working in the International Health Division's laboratories in New York, was resisting Veldee's proposal. Basic principles and human lives were at stake. The Rockefeller scientists

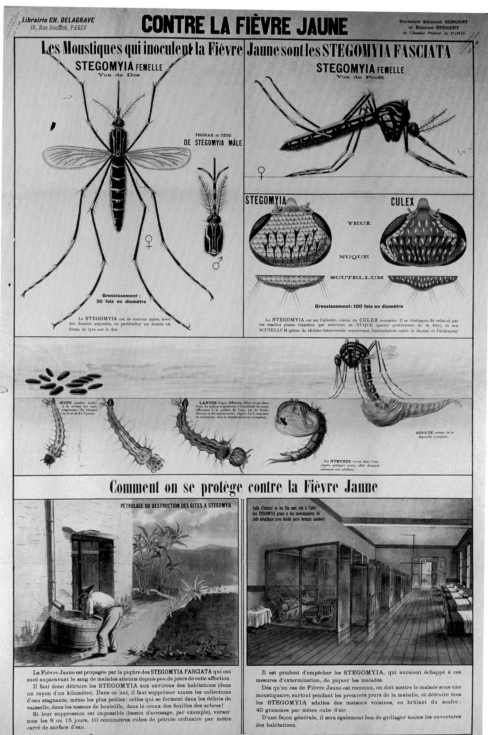

Chapter Six: Knowledge

weren't sure that commercial companies could be trusted to manufacture a vaccine that was still very difficult to preserve. Even more importantly, Fosdick was appalled by the notion that commercial companies should be allowed to profit from the Foundation's enormous investments of money and lives in path-breaking medical research. In the culture, there was still a deep uneasiness with the idea that private interests should profit from the illnesses of others.

The Fight Against Yellow Fever

A scourge on human populations for centuries, yellow fever is endemic in tropical and subtropical areas of Africa and Latin America. The disease damages internal organs and frequently leads to severe bleeding and death. As the disease attacks the liver, victims frequently see their skin turn yellow or jaundiced—a condition that gave rise to the name "yellow fever" or "yellow jack."

For centuries, as epidemics ravaged cities, doctors and scientists were unable to identify the source of the disease or its method of transmission. A Cuban doctor and scientist, Carlos Finlay, first suggested in 1881 that mosquitoes transmitted yellow fever. A team of American doctors, led by United States Army Surgeon Walter Reed, proved this theory correct in 1900. They also demonstrated that the disease was transmitted by a particular kind of mosquito, the Aedes aegypti. With this information, physician and later Rockefeller Foundation scientist William Gorgas organized to eradicate the Aedes aegypti in Cuba and Panama by attacking their breeding sites. The campaign was so successful that it stopped the devastating loss of life among canal workers and allowed for the construction of the Panama Canal.

The Rockefeller Foundation launched its fight against yellow fever in 1915, when Wickliffe Rose, the head of the International Health Board, made the brave, or perhaps foolish, decision to go beyond the fight against hookworm—which had a known cure—to tackle two diseases that had no known cure: malaria and yellow fever. Rose was responding to the concerns of officials in the United States, as well as in Hong Kong and Singapore, who feared that the opening of the Panama Canal would lead to epidemics of yellow fever in regions that had not previously been affected. Rose and other leading public health officials, including Gorgas, who had been promoted to Surgeon General of the U.S. Army, believed they could take the eradication campaign to other affected cities and countries. Delayed by World War I and negotiations with local authorities, these efforts proved

Cuban doctor Carlos Finlay first suggested that yellow fever was transmitted by mosquitoes. A team of researchers led by Walter Reed identified Stegomyia (later known as Aedes aegypti) as the carrier. (National Library of Medicine.)

Hideyo Noguchi (left) was internationally recognized for his work on syphilis, snake venom, and spirochaete bacteria when he turned his attention to yellow fever. (Rockefeller Archive Center.)

successful in Guayaquil, a key port in Ecuador that served ships headed for the Panama Canal.

Meanwhile, researchers at the Rockefeller Institute, including Hideyo Noguchi, were working on isolating the pathogen for yellow fever in order to find a way of arresting its attack on the body. In 1918, Noguchi, who had earned considerable respect for his work on syphilis, snake venom, and the spirochaete bacteria, claimed to have found a bacterium that caused yellow fever. Noguchi said that he had developed a vaccine that inoculated guinea pigs. Preliminary tests on human subjects yielded impressive results. After the Rockefeller Institute began producing large quantities of vaccine, inoculation campaigns in Mexico and Peru in 1921 seemed equally promising. Leaders at the Rockefeller Foundation, the Rockefeller Institute and the International Health Board were ecstatic.

Exuberance was followed by dismay, however, when researchers with the International Health Board's West Africa Yellow Fever Commission discovered in 1926 that most of Noguchi's results could not be replicated in Africa. They concluded that the disease in Africa was fundamentally different from yellow fever in South America. Further experiments with rhesus monkeys appeared to suggest that Noguchi was wrong in his identification of the pathogen for yellow fever. Noguchi, shamed by the discovery, sailed for West Africa to address the situation himself, but was infected with the disease in the lab and died. Noguchi was not the only scientist taken in the battle against yellow fever. Five other Foundation staff members gave their lives in the fight. Their work, however, led to critical breakthroughs.

Continuing research seemed to suggest that there were at least two ways in which yellow fever was transmitted. On one hand, the aegypti mosquito traveled mostly from people to mosquito to people

Louise Pearce, a physician and researcher, went to the Belgian Congo in 1920 to field test a new drug, Tryparsamide, developed by the Rockefeller Institute for the treatment of African sleeping sickness. The Rockefeller Institute patented the drug to guarantee safe production and distribution. (Rockefeller Archive Center.)

in urban areas, often infecting all of the members of a household. Alternatively, so-called jungle yellow fever was carried by monkeys and opossums and transmitted by jungle mosquitoes. A crucial development came on June 29, 1927, when one of the Foundation's scientists at the Yellow Fever Laboratory in Lagos, Nigeria, isolated the yellow fever virus from an African man named Asibi. Scientists were able to attenuate this strain and mix it with human serum recovered from yellow fever victims to create a crude vaccine that could protect workers in the lab.

Dr. Max Theiler, a young South African researcher who had studied at the London School of Hygiene and Tropical Medicine, had focused on yellow fever as a virus long before others accepted this theory. Invited to join the staff of the International Health Division under Dr. Wilbur A. Sawyer, he continued his research and was able to develop a new vaccine, based on the Asibi virus strain, that did not use human serum. Labeled 17D, the vaccine was first tested on human subjects in November 1936. After successful trials, the vaccine soon went into mass production. In 1938, more than a million people were vaccinated. By this time, the fight against yellow fever had absorbed over half of the IHB/IHD's disease budget and cost nearly $14 million. In 1951, Theiler would win the Nobel Prize in Physiology or Medicine for his effort to isolate the virus and develop the vaccine.

The importance of the Foundation's breakthrough could hardly be overstated. With the advent of World War II, Allied forces coming from areas where the disease was not endemic were hugely susceptible and could be killed in massive numbers. The soon-to-be Allied governments were desperate to obtain millions of doses of the vaccine. But who would control the rights to yellow fever vaccine? And who would take charge of its production?

When the Rockefeller Institute was founded in 1901, its charter included language that made "all discoveries and inventions" by employees the property of the Institute to "place at the service of humanity in accordance with the beneficent purposes of the founder." This philosophy permeated the field of medical research in the first half of the twentieth century, especially when researchers received funding from either the government or non-profit organizations. The first patent for the production of insulin, for example, was sold by the inventors to the University of Toronto for one dollar.

Rockefeller philanthropists recognized, however, that there was a useful purpose to patenting, particularly when it came to ensuring public safety. The ability to control the production of a vaccine or a drug ensured that it would be made properly. Early in the history of the Rockefeller Institute, scientists developed a new arsenic compound known as Tryparsamide that proved effective in treating African sleeping sickness, a disease that killed hundreds of thousands of people in Africa. The Rockefeller Institute patented the formula "to control the manufacture and sale for the protection of the purity of the product."

Max Theiler, a scientist working in the Rockefeller Foundation's International Health Division, developed the first yellow fever vaccine. In 1951 Theiler was awarded the Nobel Prize for his work. (Rockefeller Archive Center.)

In the early 1930s, as Rockefeller Foundation scientists were hard at work on the yellow fever vaccine, there was a great deal of interest in the research community in the idea of funding basic research with proceeds received from patents. The Rockefeller Foundation was skeptical. As President Max Mason wrote to Dean C. S. Slichter [at the University of Wisconsin], the Foundation was concerned that if this idea caught on it would inhibit the publication of research and lead to greater secrecy in the scientific community, which would slow the pace of discovery and innovation "to the great detriment of the scientific spirit." This would be compounded by the growth of patent litigation that would require

Max Mason, a distinguished mathematical physicist and former president of the University of Chicago, became president of the Rockefeller Foundation in 1929. Mason feared that patenting would slow the pace of scientific discovery and innovation. (Rockefeller Archive Center.)

expert testimony and take researchers away from the lab. Mason believed that support for pure research by government and private donors would also suffer "if the idea becomes spread that such research is capable of commercialization for its own support and that this process is advisable."

In 1932, program officer Robert Lambert echoed these ideas when he wrote to Dr. Claus Schilling at the Koch Institute to say: "Since the Foundation's aid to research is based on the principle that any advance in knowledge should be made known freely to all the world, the officers are not at liberty to take any step which might appear to be out of accord with that principle. Furthermore, as a matter of policy, we do not undertake to act as intermediaries in negotiations between scientists and governments regarding the application of scientific discoveries, however much we may wish to see the best use made of any such advance in knowledge." Nevertheless, as late as 1933, the Foundation had no policy on patents.

As the Foundation continued to the wrestle with the issue, other perspectives came to the fore. Vannevar Bush, writing as Dean of Engineering at MIT, pointed out to Max Mason that "patenting for control, especially on medical matters, is oftentimes essential." Moreover, clear patent control was essential to attracting funding for development. Bush conceded that he was "struggling to crystallize my ideas" on whether or not educational institutions should patent discoveries as a strategy for funding further research. "From one point of view there is a danger that revenue from patents might alienate the beneficiaries of educational institutions. On the other hand there is certainly a possibility that some types of men would incline strongly to support institutions which showed an ability to take care of their own affairs."

In 1937, the University of Cincinnati considered adopting a policy to patent discoveries coming from its labs. The Rockefeller Foundation, which provided grant money to the university's department of neurology, requested that the university notify the Foundation if the university intended "to operate these patents for the purposes of securing income from them." Alan Gregg believed that the Foundation's trustees should at least be informed if the

Chapter Six: Knowledge

"GOLDEN RICE" AND THE ROLE OF INTELLECTUAL PROPERTY

Preschool children in poor communities in developing countries often die because they don't get enough Vitamin A. One study in Indonesia in the 1980s showed that mortality rates among children could be reduced by 30 percent if they received sufficient doses of this critical vitamin.

Rice is the leading staple in the diets of many poor children around the world, but rice does not contain Vitamin A or its precursor, beta-carotene. After the Rockefeller Foundation launched its rice biotechnology program in 1985, the development of a new breed of rice with beta-carotene became a major focus.

Research by two European scientists—Dr. Ingo Potrykus and Dr. Peter Beyer—led to a fundamental breakthrough. By genetically engineering rice that incorporated daffodil genes, these researchers were able to create "golden rice," a breed rich in the beta-carotene needed for Vitamin A.

Intellectual property controls threatened to constrain the widespread production, safety testing, and dissemination of golden rice. To resolve these issues, the researchers, with the Foundation's consent and encouragement, entered into a partnership with Zeneca, a large pharmaceutical and agribusiness. The agreement allowed public-sector breeding programs to make golden rice seeds available to resource-poor farmers in developing countries at no additional cost. Zeneca (today Syngenta) also provided resources to the Humanitarian Project, founded by the inventors to continue their research.

This innovative partnership should enable millions of the world's poorest children to enjoy better health and a higher quality of life.

Foundation had provided the initial capital for the discovery. Warren Weaver, director of the Natural Sciences Division, wrote in a letter to a grantee at the University of Virginia: "When people ask us questions about possible patents arising in connection with work which we have supported, in whole, or in part, our reply is, in effect, to tell them to use their own best judgment. If their judgment should turn out to be notoriously bad or clearly selfish, this would probably be reflected in our future relations."

One solution to this dilemma was available through the Research Corporation for Science Advancement, established in 1912 by Professor Gardner Cottrell at the University of California, Berkeley. Cottrell had invented a device to reduce air pollution by removing particles from a flowing gas. With profits from this device, the Research Corporation funded research by other scientists. By 1937, with an agreement with MIT, the Research Corporation began to manage patents for educational institutions.

All of these conversations were ongoing as the Rockefeller Foundation struggled to standardize the preparation of the yellow fever vaccine in 1938. That fall, the U.S. pharmaceutical company Sharp and Dohme was the first commercial company to indicate an interest in manufacturing the vaccine. The Rockefeller Foundation expressed concern over whether the vaccine would be created with high standards. The U.S. Public Health Service offered its reassurance: "Yellow fever vaccine comes within the scope of the Biologics Act and can be marketed only with the approval of the Treasury Department thru the Public Health Service." The government promised that the company's vaccine "will not be marketed unless it complies with the requirements of the Treasury Department [which oversaw the PHS]."

The Rockefeller Foundation, however, remained concerned. Scientists in the labs felt that the production process had not been perfected. To be effective, the vaccine needed to contain a live virus. To keep the virus alive while the vaccine was being shipped, it had to be kept cool and maintained in dry form. The situation made the vaccine unlike any other vaccine then available. These factors led the Foundation's scientists to believe "that the manufacture of this

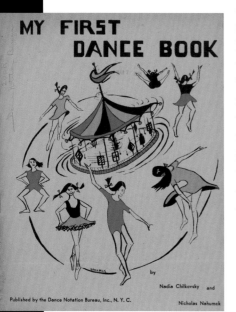

MY FIRST DANCE BOOK

by Nadia Chilkovsky and Nicholas Nahumck

Published by the Dance Notation Bureau, Inc., N.Y.C.

1954
New grants for dance and music reflect the Rockefeller Foundation's expanded interest in supporting the arts and culture. (Dance Notation Bureau. Rockefeller Archive Center.)

TIMELINE

product on a commercial basis is somewhat premature." If Sharp and Dohme wanted to go ahead, the Foundation wanted to make sure they didn't link their product to the Foundation. In response, the government reiterated that Sharp and Dohme would only be licensed to produce and sell the vaccine if the U.S. Public Health Service approved its vaccine and "no responsibility, even by implication, will attach to the Rockefeller Foundation."

While these conversations were taking place, the debate over patenting continued at the Rockefeller Foundation. By 1940, Raymond Fosdick hoped to resolve the issue by creating a joint committee of trustees and officers to study the problem. Members were appointed and the committee met, but no minutes or report were ever issued. The debate stalled as the world became increasingly embroiled in war.

The government and the research community seemed to switch direction in 1940. The U.S. Public Health Service considered establishing a production facility in Bethesda, Maryland. In June, the Division of Medical Sciences of the National Research Council asked the IHD to provide and maintain a supply of 100,000 doses of yellow fever vaccine for the armed forces of the United States. An empty floor in the North Building of the Rockefeller Institute was allocated for this work and for the production of influenza vaccine. Dr. Kenneth Goodner was appointed director of the new manufacturing division. The effort was supposed to be temporary, until the government could establish vaccine production facilities of its own.

For the American military, the request for a standby supply of yellow fever vaccine was precautionary. In Africa, however, where British troops were already fighting, the need for the vaccine became urgent late in 1940, when an outbreak of the disease swept through the Sudan. By January 1941, the British government was asking for 50,000 doses a week. But the lack of refrigerated shipping options made this almost impossible.

As demand for the vaccine surged, the U.S. Surgeon General wanted to license commercial manufacturing. The government asked the Rockefeller Foundation to train two scientists from these commercial firms in its labs. The Foundation demurred, saying space was already tight. They suggested it wasn't really necessary. The procedure had been published, and a competent biological company would be able to do it. Milton Veldee, the chief of the Division of Biologics at the U.S. Public Health Service, agreed. Nevertheless, the Foundation was clearly not pleased at the prospect of commercial firms entering the field. So Foundation president Raymond Fosdick went to see the Acting Surgeon General, Warren Fales Draper and waited as Draper talked to his staff on the phone.

With war raging in Europe and North Africa, Acting Surgeon General Warren Draper was under pressure to obtain millions of doses of yellow fever vaccine to inoculate U.S. recruits and British forces. (National Library of Medicine.)

A graduate of Harvard Medical School, the fifty-seven-year-old Draper had spent much of his career in the U.S. Public Health Service. He understood the bureaucracy. When Draper got off the phone with Veldee, Fosdick made it clear that the Foundation was already working with production facilities in the United Kingdom, South Africa and Brazil to meet the world's needs for the vaccine. It could and would produce enough yellow fever vaccine to meet the needs of the United States. The Foundation was happy to do so as "our contribution to the cause of national defense." Draper accepted Fosdick's offer, which ended the talk of bringing commercial firms into the process.

True to Fosdick's expression of patriotism, the Rockefeller Foundation agreed to supply the vaccine for one dollar a year. In 1941, before the U.S. entered the war, more than 2 million doses were made and shipped, primarily to Africa but also to India. Another 1 million doses were delivered to the U.S. Army and Navy. Foundation staff worked all year long—Sundays and holidays included. Some shipments were lost when transport ships were torpedoed or delivery planes crashed. The cost of each dose was approximately three cents.

The Rockefeller Foundation continued its efforts as the U.S. government equipped its Public Health Service laboratory in Hamilton, Montana, to manufacture the vaccine. Meanwhile, in Britain and Brazil, two other laboratories, Wellcome Research Institute and the Yellow Fever Laboratory in Rio de Janeiro, were producing vaccine. And in South Africa, efforts were being made by the South African Institute for Medical Research to begin manufacturing. A similar effort was underway in India. The government of the Netherlands East Indies was also interested in manufacturing.

The Foundation's vaccine production ran into a major problem when U.S. Army service members who had been inoculated became sick and jaundiced. The jaundice problem led the Rockefeller Foundation to modify its strategy for the production of the vaccine, eliminating the use of human serum. It also led to an institutional change. In the wake of this incident, the Surgeon General of the Army suggested that the Rockefeller Foundation's laboratories should obtain a license from the U.S. Public Health Service to produce the yellow fever vaccine. Dr. Johannes H. Bauer, who worked in the yellow fever lab, agreed to this idea and wrote to the director of the National Institute of Health

One hundred doses of yellow fever vaccine prepared by the International Health Division of the Rockefeller Foundation in its New York laboratories. In 1939, the IHD's scientists feared that the production process was not stable enough to turn over to commercial manufacturers. (Rockefeller Archive Center.)

ELLOW FEVER VACCI

Date of Preparation

nts with 55 cc. of sterile pho
use 0.5 cc. per person for
dry vaccine should be stored
ing in salt solution it m
e hours and any resid

LABORATORIES OF THE
ATIONAL HEALTH DIVISION
EFELLER FOUNDATION, NE

STERILE PHYSIOLOGICAL SALT SOLUTION

55 cc.

LABORATORIES OF THE
INTERNATIONAL HEALTH DIVISION OF THE
ROCKEFELLER FOUNDATION, NEW YORK

Form No. 409

21744c

in May 1942. The licensing process led to a full write-up of the new methods used for producing the vaccine. It also led to a major overhaul of equipment and procedures in the lab. But it still did not lead the Rockefeller Foundation to secure a patent on the vaccine.

In fact, by June 1942, the issue of patenting was still unresolved within the Foundation. Writing to Linus Pauling, Warren Weaver confessed that the staff at the Foundation was divided over the issue: "The medical people here have taken a strong position against patents as such." In Weaver's Natural Science Division, the *laissez faire* attitude of the 1930s persisted. Weaver was concerned that Pauling's work related to hemoglobin, if patented, would have implications for medicine, so he noted that his division would be more careful.

When the war ended, the Rockefeller Foundation abandoned the business of producing yellow fever vaccine, and the U.S. Public Health Service took over. The Foundation characterized the effort "as a war measure to supply the army and the navy." No commercial entity stepped into the field.

In 1949, the Rockefeller Foundation was again forced to wrestle with the issue when the National Research Council launched a survey of educational and philanthropic organizations on the patent issue. President Chester Barnard deemed it unacceptable for the different divisions in the Foundation to have different policies, although he pointed out that, "as things have turned out, there has been very little difference in the practice of the two divisions." Barnard believed that the problem was less urgent than it had been a decade earlier because of the development of the Research Corporation and other nonprofit patent management organizations. He noted that the Research Corporation's practice included provisions for the discoverer to receive "some modest return" from his or her discovery, which the Rockefeller Foundation did not think improper.

Barnard's letter, however, did not completely reflect the sentiment of the organization or the field. One staffer said that a conference sponsored by the National Research Council in 1949 to address the patent policies and practices of educational institutions "reflected complete confusion and a perfect welter of policies and

1954

Ralph Ellison receives a Rockefeller Fellowship to support his literary work. Ellison was among a distinguished list of novelists and playwrights who received literature fellowships in the 1950s and 1960s. (Rockefeller Archive Center.)

lack of policies." Within the International
Health Division, according to the director, George K. Strode, "We believe that
scientific advances in the field of medicine
should be freely available to all." Strode
acknowledged, however, the issue of
control. "We recognize that there are some
in the world who would exploit the scientific work of others through the patent
device and in consequence we would not
condemn the device if used to protect the
welfare of man." Strode noted, "The IHD
could have patented its yellow fever vaccine; instead it published full particulars
concerning the vaccine and thereby made
it impossible for others to patent it."

Linus Pauling's work with hemoglobin
was supported by the Rockefeller
Foundation. Warren Weaver feared in
1942 that Pauling (right) would seek
to patent his work, which would have
serious implications for medicine.
(Rockefeller Archive Center.)

In 1950, the Foundation finally turned
to its attorney, Chauncey Belknap, to
articulate a patent policy, but even he
was unsuccessful. The officers of the
Foundation agreed in November 1950 that "We have a policy
of having no policy but to deal with each case as it arises."
And Belknap wrote "I am glad we are not going to try to
solve the insoluble by laying down a uniform patent and
copyright policy for the Foundation."

But the dilemma over patents did not die. As the
Foundation's work in agriculture in Mexico progressed in
the 1950s, the development of new seed varieties raised the patent question
again. When one of the Foundation's scientific consultants, P.C. Mangelsdorf,
obtained a patent for corn that didn't need to be de-tasseled, and filed it with the
Research Corporation, the move made officials at the Rockefeller Foundation
uneasy. Warren Weaver said that the Foundation "would be criticized for its
part in what would be described as an effort to develop corn in Mexico in order
to produce revenue for one of our consultants."

Weaver continued to express concern on this issue. In 1956, he wrote a
memo to George Harrar regarding a potential patent for the development of a
solar energy project at the University of Wisconsin. Although the investigators
proposed to have a nonprofit patent management entity hold the patent,
Weaver noted that "It would be completely anomalous if solar cookers in India,
for example, cost 50 cents extra because of [the patent]." Weaver's angst was

important. The world was entering a new era where the control of information and knowledge would play a critical role in dividing the haves and the have-nots.

Over the next three decades, however, the Foundation maintained a flexible approach to its patent policies. Then in 1984 the Foundation adopted a formal policy "to ensure that the results of Foundation-supported research are made available widely for the betterment of mankind throughout the world." The policy sought to channel the financial rewards from Foundation-sponsored discoveries, inventions or developments back into research for the public interest. The policy affected all of the Foundation's grant programs. It meant, for example, that researchers working on rice biotechnology projects funded in whole or in part by the Foundation would share their discoveries in developing countries with "zero royalty use."

IDEAS IN A KNOWLEDGE ECONOMY

The evident tensions over patenting vaccines for yellow fever, encephalitis, and other diseases marked the beginnings of a broader movement from an industrial to an information- or knowledge-based global economy in the late twentieth century. This transition accelerated with the proliferation of computers and networked global information systems. It permeated the health sciences as biotechnology led to the patenting of life forms. In 1999, staff at the Rockefeller Foundation recognized that "debates around intellectual property rights will be core to the distribution of wealth and poverty in the next century."

Foundation president Gordon Conway drew attention to the issue that year when he appeared before the board of directors of Monsanto and urged them to "disavow use of the terminator technology to produce seed sterility." Conway then went public with his recommendations the following day. In the moment, Conway's confrontation sparked animosity, but Monsanto agreed to study the issue. In October, in a public letter to Conway, Monsanto's CEO announced that the company would not commercialize sterile seed technologies designed to force farmers to buy new seed every year. This was a preliminary victory for the Foundation and for the advocates of less restrictive applications of intellectual property rules in developing nations, but it was only the beginning of a much larger fight.

In April 2002, to address these issues, the Foundation's board of trustees approved a new initiative entitled "Charting a Fairer Course for Intellectual Property Policy." The project brought together officers from each of the Foundation's main programs at that time, including Global Inclusion,

In 1999 Rockefeller Foundation president Gordon Conway challenged Monsanto's use of so-called "terminator technology" to produce seed sterility. (Rockefeller Foundation.)

Creativity & Culture, Food Security, Health Equity, the Africa Regional Program, and the Program-Related Investment team in ProVenEx. Over the next two years, the team worked closely with grantees and analysts—including HIV/AIDS activists, small-scale farmers, plant breeders, and indigenous peoples—to identify ways in which the Foundation could support changes in intellectual property policy that would benefit poor and excluded people.

The team outlined the challenges. International trade agreements provided for high levels of intellectual property (IP) protection in the developed world and played a major role in directing capital into research. But these incentives favored markets that promised the highest return, and arenas that might offer the greatest benefit to the poor were often neglected. Meanwhile, "IP monopolies" often resulted in high prices for drugs or seeds that put these products outside the reach of developing nations. Even when researchers sought to address the needs of the poor, they were often stymied by "patent thickets" that made it difficult for independent researchers to work in the arena. The group pointed out a number of ironies and inequities in the situation. Many agro-biotechnology and pharmaceutical products had been derived from genetic material and traditional knowledge originating in developed countries. Intellectual property laws rarely provided any compensation to developing nations for these contributions.

The group also concluded that many of the Foundation's grantees that were struggling with these issues were making a difference. "A deeper and more nuanced understanding of the role of IP in development is emerging," the team concluded in 2004. New policies were also emerging that would lift patent protections to allow greater access for developing countries to medicines essential for the treatment of HIV/AIDS and neglected diseases such as TB and malaria.

This work led to new grants in various program areas to support "more progressive IP practices." Moreover, the organization's learning in this realm, combined with a history of emphasis on the open dissemination of knowledge stretching back to the development of yellow fever vaccine and more, positioned the Rockefeller Foundation to be an effective broker between groups promoting policy change in the intellectual property arena and those institutions in academe and the private sector focused on research and innovation.

GRANTEES

What makes a relationship with grantees successful?

In keeping with the decision to make grants rather than operate programs for the long term, foundations confront the question of how to work with grantees. These challenges begin with the first inquiry. New foundations quickly discover that the volume of requests for aid can be overwhelming. Articulating specific programs can help to narrow the pool of serious applicants, but they may also constrain the foundation by discouraging innovators who might have projects the foundation hadn't even imagined.

As they seek to focus their programs to achieve tangible objectives and goals, foundations often discover that the kinds of grantees or projects they want to support don't exist. Some foundations are tempted to establish and run these projects on their own. Others look for partners or collaborators who can help create the necessary institutions capable of pursuing the work in the field that will achieve the goal.

All of these approaches raise issues for board members and staffers. If the foundation funds grantees who come "over the transom," will the foundation develop the kind of relationship with a grantee that leads to long-term transformation? If the foundation creates and launches a program on its own, is it really prepared to be the operator for the long term? If the foundation helps to create a new agency, what responsibility does it have to provide sustaining support that will allow the institution to achieve long-term stability? Inevitably, foundations are also forced to consider the question of when engagement becomes interference.

All of these issues ultimately focus on questions of success or failure. If foundations provide venture capital to the social sector, they have to expect high rates of failure, but they also need to invest in evaluation efforts that will yield lessons even from initiatives that don't work. They have to ask themselves, how long does it take to give a grantee a fair shot at getting off the ground? How long before sustainable resources come to the table?

At some point, funders almost always want the grantee to become independent. Negotiating the end to the relationship can be difficult, however, especially when the funder has been deeply involved in the development of the project or program. Funders have to wrestle with their moral responsibilities in the situation. Grantees have to confront the harsh reality as to whether the project is actually viable.

The Rockefeller Foundation has faced all of these issues time and again over the course of a hundred years. In the middle of the twentieth century, the Foundation's philosophy was crystallized in a famous memo entitled: "How Do You Do, Dr. X?"

GRANTEES

How Do You Do, Dr. X?

In 1952, Warren Weaver, the head of the Rockefeller Foundation's Division of Natural Sciences, wrote a striking memo entitled "How Do You Do, Dr. X?" The ten-page document provided new staff with a guide to interacting with visitors who came to the door hoping to receive a grant from the Rockefeller Foundation. The title alone spoke volumes about the kinds of applicants who frequented the Foundation—academic scientists and researchers immersed in the deep search for knowledge that might advance civilization. In many ways the document amplified a short handbook Weaver wrote in 1946, called "N.S. Notes on Officers' Techniques." Both provided extraordinary insight into the culture of the Foundation and its attitude toward applicants and grantees.

Weaver began his memo with a statement on "The Least They Can Expect." Everyone who came to the Rockefeller Foundation deserved to be treated with courtesy and "should leave with the feeling that he has had a fair reception." He admonished the staff to listen more than talk. As he wrote in Officers' Techniques, "in the language of radiation theory, be very good absorbers and poor emitters." He advised officers to ask everyone before they left if they had been given a chance to say the things they wanted to say. Whenever someone actually met with an officer, the meeting should be recorded in the voluminous diaries that all officers kept describing the people and places they encountered as part of their work. (These diaries

constituted a key element within the Foundation's
enormous information system that constituted one
of its primary sources of ongoing innovation.) These
diaries were widely shared and made available to the
officer's colleagues in the division as well as to the central
administrative team. If a copy of a diary entry needed
to be directed to a particular staff member, secretaries
inserted a carbon when they typed up the entry so that it
could be initialed to the proper individual.

Weaver described the standard method for routing inquiries, which
involved a sometimes difficult process of judgment as to whether, for
example, a proposed project related to human genetics (Medicine and Public

Warren Weaver, director of the
Foundation's Natural Sciences division
for 27 years, was an accomplished
mathematician in his own right. Weaver
immersed himself in the work of the
Foundation's grantees and played a
profound role in the development of
the field of molecular biology.
(Rockefeller Archive Center.)

The Rockefeller Foundation moved to the newly constructed Rockefeller Center in New York in the summer of 1933. The new facilities provided ample space for the Foundation's growing staff and room to greet potential grantees and dignitaries. (Rockefeller Archive Center.)

Health) or genetics at the molecular level (Natural Science). While officers weren't cross-trained in one another's disciplines, they were asked to listen to and take notes on visits by applicants to other divisions if no one else was available. Weaver conceded that many projects were interdisciplinary and should involve program officers from different divisions. The Foundation also tended to put the relationship ahead of the discipline, so if one program officer had been working with a researcher, he or she would continue even if the new project seemed to fall into a different discipline.

Visitors would often want to know how to apply for a grant from the Rockefeller Foundation, and were surprised to know that there was no formal application form; nor was there any special calendar. "We do most of our work during the academic part of the year," Weaver noted. (Staff were generally not in the office in the summer, when they were traveling to visit grantees.) But the lack of a specific application form did not mean that the Rockefeller Foundation took the process of applying or decision-making lightly. Instead of receiving forms, Rockefeller program officers preferred to ask a potential applicant to "talk about his ideas while he is at RF. What is he doing? What does he want to do? What does he need in order to do what he wants to do?" Eventually, Weaver said, these ideas should be put into a letter that should be sent to the Foundation. "The letter does not need to be long or complicated," but Weaver said it should include a c.v. and a list of publications for key personnel. It should also include a descriptive statement of the problem or field of inquiry (at least a page, but no more than five).

Weaver was very prescriptive about the structure of this statement: the first several paragraphs should be written for a layperson's understanding so that it could be included in packets for the Board of Trustees. "We also find this most illuminating about the applicant himself." In the rest of the description, the applicant was invited to "let yourself go and get more technical for two or three pages of description." The applicant needed to provide a budget detailing what funds would be provided from the host institution. The Foundation also wanted to know "what hopes of continuity" there were for work that might follow the end of a Foundation grant, and what physical facilities were available for the project. If the responses provided to all of these questions piqued the interest of the Foundation's officers and fit with a program, then the applicant might be invited to submit a formal request. This request had to come from the highest authority within the applicant's institution (for example, the president of the university). Weaver advised new program officers to tell applicants that the Rockefeller Foundation rarely made a decision on the basis of written information alone. If the project had merit, "one of the officers will visit the man in his own laboratory, to meet his people, and to see with his own eyes the circumstances, handicaps, and progress of his work."

> "Almost everyone knows that we do make exceptions."
> *Warren Weaver, 1952*

One of the toughest but most routine jobs facing any officer was to say no or decline an application. The easiest answer was always to say that a proposal did not fall within the scope of the Foundation's program, but, as Weaver noted: "Almost everyone knows that we do make exceptions," so the pat answer didn't work. Rockefeller program officers had to say that the proposal did not fall within the program *and* the Foundation did not choose to make an exception in this case. But Weaver said that applications should never be declined too quickly; there should always be sufficient time "for us to roll the

TIME
THE WEEKLY NEWSMAGAZINE

ALFRED KINSEY
Reflections in the mirror of Venus.

matter around in our minds, and be perfectly sure that the obvious necessity for declination is indeed inescapable." In a rephrasing of the classic advice that it is always easier to change "no" to "yes" than the other way around, Weaver cautioned against ever expressing encouragement or optimism with regard to an application. "If you are conservative and the man gets the grant, he is happy, satisfied, and thinks the officers very stout fellows; but if you are the least bit optimistic and he does not get his grant, then he is likely to feel you have let him down."

Weaver's instructions to new program officers also crystallized the Rockefeller Foundation's philosophy of grantmaking, which echoed many of the principles laid down by John D. Rockefeller, Frederick Gates, and Jerome Greene in the earliest days of the Foundation's life. The Foundation did not "give money to completely unattached persons. We give money to institutions for the use of people." The Foundation generally did not provide support to pay for buildings, publications, or "major salaries" and overhead that would be part of an institution's general administrative cost. The Foundation did not fund expeditions. (Weaver conceded this might be institutional cowardice, but the Foundation did not want to be held responsible in the event of a tragic accident.) The Foundation did not provide funding for people to go to general conferences, but it would fund small groups of people to come together to focus on a specific problem.

Weaver explained that the Rockefeller Foundation gave money in several different ways. "Appropriations" were made by the trustees. These were generally large grants given to major projects. "Officer's actions" included grants-in-aid or fellowships and could be decided by staff. These kinds of grants could be decided in a week or, "if in a great rush," in a day or even an hour. But they could not extend for more than three years or be worth more than $10,000 (in 1936 dollars). The Foundation also allowed for very small "allocations" of up to $500 conferred by an individual program officer. Weaver gave an example of a Swedish researcher visiting the United States who stopped off at Bell Laboratories and discovered they were making a device that

Alfred Kinsey and his team of researchers investigating human sexuality received indirect support from the Rockefeller Foundation through grants provided to the National Research Council's Committee for Research on Problems of Sex. Kinsey's research was controversial inside and outside of the Foundation. When Congressman B. Carroll Reece launched an investigation into the work of private foundations, he attacked the Rockefeller Foundation for supporting Kinsey's work. Months after Kinsey appeared on the cover of *TIME* in 1953, the Rockeller Foundation decided to end its support for Kinsey's work. (TIME magazine.)

was not yet on the market, that he needed for his research. The Foundation might provide a small allocation to allow him to purchase and ship some of these devices back to Sweden. "This is admittedly 'chicken feed,'" Weaver wrote, "but it may keep a very good rooster alive and crowing."

People understood that the Rockefeller Foundation was well-placed at the center of many networks of information and influence. In the 1930s, they would arrive in the office hoping to benefit from these networks. Deans of graduate schools, research directors, college presidents, and scientists would drop by every time they were in New York, "presumably on the hypothesis that presence, rather than absence, makes the heart grow fonder." Sometimes people came looking for a job. Other times they came looking for employees. Weaver wisely counseled program officers to avoid recommending people for positions. "At the worst there might be an assumption that we have a special interest in the person, and that therefore there is some implication of future support from us. At the least, we may very likely be hurting the institution the man leaves."

> "This is admittedly chicken feed, but it may keep a very good rooster alive and crowing."
> *Warren Weaver, 1952*

The informal and relationship-based approach to grantmaking articulated in "How Do You Do, Dr. X?" carried on for decades after Warren Weaver retired. Even in 1983, when the Foundation received roughly 8,000 proposals per year, the section in the annual report titled "Applications" began as it had for decades: "No special form is required in making a request for Foundation aid." Applicants were still encouraged to send a letter to the foundation with a description of the project, a comprehensive plan and budget, and a listing of the applicant's qualifications and accomplishments.

Increasingly, however, the process of selecting grantees evolved along the deeper path worn by the Foundation's program officers as they traveled the globe gathering information. The networks they created provided a rich asset to be mined and developed to meet the Foundation's increasingly targeted goals. By the start of the new millennium, grantees were increasingly seen as partners in the process of philanthropy, and the Foundation devoted significant resources to the processes of identifying and shaping collaborations. Though the Foundation remained eager and open to input from a wide variety of constituencies, the typical Dr. X was far less likely to be seen as the primary grantee. The Foundation's new collaborators were more likely to be working with or in communities around the world.

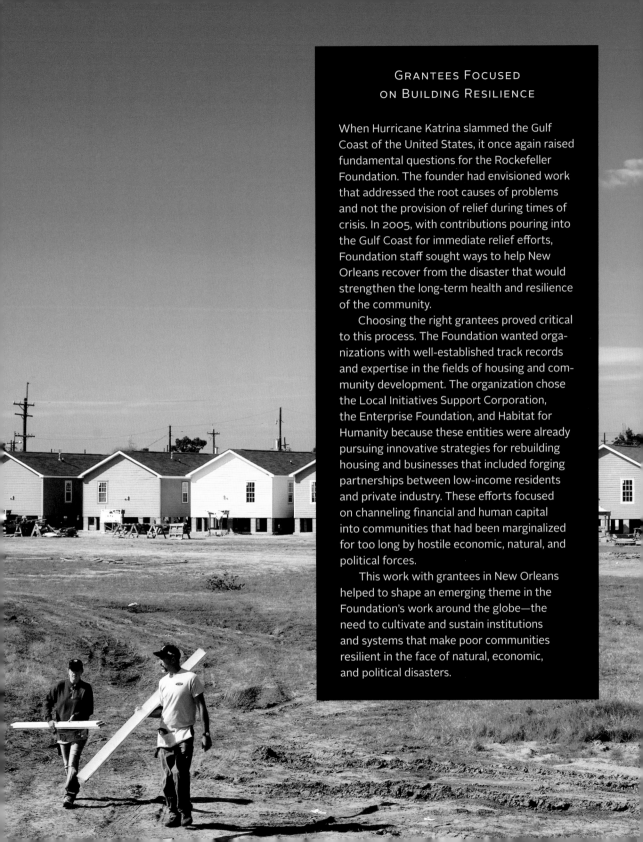

GRANTEES FOCUSED
ON BUILDING RESILIENCE

When Hurricane Katrina slammed the Gulf Coast of the United States, it once again raised fundamental questions for the Rockefeller Foundation. The founder had envisioned work that addressed the root causes of problems and not the provision of relief during times of crisis. In 2005, with contributions pouring into the Gulf Coast for immediate relief efforts, Foundation staff sought ways to help New Orleans recover from the disaster that would strengthen the long-term health and resilience of the community.

Choosing the right grantees proved critical to this process. The Foundation wanted organizations with well-established track records and expertise in the fields of housing and community development. The organization chose the Local Initiatives Support Corporation, the Enterprise Foundation, and Habitat for Humanity because these entities were already pursuing innovative strategies for rebuilding housing and businesses that included forging partnerships between low-income residents and private industry. These efforts focused on channeling financial and human capital into communities that had been marginalized for too long by hostile economic, natural, and political forces.

This work with grantees in New Orleans helped to shape an emerging theme in the Foundation's work around the globe—the need to cultivate and sustain institutions and systems that make poor communities resilient in the face of natural, economic, and political disasters.

A s the Foundation focused on grantmaking in the 1930s, the organization's strategies for identifying and working with grantees evolved as well. As Warren Weaver and Raymond Fosdick explained in 1936, using as an example the program in experimental biology (the field was later known as molecular biology), grantees surfaced primarily in three different ways. The greatest number of applications came from people who learned about the Foundation by reading a newspaper or magazine article or one of the Foundation's annual reports and contacted the Foundation asking for support. Most of these applicants, as Fosdick put it, "are quite outside our program and can be handled [rejected] quickly." If the Foundation had an interest in the application, officers would visit the institution and its laboratories, meet all the workers, and listen to explanations of the work and the need before they would recommend a grant for approval.

Other projects came forward through the conduit of a national or international science committee focused on a particular academic discipline. The National Research Council Committee for Research in Problems of Sex, for example, would identify and recommend projects to the Foundation. This group solicited projects informally without a defined application process. The National Research Council Committee on Radiation, however, published an invitation for grant applications, reviewed these applications, and then forwarded recommendations to the Rockefeller Foundation.

Finally, a third group of applications came as a result of the Foundation's continuous contact with the field. In formal and informal meetings in laboratories, universities, and conferences, program officers were constantly talking to potential applicants about work in the field. (From the time the program in experimental biology was launched in April 1933 to March 1936, Foundation staff paid 531 visits to 312 laboratories or institutions in 65 cities in 17 countries in Europe and more than 75 institutions in the United States, many of them multiple times).

1956

Following the recommendation of President Dean Rusk, the Board of Trustees launches a major new initiative to help developing nations in Latin America, Asia, the Middle East and Africa. (James S. Wright. Rockefeller Archive Center.)

TIMELINE

Chapter Seven: Grantees

Sustained relationships with grantees were at the heart of the Foundation's success. Fosdick and Weaver pointed out that in the sciences, particularly, the Foundation often started small with a particular researcher or institution. Fosdick used the example of three primary researchers at the Rothschild Institute for Physico-Chemical Biology in Paris. Back in the 1920s, the International Education Board had provided a series of fellowships to scientists Rene Wurmser, Boris Ephrussi, and Emmanuel Fauré-Fremiet, who later became affiliated with the Rothschild Institute. The fellowships allowed them to travel and collaborate with researchers in other European and American institutions. These fellowships culminated in grants-in-aid to support their research. During all this time, Foundation program officers were in contact and made visits to their labs. Familiarity "rooted in the established Foundation habit of frequent visits" helped build a shared vision for the research and a base for the Foundation's support, culminating in a major grant in 1936 to support the work of all of these men at the Rothschild Institute.

Fosdick summarized the Foundation's grantmaking strategy in a letter to Karl Compton, the president of MIT, in December 1943. He noted that the Foundation, like similar organizations, adopted rules and principles as a way of narrowing the totality of requests so that they could be dealt with competently. "But the deeper significance is that the principles, if wisely chosen, can give steadily accumulating significance to what would otherwise be only a scattered sequence of unrelated episodes. The Rockefeller Foundation has, in actual fact, made little use of rules; but it has not hesitated to formulate principles."

EVALUATION

In the late 1930s, Raymond Fosdick wrote a note to Alan Gregg wondering if the $160 million the Foundation had spent had made a difference. The note revealed Fosdick in a vulnerable moment, but it was the kind of moment that visits almost everyone in philanthropy.

For years the Rockefeller Foundation had relied on a very subjective system of evaluation. Program officers visited grantees and talked to peers in the same discipline. They wrote long memoranda for grant files and officer diaries. These efforts generated a great deal of paper, but surprisingly, given the Foundation's attention to systems and the rationalizing principles of science, there was little theoretical or formal basis for evaluation. In part this reflected the philosophy of the foundation. As Lindsley Kimball, the Foundation's vice president for administration

explained to visitors from the fledgling Ford Foundation in 1952, it was the Foundation's job to thoroughly vet the applicant and the project before funding. But once the decision was made, the Foundation believed it should "let the chips fall where they may." Although the Foundation kept track of expenditures as compared to the grantee's budget, the grantee was responsible for execution and the Foundation "should interfere as little as possible in the grantee's operations." Rockefeller believed that contacts in the field were more useful than any detailed narrative reports by grantees. When grantees wanted additional money, however, evaluation of past performance played a critical part in the Foundation's deliberations. In these cases, as Kimball reported, a complete evaluation was performed by the staff.

In this arena, the Foundation was not out of step with its peers in the philanthropic community. At Ford, for

Fire destroyed the main building at Wellesley College in 1914. The Rockefeller Foundation pledged $750,000 to help with reconstruction, but only if the college could raise the additional $1.25 million needed for the project. Local giving by those who cared about the outcome of a project was critical to the Foundation's philosophy of grantmaking. (Wellesley College Archives.)

Chapter Seven: Grantees

example, in the 1960s, "Large programs were continued for many years without thorough assessments." Meanwhile, project and grantee evaluations were often stored in the Foundation's archives without reflection. In 1990, Foundation President Peter Goldmark said that "effectiveness" was "one of the most perplexing issues for foundations." That year the Rockefeller Foundation decided to institute a new system of regular evaluation. As Goldmark told the public, "We are determined to bring rigor and tenacity to this effort." Under Judith Rodin's leadership, monitoring and evaluation were built into every major initiative of the Foundation.

Long-Term Support

In 1914, a fire swept through the main wood and brick building of Wellesley College. After reading about the disaster in the paper, Jerome Greene wrote to John D. Rockefeller to ask whether the newly created Rockefeller Foundation might come to the rescue of the college. Greene noted that "the behavior of the girls in the fire offers good evidence that Wellesley is an educational institution in the best sense of the term." Greene then suggested that "while our attention is rightly given in the main to plans carefully thought out with coolness and deliberation I think we may well consider the good we can occasionally do by an act that will convey no less the impression of generous sympathy than of mature judgment."

Shortly afterward, Bishop William Lawrence, a fundraising innovator and a Wellesley trustee, arrived at 26 Broadway to make a personal appeal for the college and its 1,500 female students. Before the fire, the General Education Board had promised $200,000 towards Wellesley's effort to raise $1 million for its endowment. John D. Rockefeller Jr. was sympathetic—so sympathetic, in fact, that when he did not receive a written proposal within the week, he wrote to Lawrence to say "we have been

Bishop William Lawrence was an early innovator in the field of fundraising, especially in the arena of endowment building. In negotiating with Lawrence over the Rockefeller Foundation's grant to Wellesley, John D. Rockefeller Jr. helped provide structure and incentives for Lawrence's campaign. (Library of Congress, Prints & Photographs.)

Docherty Peeter Weston Johnson Wilson Mieldazis Craig Magoon Tiedeman Boyd Lenert Bedell Knight Taylor Cox Conrad Cassidy

Holmes Becker Cort Taliaferro Hegner Augustine Root Simon Hoffman

International Health Board Class - Medical Zoology
Johns Hopkins School of Hygiene, January 1922

waiting the receipt of this letter before advising you of the decision which we have reached. I assume I will hear from you shortly."

To save the college, Wellesley's trustees launched a capital campaign to raise $2 million for buildings and an endowment fund, and at a meeting on April 2, the Executive Committee of the Rockefeller Foundation agreed to contribute $750,000 contingent upon the college's ability to raise the balance. The point of the gift: to provide physical and financial resources that would allow the college to fulfill its mission through good times and bad times ahead.

Junior's good-news letter to Lawrence reveals the way in which the Rockefeller Foundation was already seeking to engage with grantees as well as provide them with resources. Lawrence had told him that the trustees were inclined to lower the total campaign goal to $1.8 million,

Endowment gifts were frequently offered to universities in the early days to encourage a long-term commitment to new programs. Rockefeller Foundation grants helped build and endow the School of Hygiene and Public Health at Johns Hopkins University, which opened in 1918. (Rockefeller Archive Center.)

but Junior suggested they stick with the original goal in case costs rose. If the construction project came in on budget, then they would have an additional $200,000 for the endowment. He also suggested they raise the money in one campaign, rather than go for building money first and endowment money second. If they split the campaigns, fundraising would peter out once the building goal was met, and "you will be obliged to plod along on the endowment as you have done in the past, without the additional incentive and leverage which the recent fire will give." He also pressed Wellesley to set a definite end date to the campaign to bring a sense of urgency to the effort.

In expressing gratitude for the gift, Bishop Lawrence noted that aside from the money itself, the Foundation's endorsement would help the capital campaign immensely. In this case, Junior's advice hit home. Wellesley launched an aggressive campaign and surpassed their goal by $100,000 on December 31, 1914.

For the first two decades of the Rockefeller Foundation's history, Rockefeller money flowed heavily from the Foundation, the General Education Board, the International Education Board, and the Laura Spelman Rockefeller Memorial to provide endowments for leading institutions. This strategy sparked some controversy among board members, however. Frederick Gates, for example, resisted the idea of making large contributions to endowments. In 1913, he wrote, "It seems to me that if there were no other objection to our giving to endowments—and there are many—this one objection, that we would not be able to have influence in the conduct of the institution proportionate to the weight of our gift, once it is out of our hands and built into an endowment, would be in itself a fatal objection. To have a voice in the conduct of institutions, to observe annually whether or not they are fulfilling their mission, are doing effective work, are meeting the needs of the community which they are set to meet, is both a healthful influence on the institutions themselves and a perfectly just and necessary protection to the Foundation." Indeed, Gates believed this kind of oversight represented a critical social role for the Foundation, protecting other givers who didn't have the time for this kind of due diligence.

On the other hand, large gifts to major institutions, in the minds of some, represented exactly the kind of wholesale philanthropy that Gates believed was necessary, given the scale at which the Rockefeller Foundation was operating. In 1928, for example, as the Foundation considered cutting back considerably on its institutional support programs, Roger Greene, the head of the China Medical Board, protested to President George Vincent. The Foundation's intended shift to an emphasis on the advancement of knowledge would demand specialized staff with a high level of scientific knowledge to assess the proposals by scientists working on the cutting edge of knowledge. Moreover, many of these grants would be small because "a great investigator frequently needs no more to carry his work over a critical point." Processing and judging large numbers of small grants would increase the Foundation's need for staff and grow the operating budget. In contrast, Greene pointed out, giving large, unrestricted grants for research to universities and special institutes would require only a modest staff at the Foundation. He suggested that picking a handful of top universities would be a good policy. Greene also believed that this policy would help to sustain these educational institutions, which he believed was important to the Foundation's mission and goals. "We have felt that American university presidents had to do too much in the way of money raising," he wrote to Vincent, "but have we done anything to lessen that burden? We have rather encouraged them to take up new projects which otherwise they might not have attempted."

In general, the Rockefeller Foundation made endowment gifts in the same spirit as John D. Rockefeller had made his gifts to the Rockefeller Foundation—with great license to the trustees of the grantee institution to do with the money as they saw fit, and according to their charitable mission. In April 1934, a trustee resolution made these guidelines explicit. Institutions that had received endowment gifts from the Foundation were free to merge or consolidate with other institutions and to take the endowment with them. If, after ten years, a better purpose akin to the original purpose had emerged for the income from the funds, they were free to redeploy the income. After fifty years, they could use both the income and the principal for other needs "closely akin to the original purpose."

Support for Overhead

In the case of the Rockefeller Foundation, many of its grantees during the first seventy-five years were universities or institutions of higher learning. An issue that emerged in the 1950s was the increasing tendency of universities to include within their budgets a percentage for overhead and university administration. The Foundation wrestled with whether or not it was willing to pay for this. In 1958, President Dean Rusk worried: "What happens to research if overhead commissions become an important part of the general support of our key universities. Couldn't this become a large and pretentious racket, with the tail wagging the academic dog?" He suggested that university administrators might propose mediocre research projects just "to pay heat and light bills." Rusk thought it might be better for the Foundation or other philanthropists to simply contribute to university

operating budgets. "Unless there is some evidence of inspired curiosity, why not put up the 25 percent and save the 75 percent wasted upon mediocre 'research.' I'm fearful of entering this jungle."

In fact, the Rockefeller Foundation had been in this jungle for quite some time. In 1913, Jerome Greene suggested that it would be "unwise for an institution like the Rockefeller Foundation to assume permanently or indefinitely a share of the current expenses of an endowed institution which it does not control." Greene understood that the question of control had at least two dimensions. One related to program, the other to administration. John D. Rockefeller had supported the mission and program of the University of Chicago, but he was constantly frustrated by the expectation that he would cover the institution's rapidly growing budget in the early years when he had no control over spending.

After World War II, this issue appeared in a new context as many universities and research institutions began to insist that they could not support externally funded research projects without a contribution to the

John D. Rockefeller's gifts to create the University of Chicago have been described as his first great adventure in giving. (Hans Behm, Library of Congress, Prints & Photographs.)

26 Broadway,
New York.

May 15 th 1889.

Rev. Fred T. Gates, Cor. Sec'y,

American Baptist Education Society.

My dear Sir:

I will contribute six hundred thousand dollars, ($600.000#) toward an endowment fund for a college to be established at Chicago, the income only of which may be used for current expenses, but not for land, buildings or repairs, providing four hundred thousand dollars, ($400.000#) more is pledged by good and responsible parties, satisfactory to the Board of the American Baptist Education Society and myself, on or before June 1st 1890; said four hundred thousand dollars, or as much of it as shall be required,

26 Broadway,
New York.

In 1890, Rockefeller pledged $600,000 to help create the University of Chicago. The gift was contingent upon the American Baptist Education Society's efforts to raise an additional $400,000. By 1910, after making his final gift, Rockefeller had contributed $35 million to the university. (Rockefeller Archive Center.)

to be used for the purpose of purchasing land and erecting buildings, the remainder of the same to be added to the above six hundred thousand dollars, as endowment.

I will pay the same to the American Baptist Education Society in five years, beginning within ninety days after completion of the subscription as above, and pay five per cent. each ninety days thereafter until all is paid; providing not less than a proportionate amount is so paid by the other subscribers to the four hundred thousand dollars; otherwise this pledge to be null and void.

Yours, very truly,

Jno. D. Rockefeller.

university's overhead. MIT offered a case in point. Given the magnitude of externally funded research carried on at MIT, the institution asserted that it was not able to pay the incremental administrative costs of these projects out of its own endowment. Moreover, the university said that the endowment funds were not given to support research, but rather for "educational purposes of a different nature." Thus it developed a policy that all projects and grants had to "cover the total cost of a research project on a no-loss, no-gain basis."

Unfortunately, detailed cost accounting necessary to allocate costs appropriately was almost impossible. Thus indirect charges were levied based on a percentage of the total cost of the project. MIT calculated that indirect expenses normally fell within a range of 15 to 25 percent of the total direct costs for the project. MIT based this range on years of experience with government-contracted work.

The Rockefeller Foundation also recognized this issue in the 1950s in the context of its fellowship program by giving a general, unearmarked grant, over and above the cost of tuition, to each institution that received a fellow. A similar issue came up in the context of paying for the salaries of principal investigators on grants. Warren Weaver outlined what he saw as the prevailing practice in 1952. With developmental grants where the Foundation was looking "to build up a certain general field of activity in some institution," it had become standard practice to pay for major salaries in the beginning and then to taper off. This was done in the field of psychiatry, for example. But Weaver pointed out that these kinds of grants marked the exception rather than the rule in the Natural Sciences and Medicine and Public Health Divisions. In Humanities, the institutional structures and prevailing practices were different. As Joseph Willits, the director of the Social Sciences Division, pointed out, often the payment of a salary for a principal offered the only way in which an academic could buy release time to work on a project.

1963
University Development program begins. The effort seeks to promote economic and social well-being by enhancing higher education and research in African, Asian, and Latin American nations. (Ted Spiegel. Rockefeller Archive Center.)

When the Board of Trustees conducted a five-year review of the Foundation's programs in 1958, the issue of whether to pay overhead to grantee institutions merited special attention. To the trustees, the solution lay in a shift of the Rockefeller Foundation's program away from project-specific funding to more general support for institutions. In part, the trustees felt that the

TIMELINE

new governmental funding agencies would be increasingly responsible for specific projects. The report approvingly quoted trustee Dr. Lee DuBridge's argument that requests for project support should always come through the university administration, with indirect costs clearly articulated so that the Foundation could judge the real commitment of the institution to the project.

In 1958, Dean Rusk summarized the Foundation's current philosophy on overhead by saying that when the Foundation initiated a project and asked an institution to be the implementer, the Foundation normally accepted "an obligation to pay the full costs." Where the grantee came to the Foundation looking for support, costs for specific project facilities, support staff, or personnel benefits were allowed. But the Foundation did not allow a surcharge as a contribution toward the general costs of the institution involved. Rusk wanted institutions seeking general operating support to apply for it specifically, but they were unlikely to get it. Although the Foundation and the General Education Board had given nearly $250 million to the endowments of forty-one American universities over the history of the institution by 1958, it was increasingly reluctant to help build endowments, preferring targeted programs that would yield demonstrated results.

University of Chicago President Harry Pratt Judson with John D. Rockefeller Jr. (Rockefeller Archive Center.)

As a consequence of its history, the Rockefeller Foundation is still well-placed at the center of many networks of information and influence, as Warren Weaver pointed out in 1952. These networks, anchored in relationships with grantees past and present, represent one of the Foundation's key assets as it seeks to address the challenges confronting the poor and vulnerable around the world. Although "Dr. X" rarely arrives unannounced anymore, the attitude of listening and being open to ideas that come from grantees and partners has played a critical role in paving the way for successful collaborations, especially with other funders in the world of philanthropy.

Recognizing Genius

For more than a century the Nobel Prize has been associated with profound discovery. Often this recognition comes to the discoverer long after the path-breaking work has been completed. In contrast, fellowships awarded by the Rockefeller Foundation and other grantors are often given early in someone's career. They provide resources to enable further study or training, equip a lab, or perform experiments. Timing is everything. Even small grants given at the right moment can make an enormous difference.

As of 2012, at least 221 Nobel Prize winners have received support from the Rockefeller Foundation or its sister philanthropies. They come from all over the world and reflect not only the spectrum of human understanding, but also humankind's eternal ambition to live in a peaceful world. (Data provided by the Rockefeller Foundation.)

1903	1904	1907	1911	1912	1914	1914
1927	1927	1929	1929	1929	1930	1931
1938	1938	1939	1939	1939	1943	1943
1947	1948	1948	1949	1949	1950	1950
1956	1956	1957	1957	1958	1958	1958
1962	1962	1962	1962	1963	1963	1964

1970	1970	1970	1970	1970	1971	1971	1972	1972	1972	1972	1973	1973
1977	1977	1978	1978	1979	1979	1979	1980	1981	1981	1982	1982	1982
1990	1991	1992	1993	1993	1994	1994	1994	1995	1995	1995	1996	1996
2002	2002	2002	2003	2003	2004	2004	2005	2005	2006	2006	2006	2007

42 CHEMISTRY   48 ECONOMICS   7 LITERATURE

© The Nobel Foundation

1915 1915 1918 1918 1920 1921 1922 1922 1922 1923 1924 1925 1926

1932 1932 1932 1933 1933 1934 1934 1935 1935 1936 1936 1936 1937

1943 1944 1944 1945 1945 1945 1945 1946 1946 1946 1946 1947 1947

1951 1951 1951 1951 1952 1953 1953 1954 1954 1954 1954 1955 1955

1959 1959 1959 1959 1959 1960 1960 1960 1960 1961 1962 1962 1962

1964 1964 1965 1965 1967 1967 1967 1968 1969 1969 1969 1969 1969

1973 1973 1974 1974 1974 1974 1975 1975 1976 1976 1976 1977 1977

1982 1983 1983 1984 1985 1985 1986 1986 1986 1987 1988 1988 1989

1996 1997 1997 1997 1998 1999 1999 1999 2001 2001 2002 2002 2002

2008 2008 2008 2009 2010 2010 2010 2010 2010 2011

71 MEDICINE   18 PEACE   35 PHYSICS   221 TOTAL

COLLABORATION

How do we collaborate?

Foundations often act with a great deal of autonomy. Protected by endowments and self-perpetuating boards, they can, if they choose, spend their time soliciting and reviewing grant proposals, writing checks, and reading evaluations without ever thinking about what their peers are doing. Only the donor's intent and a desire to be effective compel foundations to work closely with grantees or other funders.

In a world where philanthropic dollars represent only a small share of the available capital, foundations seeking to maximize the impact of their grants and contributions must be able to collaborate with grantees, governments, and other potential funders. By pooling resources, they can minimize the risk that any one funder takes on a social venture. They also benefit from information sharing that allows ideas to be tested from multiple points of view. Finally, collaboration reduces the likelihood of creating redundant organizations or facilities in a given community or social sector.

Collaboration is not easy. It demands alignment of the goals of multiple institutions and a process for shared decision-making. Within the context of a single organization there are hierarchies for resolving differences. Ultimately, a president or board of trustees must decide. Within the context of a collaboration, however, lines of authority are often less clear and decisions must be negotiated. The costs of communication and coordination go up, and decision-making slows.

Collaboration is also shaped by the partners a foundation chooses. At one end of the spectrum, some foundations make grants and never expect more than a thank you letter and a summary report when the project is finished. But other philanthropic organizations see grant-making as an active partnership between the foundation and the grantee, with the foundation supplying intellectual and social capital as well as financial resources.

Many projects or initiatives require the cooperation and assistance of government agencies. In this arena, the foundation has to understand the political factors that shape the government's ability to act. The foundation also has to avoid getting trapped within the government's political constraints.

In recent years, with a growing recognition that the private sector represents a powerful force for innovation and a deep source of capital, many foundations are looking to partner with private-sector corporations or companies in an effort to achieve a "double bottom-line" impact, producing both a social and financial return. Culturally, these collaborations are often difficult because the motivations of the organizations are not the same. Companies must deliver profits to their owners. Foundations seek social returns on the investments made by their donors. Nevertheless, as authors Matthew Bishop and Michael Green report, there is great potential for what is sometimes called "philanthrocapitalism."

COLLABORATION

NO LONGER THE BIGGEST

In December 1946, Wyman P. Fiske came to New York to meet with Warren Weaver. A tall, heavy man in his late 40s, with a law degree as well as an MBA from Harvard, Fiske was a former accounting professor at MIT who knew something about philanthropy. He had developed and directed the Sloan Fellowship Program since 1939. Nevertheless, he had a lot of questions.

In Michigan, the founder of the Ford Motor Company was near death. Years earlier, after Congress voted to tax estates of over $50 million at a rate of 70 percent, Henry Ford had created the Ford Foundation. To avoid paying an estimated $321 million in federal estate taxes, Ford and his son Edsel had willed most of their shares in the Ford Motor Company to this new institution. While the two men were still alive, the foundation gave an average of $1 million a year to Michigan charities. But with Ford's death, the foundation would become the richest in the world, with assets valued at nearly $500 million ($4.67 billion in 2011 dollars), almost four times the net worth of the Rockefeller Foundation. With these assets, the Ford Foundation needed a program. They had asked Fiske to develop a plan.

Fiske had a lot of ideas. He was very interested in a program focused on training leadership in business as well as in "national life." He and Weaver talked generally about the idea of "cooperation." At one point, Weaver suggested that Ford might think of funding fields of science that had little

Scions of two of America's most successful entrepreneurs: Edsel Ford and John D. Rockefeller Jr. To avoid enormous inheritance taxes and a forced sale of Ford Motor Company shares in the 1930s, Edsel and Henry Ford established the Ford Foundation. (Rockefeller Archive Center.)

contact with natural sources of support; he included mathematics and astronomy in this category. He joked later to his colleagues that mathematicians might even be able to help Ford Motor develop an efficient spring suspension system for its cars.

Over the next several months, Fiske frequently returned to the Rockefeller Foundation to pick the brains of its top officers. He wanted to know about different programs and generally about operations. He and Weaver talked about the influence of donors and their families on a foundation's work and program. Fiske believed the Ford Foundation would need to move its offices out of Detroit.

The Rockefeller Foundation's officers were at least a little skeptical of Fiske's efforts, concerned that he was naïve and knew little about the actual work of giving money away. Over lunch with Alan Gregg, the head of the Foundation's medical division, Fiske talked about "the science of man" concept. He was also interested in "the present state of morals and ethics," a topic that was important to Chester Barnard and the Foundation board. After Weaver met with him again on March 7, 1947, he noted that Fiske continued to show "a considerable but rather formless enthusiasm for the social sciences and for the development of 'leadership.' He also intends to recommend a little of almost everything else." To borrow from Frederick Gates, there was a danger that the Ford Foundation might fall victim to "scatteration."

All of the Foundation's officers, however, recognized the weight of Fiske's task. As Alan Gregg wrote in his diary, "I do not know that I have seen, aside from wartime conditions, as large an opportunity confronting an individual as that which [Fiske] confronts." What is less clear is whether the Foundation's officers realized how Henry Ford's death would signal the beginning of a new era for the Rockefeller Foundation.

Over the years, the Rockefeller Foundation had collaborated with other major philanthropic organizations, especially the Carnegie Corporation. But in the postwar era, the scale and complexity of the world's problems, combined with the relative paucity of philanthropic dollars in the context of these challenges, forced the Foundation to find new ways to partner with other foundations. Much of what the Rockefeller Foundation learned in this era, it learned in working with Ford.

Henry Ford's death in April 1947 forced the Ford Foundation to get serious about the future. Wyman Fiske was quickly pushed aside. In December 1948, Henry Ford II announced the formation of an eight-member study commission under the leadership of H. Rowan Gaither Jr., a San Francisco attorney who had served as the assistant director of the Radiation Laboratory at MIT during World War II, and would soon help found the Rand Corporation. Less than two years later, the Commission released its recommendations for the policy and program of the foundation.

The proposed program was organized around five core initiatives: 1) to promote world peace and establish a world order of law and justice; 2) to secure greater allegiance to basic principles of freedom and democracy; 3) to advance the economic well-being of people everywhere; 4) to strengthen educational opportunities to promote equal opportunity and allow individuals to realize their potential; and 5) to increase knowledge of factors that influence or determine human conduct and extend that knowledge for the benefit of individuals and society. In keeping with the traditions developed by the Rockefeller Foundation and Carnegie Corporation, the Ford Foundation's objectives were broad and comprehensive, providing a great deal of room for staff and future trustees to be opportunistic and respond to emerging challenges.

Through the 1950s, the Ford and Rockefeller Foundations found many reasons to work together.

1970
Norman Borlaug wins the Nobel Peace Prize for his work with the Rockefeller Foundation's Conquest of Hunger program.
(Rockefeller Archive Center.)

COLLABORATION ANCHORED IN HISTORY

When Bill Gates established the foundation that would bear his name in 1994, he asked his father to manage the new organization. To understand the challenge, William H. Gates Sr. began reading about the Rockefellers and the Rockefeller Foundation. What he learned surprised him, and his discoveries would help pave the way for a collaboration anchored in the confluences of history.

"Every corner we've turned in the field of global health," Gates Sr. writes in his book *Showing Up for Life*, "we've found ourselves building on efforts the Rockefeller Foundation had helped launch and fund in the 1980s."

If you want to pursue "audacious goals," Gates writes, "you need like-minded partners with whom to collaborate. And we learned that such goals are not prizes claimed by the short-winded. The Rockefellers stay with tough problems for generations."

These were the insights that helped pave the way for the Alliance for a Green Revolution in Africa. "We expect that, over time, African farmers will be able to produce two or three times as much food as they are growing now," Gates says, "and sell what they don't need. All this should help tens of millions of people in sub-Saharan Africa lead more prosperous lives."

Chapter Eight: Collaboration

After Dean Rusk became president in 1952, the Rockefeller Foundation's interest in the developing world coincided with the Ford Foundation's objectives to promote world peace and strengthen the institutions of democracy at home and abroad. As the two largest private foundations, Ford and Rockefeller also strategized their response to Congressional investigations into philanthropy launched in 1952.

Ford and Rockefeller worked together particularly on agriculture programs. Even before Rusk officially assumed his position at the Rockefeller Foundation, Foundation officials had concluded that collaboration with other foundations would be critical to the success of its programs in the future. Rusk met with Ford Foundation's staffer John B. Howard in April 1952. The two men talked about a variety of subjects, including Rockefeller's plans to develop hardier food crops in India and Southeast Asia. Howard told Rusk that the Ford Foundation would be very interested in this initiative.

Through the mid-1950s, staff at the Rockefeller Foundation studied a variety of options for developing rice research in Asia. Meanwhile, the Ford Foundation invested heavily in development projects in India between 1951 and 1953 that met with only limited success. Staff work and the exhortations of John D. Rockefeller 3rd raised the Ford Foundation's interest in population and food production issues. Then, in August 1958, senior officials from both foundations met to discuss grants they were considering making to the College of Agriculture at Lyallpur in Pakistan. At this lunch, the conversation turned to the idea of developing a single international institute to focus on rice research.

From this initial conversation, it took just over a year to work out the details with the Philippine government to establish in Los Baños the International Rice Research Institute (IRRI), which was formally created with a memorandum of understanding signed in December 1959. To get the institute off the ground, the Ford Foundation agreed to provide capital and the Rockefeller Foundation assumed a substantial burden to pay for staff and programming. Dean Rusk believed that the cooperation of Ford and Rockefeller internationalized the project and made it seem less like a national effort on the part of the Philippines. Although he highly doubted the possibilities for securing cooperation among the Asian nations, Rusk believed the foundation-led institute would enjoy more success than any analogous effort launched by national governments or even international agencies.

Cooperation on IRRI opened the door in the 1960s

At the International Rice Research Institute (IRRI), sponsored by the Rockefeller and Ford Foundations, researchers looked for new ways to control pests affecting rice crops. (Rockefeller Archive Center.)

Research on barley helped lead to the development of the International Center for Tropical Agriculture in Colombia with sponsorship by the Ford and W.K. Kellogg Foundations. (Rockefeller Archive Center.)

for continuing partnerships between Ford and Rockefeller, especially in agriculture. Indeed, by 1963, Foundation president J. George Harrar was actively negotiating with Ford for joint support of three international institutes including IRRI, the Arid Lands Research Institute and the International Institute of Tropical Agriculture. For its part, the still-developing Ford Foundation benefited from the Rockefeller Foundation's experience and connections in the world of scientific research. Meanwhile, the programs initiated by the Rockefeller Foundation were more ambitious than they might have been thanks to the Ford Foundation's participation.

Lingering Uncertainty

D espite their cooperation on IRRI, however, Ford and Rockefeller Foundation staffs were still uncertain about how to work together. In 1960, for example, Robert Morison, who directed the Rockefeller Foundation's Medical and Natural Sciences Division, had raised a cautionary flag when one of his staff asked about cooperating with the Ford Foundation. From Morison's point of view, there were practical and ethical issues to be resolved.

Morison noted that things shared in confidence by grantees or others in the Rockefeller Foundation's network should not be passed on to other foundations. He also said the Foundation should avoid "the impression that we are in any way putting pressure on another foundation to do what we want them to do." He further suggested that "it is important to avoid doing anything which might be interpreted on the outside as undue collusion between two large foundations with unusual power." Morison conceded that there was no equivalent in the philanthropic world to the antitrust laws that applied in business, "but from time to time in the past the public has worried about the amount of power over cultural activities placed in the hands of a few foundation officers and trustees."

Morison determined that it was appropriate for Foundation staff to share their appraisals of the institutional capacities of organizations that had applied to the Ford Foundation for funding, but that it was "probably not wise, except under extraordinary circumstances, to travel around with the representatives of other foundations or to give the impression that we are making a sort of joint appraisal." Morison didn't want grantees to think that the Rockefeller Foundation might become a conduit or an advocate for grants from the Ford Foundation.

Robert S. Morison succeeded Warren Weaver as director of the Division of Medical and Natural Sciences. As collaboration with the Ford Foundation developed, he and other staff had to define the boundaries for the working relationship between the two organizations. (Rockefeller Archive Center.)

Resolving protocol issues was one thing, but the Rockefeller Foundation also struggled with the idea that it was no longer the biggest foundation on the planet. The birth of the Ford Foundation foreshadowed an important question that would confront the Rockefeller Foundation in the second half-century of its existence. When it was no longer the largest private foundation, or even the second largest, how would it continue to exercise influence? Asked to look ahead twenty years in 1960, Charles Fahs, the director of the Humanities program, suggested that it would have to be through "intellectual leadership and by imagination and courage on the part of both officers and Trustees." He said that with the growth of other American foundations, the Rockefeller Foundation could withdraw from fields that others were likely to serve, and focus on problems that others "are unwilling or unable to tackle."

Indeed, cooperation with Ford in the 1960s opened the door to other collaborations. Out of a Bellagio Conference came the establishment in 1971 of a consortium known as the Consultative Group on International Agricultural Research (CGIAR). The Foundation teamed with Ford and Kellogg to finance the International Center for Tropical Agriculture (CIAT). With Canada's International Development Research Centre, the Foundation embraced a number international agricultural initiatives. In the U.S., the Foundation worked with the Kresge Foundation to support environmental programs at Michigan State University and Woods Hole, Massachusetts, and to help finance a building at CIAT. Rockefeller also helped connect Kresge with New York University to finance a new medical building. These collaborative projects led to the development of a more collegial relationship between the two foundations, especially on environmental programs. Rockefeller staff provided leads to Kresge regarding potential grantees working on projects that complemented the joint projects they funded.

COOPERATING WITH SMALLER FOUNDATIONS

The emergence of the Ford Foundation in the early 1950s posed one kind of challenge to the Rockefeller's Foundation's role in the philanthropic community. The proliferation of thousands of smaller private foundations raised another. Through the 1960s, a series of Congressional investigations focused on abuses of the tax code perpetrated by some private foundations as well as the lack of public information about the work of foundations in general. The Rockefeller Foundation defended itself and the principles of philanthropy during these hearings, but some people expected more as the foundation community sought to pull together and establish standards and best practices that would stave off further attacks.

The Rockefeller Foundation was deeply ambivalent about some of these efforts. In 1972, for example, the Commonwealth Fund sought to recruit Rockefeller and Ford to take part in a study of the administrative expense of leading foundations. Both Rockefeller and Ford hesitated, fearing that they would not necessarily agree with the report's findings. Rockefeller trustee Robert Goheen pressed John Knowles to get involved, suggesting that in this new world the Rockefeller Foundation should be a leader in dealing with foundation management issues. Frederick Seitz, the head of Rockefeller University, wrote to Knowles to suggest that the Rockefeller Foundation had to "exhibit rational leadership" to protect its own interests and the field. In 1973, the Rockefeller family offices helped fund a study, by Harvard Professor Martin Feldstein, of the economic effects of charitable contributions on tax policy and social welfare in the United States. Feldstein's report bolstered the philanthropic community when it demonstrated that tax deductions produced far more dollars for social welfare programs than conventional government programs.

Some staff imagined a leadership role for the Rockefeller Foundation that went beyond these defensive actions in the public policy sphere. In 1972, for example, vice president Sterling Wortman proposed that the Foundation begin to systematically track the interests of smaller foundations to "become a broker for ideas as well as for funding of worthwhile proposals." Wortman proposed that the Foundation experiment with such an initiative, trying it for three years to see if it worked. Wortman also wanted to use this program as a vehicle to begin to strengthen weak relationships with foundations in Europe. The plan was not approved.

The Rockefeller Foundation's Bellagio Center has played a key part in the effort to convene stakeholders and design innovative solutions to global challenges. Among many historic moments, a 1971 conference led to the formation of the Consultative Group on International Agricultural Research (CGIAR). (Rockefeller Archive Center.)

T he expansion of the philanthropic community accelerated with the boom of the 1980s. By 1987, with $1.6 billion in assets, the Rockefeller Foundation was ranked seventh among the largest foundations in the United States. These changes created obvious new realities. As Peter Goldmark said to a gathering of philanthropists on the occasion of John D. Rockefeller's 150th birthday in 1989, Rockefeller and his philanthropies had had the audacity to set out "to tackle global problems single-handedly: eliminating hookworm and yellow fever, or creating the entire field of public health. Today no one in this room represents an institution that can single-handedly wrestle to the ground a global problem. That day is long past. And we in philanthropy are all faced with the requirement to build partnerships more daring, more disciplined, more generous, than anything we have ever done before."

Goldmark and his fellow CEOs at the Ford Foundation (Franklin Thomas and later Susan Berresford), the MacArthur Foundation (Adele Simmons), and Pew Charitable Trusts (Rebecca Rimel) formed a group engagingly known as "the Four Musketeers" to try to develop a structured dialogue regarding ways in which they might collaborate on common goals. The W.K. Kellogg Foundation (William Richardson) joined the group in 1995. To strengthen the framework for collaboration throughout their organizations, the group sponsored a "Multi-Foundation Training" session in 1995 that was in reality a conversation about priorities, impact and opportunities for collaboration. This group would also provide a useful sounding board for the Rockefeller Foundation board of trustees in 1997 as it began the search for a new president, after Goldmark announced his departure at the end of the year.

The foundations represented in the Musketeers group were among the largest in the country, but they would soon welcome a newcomer to the philanthropic community. It is in the nature of philanthropy's relationship to capitalism that new foundations will be born that surpass their predecessors in wealth. So in 2000, with the creation of the Bill & Melinda Gates Foundation (with an initial endowment of $16 billion that quickly grew to $36.3 billion by the summer of 2011), a new institution was created with enormous potential.

1978
Rockefeller Foundation helps to convene the first meeting of the Great Neglected Diseases Network. (Rockefeller Archive Center.)

In 2006, the Rockefeller and Gates Foundations launched a partnership to create the Alliance for a Green Revolution in Africa (AGRA). The need was overwhelming. Three hundred million Africans went without sufficient food each day. Modest investments and improvements in farming practices were expected to triple or quadruple the levels of production. The Gates Foundation initially committed $100 million over five years, and the Rockefeller Foundation provided $50 million. AGRA represented the Gates Foundation's first "venture into poverty and development after years of focusing largely on global health and education." To outsiders, as well as the partners, the collaboration was extremely promising. As the *Washington Post* reported, "the mere fact that the world's biggest philanthropist is joining with the preeminent foundation working in agricultural development is 'going to make a difference.'" Indeed, the combination of the Rockefeller and Gates Foundations on this initiative, as Melinda Gates said, reflected a shared vision "for creating lasting change that will help millions of the most vulnerable in Africa lift themselves out of extreme poverty."

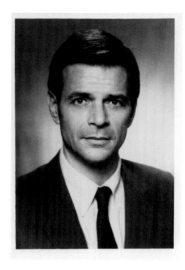

As president, Peter Goldmark worked with his peers in the philanthropic community to promote greater collaboration. (Rockefeller Archive Center.)

A Renewed Look at the Private Sector

As collaboration became increasingly important to strategy, in the 1990s the Foundation turned to the biggest source of capital in the world—the private sector. John D. Rockefeller had suggested that creative entrepreneurs in the marketplace offered the most powerful vehicle for improving the well-being of mankind. Neither philanthropy nor government had the resources to meet all of these growing needs. Moreover, as Foundation leaders increasingly recognized, the private sector offered valuable knowledge and experience to tackle some of the biggest problems facing humanity. But partnering with the private sector demanded a new way of thinking about collaboration, a way of thinking rooted in the idea of social investing.

Members of two local cassava associations gather in Malawi. Under the aegis of the Alliance for a Green Revolution for Africa (AGRA), the Foundation and its partners sought to triple or quadruple agricultural production levels in Africa to meet the needs of the continent's growing population. (Jonas Bendiksen.)

SOCIAL INVESTING

How should the Foundation's mission influence its investment strategies?

P rivate foundations have traditionally seen money from two perspectives. It is a resource given to them by the donor, and if it is meant to do good over time it must be invested in a way that will protect the value of the asset and produce annual income. This income, in turn, provides the resources the organization needs to carry out its program.

As good stewards, boards of trustees have been expected to manage their investments prudently and allocate their budgets to maximize the effectiveness of their programs. Traditionally, the social mission of the organization was not supposed to color the organization's investment strategy. Likewise, the investment of program funds was not expected to provide a financial return. As a result, for many years, the vast majority of philanthropic organizations did not make loans or invest directly in businesses. This kind of activity was unseemly, if not illegal, for a nonprofit organization. But times have changed.

Starting in the late 1960s, these assumptions began to be challenged. Foundations were asked to provide loans (investment capital) for minority businesses or housing developments in low-income communities. Activists, meanwhile, asked why foundations were investing in companies whose business practices seemed to be at odds with the work and mission of the foundation. They also asked why foundations and other entities managing public capital shouldn't provide financing to new enterprises or sectors—like renewable energy or biotechnology—that seemed to promise significant social returns. Changes in the U.S. tax code in 1969 specifically allowed foundations to begin making these kinds of Program-Related Investments.

Today, a number of philanthropic organizations practice some form of social investing. They may incorporate programmatic goals into their endowment management strategies, or they may include investment activity in their program work. Some subscribe to what has been called "socially responsible investing." They use their status as shareholders to take an activist role within the private sector or to screen out investments that might have harmful effects on society or the environment. They may also push for corporate policies that benefit the poor, the environment, or some other social good. Some institutions also practice "mission-related investing." When making investment decisions, they consider the positive impacts a company's business might have that correlate with the mission of the foundation. Taking advantage of changes in the tax code, some philanthropic entities make Program-Related Investments that provide capital to high-risk, marginalized communities, while others are engaged in "impact investing" that produces a "double-bottom line" return with social or environmental benefits as well as a return of capital or greater financial receipts.

Despite all of these innovations, this socially influenced approach to investing is still very controversial in many organizations. Some trustees continue to believe that investment policy should only be shaped by the effort to protect the value of the organization's assets and maximize the income generated within an acceptable range of risk. Many still believe that a high wall should separate the market from philanthropy.

In 1919, John D. Rockefeller Jr. disagreed.

SOCIAL INVESTING

An Activist Shareholder

On September 22, 1919, more than 350,000 steelworkers in nine American states walked off the job to protest working conditions in the nation's steel mills. The strikers wanted the workday reduced from twelve to eight hours. They wanted higher wages and the reinstatement of workers who had been fired for participating in union activity. Most of all, they wanted collective bargaining. To the surprise of many people in the United States, John D. Rockefeller Jr. quickly emerged as an advocate for the workers and the concept of collective bargaining.

Uncomfortable as a corporate board member because he shared responsibility for decisions that he could not control, Junior had resigned from the board of the Standard Oil Company and most of the other corporate boards he served on, resolved to focus his energy on philanthropy. The one board he stayed with—Colorado Fuel and Iron Company—had been an ethical and public relations disaster and confirmed his worst fears about his moral position as a board member and as a shareholder. His personal process of reconciliation with labor had convinced him that employees had a right to collective bargaining. He began to use his position as a stockholder to pressure corporations into granting these rights to workers. As he wrote to a church official, "I am now, and have long been, a believer in the moral responsibility of stockholders."

Judge gary,(right) Jno D RockfellowJr

Attending a conference in Washington in September 1919 to confront the growing issue of labor unrest in post-World War I America, Rockefeller met privately with the top executives at U.S. Steel, Elbert Gary and Henry Frick. The company's management was intent on breaking the strike and adamantly opposed the idea of collective bargaining. As a shareholder, Rockefeller hoped to convince them to recognize the workers.

Rockefeller was polite, although the atmosphere was tense. He offered examples of successful agreements between labor and management that led to increased productivity and decreased strife.

U.S. Steel's Elbert Gary with President Calvin Coolidge and John D. Rockefeller Jr. After Ludlow, John D. Rockefeller Jr. became an advocate for collective bargaining. When Gary refused to bargain with striking steelworkers in 1919, Rockefeller sold his shares in protest. (National Photo Company, Library of Congress, Prints & Photographs.)

Gary replied that he knew of more examples of failure and asserted that the principle was dangerous. Unable to make his case, Rockefeller said good-bye and expressed his hope that the situation would work out.

"If it does not," Gary responded, " it will be because you and others are advocating representation and collective bargaining."

"With every courtesy and fullest respect," Rockefeller responded. "I might say that if the outcome of the present situation is not as you and I both hope it will be, it will be due to the fact that you and other employers are unwilling to recognize and adopt the fundamental and just principle of representation and collective bargaining."

Shortly afterward, Rockefeller sold his shares in U.S. Steel. The Rockefeller Foundation liquidated its holdings in the industry, selling shares in Otis Steel and cashing out a $1 million note from Bethlehem Steel. If there was any debate over these moves with the Finance Committee of the Board, it is not recorded.

The decision to sell shares in Otis Steel may have reflected the first time that the Rockefeller Foundation wrestled with the correlation between its mission and program and its endowment. But it would not be the last time. Over the course of nearly a century, there would be many times when Foundation leaders talked about how they might promote the well-being of mankind in their role as investors. By the beginning of the 21st century, the Foundation would increasingly recognize that social investing offered a major new path for philanthropy. But it was a path that had to be opened step by step over many years.

Limitations of the Prudent Man

While Junior leveraged his position as a shareholder, the Rockefeller Foundation was more ambivalent about its attitude towards a range of investment and program strategies that would later be described under a broad category called social investing. Historically, trustees were expected to invest the assets of a trust or foundation according to the "prudent man" rule with two key goals: to produce income to meet current expenses and to preserve the corpus of the trust. Trustees and their financial advisors and attorneys generally believed that attention to social concerns would undermine this focus. In 1917, the Annual Report declared that there were things the Foundation could not "successfully or wisely do." It could not "give money or make loans to individuals, or invest in securities which have a philanthropic rather than a business basis, or assist in securing patents, or aid altruistic movements which involve private profit."

Wickliffe Rose and Thomas Debevoise, the Foundation's long-time attorney and advisor, engaged in a spirited discussion on the issue with regard to the General Education Board. In a 1925 letter, Debevoise asserted that a charitable corporation holds securities only as an investor and that "it is not equipped to direct the activities of a business corporation; that any interference by it will bring responsibilities which it cannot assume, and that its only course when it is displeased with the management of a corporation in which its funds are invested is to dispose of its investments; that while a stockholder it will never use its voting power to continue in office directors who do not show proper regard for the interests of the stockholders and public alike."

Thomas Debevoise served as outside general counsel to the Rockefeller Foundation for a quarter of a century. Debevoise argued that a foundation holds stock only as an investor and is "not equipped" to interfere with the management of a business. (Frank Ehrenford. Rockefeller Archive Center.)

As small as the foundation world was in the 1920s, however, there were examples that ran counter to Debevoise's point of view. One was the Russell Sage Foundation, which had been given specific authority by the foundation's donor to use up to one quarter of its investment funds for "social betterment." The donor had specifically stated that the returns on these investments would be less important than their social goals.

Board member Arthur Hays Sulzberger suggested in 1952 that the Rockefeller Foundation should develop housing for workers in New York City. The Foundation did not pursue this concept for a programmatically motivated investment. (Artist Benjamin Sheer. Library of Congress, Prints & Photographs.)

In 1927, during an informal conference, Debevoise pressed his points again. This time, the officers and several board members generally agreed to his principles. But Debevoise conceded that "it is also recognized that crises might arise in which the trustees might feel it their duty to take vigorous public action with respect to a given situation." Once again, forced to define its position, the Foundation came down firmly on the side of flexibility.

Though this perspective on the moral responsibilities of shareholders was not always front and center at the Rockefeller Foundation, Raymond Fosdick revisited the issue in 1940 after public controversy erupted regarding the New York Transit Company, whose stock was included in the Foundation's portfolio. In a note to Debevoise, Fosdick wrote, "I hate to have the Foundation involved in a fight over proxies, but I suppose that a tax-exempt organization has a responsibility as the owner of securities just as an individual or a business corporation has." Fosdick did not see a need to intervene in the situation, but he asked Debevoise: "How much do we know about the inside workings of the companies whose securities we hold? How much ought we to know?"

Debevoise again counseled caution. Looking through old files three years later, Fosdick found Debevoise's letter to Rose from 1925 and forwarded it to Walter Stewart, the chairman of the Foundation. "I'm not sure that I agree with Tom's doctrine," Fosdick wrote, "but it is difficult to determine what the alternative policy should be." Fosdick noted the contradictions in Debevoise's advice. How could the Foundation stay above the fray and at the same time intervene when a corporation's directors did not show proper regard for shareholders and the public? These discussions did not result in a formulation of policy towards what would today be called social investing, but they show that leaders at the Foundation were aware of the potential to do good on the investment side of the Foundation's business, as well as the expenditure side.

Board member Arthur Hays Sulzberger, the publisher of the *New York Times*, raised similar issues in 1952 when he wrote to the Foundation's new president, Dean Rusk, to suggest that the Rockefeller Foundation develop real

THE SOLUTION TO INFANT MORTALITY IN THE SLUMS

BETTER HOUSING

NEW YORK CITY HOUSING AUTHORITY ..
FIORELLO H LaGUARDIA mayor LANGDON W POST comm.

WPA WORK WPA.

estate for housing and light industry in Manhattan that would offer workers the opportunity to live close to where they worked. Rusk saw the proposal in the context of other urban initiatives focused on ameliorating problems affecting inner cities in the postwar years. He noted that it had long been the Foundation's policy to invest "on a business—not philanthropic—basis.... If RF investments were considered on the grounds of having its capital make a social contribution in addition to that which would be made by its income, such questions should be carefully explored before acting." But Rusk was leery of predicaments that might arise where the Foundation's philanthropic image would be compromised by its business investments. In real estate especially, he pointed out, "with the current social feeling against landlords, a legitimate attempt by RF to raise rents could well be met by a clamor on the part of the tenants which, as a public relations matter, RF could not ignore."

These discussions do not seem to have gone anywhere at the time. As late as 1968, research by the general counsel's office concluded that the Foundation had never made a programmatically motivated investment. That year, George Harrar asked Chauncey Belknap, the general counsel, to revisit the issue. Given the crisis in America's inner cities and the lack of investment capital in poor neighborhoods to help finance entrepreneurs, Harrar wanted to know if the Foundation could invest from its portfolio in these communities.

Belknap's report noted that the Rockefeller Foundation made frequent grants under its Equal Opportunity program to nonprofit organizations working in poor inner city neighborhoods. Moreover, in 1968 it had given

1983

Collaborative for Humanities and Arts Teaching (CHART) begins to develop teachers as key agents in school reform in the United States. (John T. Miller. Rockefeller Archives Center.)

money to two organizations—one in Harlem and the other in the Roxbury neighborhood of Boston—to help finance revolving loan funds targeted at minority business owners in inner city neighborhoods. But direct investment was a different question. According to Belknap, the Foundation had always followed generally accepted practices for charities, and the newly founded Charitable Foundations Division of the Attorney General's office of the State of New York "would be quick to pick up any deviation from what the Division regards as authorized procedure in the investment or distribution policies of a charitable corporation." In addition, Belknap wrote, "even under the most liberal standard that has been put forward, 'social

Chapter Nine: Social Investing

investments' of the type under consideration would not qualify. They would not be made with a view to fiscal return, and the realization of such a return would be largely fortuitous."

Belknap acknowledged the argument that a loan could be construed as a "new species of charitable gift" and therefore seen as within the Foundation's mission and charitable purpose. He believed there was "considerable merit in this approach, but it has never been tested in the courts and there are weighty arguments on the other side. Assistance to needy individuals has been a traditional form of charity, but assistance to needy business corporations for the purpose of helping them make a profit for the benefit of their shareholders has not so far been legally sanctioned as a permissible application of funds held subject to a charitable trust." Belknap then offered the hypothetical of two grocery stores on opposite corners in Roxbury, one financed with low-interest rate money from the Foundation. He suggested that the owner operating with market-rate loans might object to the Foundation's soft loan to his competitor as an exercise in charity. Analyzing the question from the perspective of federal regulators at the IRS, Belknap noted that the government had recently given tax-exempt status to the newly created Boston Urban Foundation, whose founding documents authorized the provision of loans "to needy individuals to start their own businesses, or acquire existing ones, in economically disadvantaged areas of Boston in which such individuals reside." The IRS ruling specifically allowed for loans to individuals, but withheld judgment on the legality of making loans to "firms, corporations, financial institutions and others."

To try and break through the IRS logjam, a nonprofit corporation sponsored by the Taconic Foundation—with support from The Rockefeller Brothers Fund, the Ford Foundation, the Carnegie Corporation of New York and seven other tax-exempt charitable foundations—created a loan fund focused on low-income inner city minority communities. After several high-level hearings, an IRS decision on the Cooperative Assistance Fund application was still pending at the time of Belknap's memo. Given the uncertainty of the situation, Belknap concluded that the Foundation should wait. Any venture down the path of social investment, at least beyond any minimal level, might jeopardize the Foundation's tax exemption.

Congress resolved this dilemma in 1969. The Tax Reform Act defined the concept of a Program-Related Investment (PRI) as any investment intended to further the tax exempt purposes of a foundation that would not ordinarily appeal to a prudent investor. Unlike a grant, a PRI could be structured with a provision for repayment and it could be made to a for profit entity whose business advanced an exempt or charitable activity or goal. The new law gave private foundations a powerful new tool as they worked to promote the well-being of humanity. The law also recognized that philanthropic organizations could make a difference by investing, as well as grantmaking.

Activist Shareholders

In the 1970s, foundations, universities and other nonprofit institutions also began to look more closely at their role as shareholders. Some refused to invest in tobacco or defense-related industries, because these businesses undermined the social goals of the foundation. Around this time, Princeton University decided that it would refuse to invest in banks that were making loans to the Republic of South Africa, because of the government's apartheid policies. This move towards activist shareholding, especially with regard to South Africa, prompted new soul searching at the Rockefeller Foundation.

Franklin Thomas had been the president of the Bedford Stuyvesant Restoration Corporation when John Knowles asked him to lead the Study Commission on U.S. Policy Toward Southern Africa. By the time the Commission was launchd in 1979, Knowles had succumbed to cancer and Thomas had been named CEO of the Ford Foundation. The Commision's report, issued in 1981, set the stage for significant changes in U.S. attitudes toward apartheid and provided guidelines for socially responsible investing in businesses in South Africa. (Georgiana Silk, Ford Foundation Archives. Rockefeller Archive Center.)

In the late summer of 1986, treasurer Jack Meyer noted a number of universities, public pension funds and foundations—including the $28 million Rockefeller Family Fund—had chosen to divest shares of companies doing business in, or with, South Africa. But the Ford Foundation, in concert with the conclusions of the Study Commission on U.S. Policy Toward Southern Africa, chaired by Franklin Thomas (and launched by the Rockefeller Foundation), had decided not to undertake a wholesale divestment. At the time, the Rockefeller Foundation already had adopted several guidelines with regard to investing in South Africa, including the Sullivan Principles and Bishop Desmond Tutu's Proposals. But there was growing pressure on American institutions to go further. Meyer outlined a number of options open to the board: maintain its policies, toughen its stance on corporate proxies to support withdrawal, begin a letter-writing campaign relative to proxies, sell securities of companies not considered to be doing enough to promote equal treatment for non-whites, or completely divest all South African holdings. Meyer concluded that selling the Foundation's South African shares would not have a significant impact. Moreover, the Foundation could do more if it remained engaged with companies doing business in South Africa. And finally, "A far more effective use of Foundation resources would be to fashion grants that directly aid anti-apartheid groups and the non-white population in South Africa." Meyer noted that the Foundation had already moved down this path, making grants worth more than $900,000 since 1982 to groups working to strengthen black-led institutions.

Meyer's memo raised concerns with other staff members. Senior vice president Kenneth Prewitt suggested that if it became public, portions of it could be taken out of context or made to sound as if the Foundation was more concerned about the cost of divestment than the welfare of black South Africans. He also urged President Richard Lyman to include a broader cross-section of the staff in a discussion of the issue so that, either way, they would feel some ownership of the final decision.

The board chose not to divest, but empowered the treasurer to review proxies for issues related to South Africa and encouraged the staff to look for new ways for the Foundation to invest in "front-line states" that bore the brunt of South Africa's troubles. But the idea of investing capital in ways that aligned with the Foundation's mission and produced both a social and a financial return did not die.

Recruited to the Rockefeller Foundation by Richard Lyman in 1985, Kenneth Prewitt served as senior vice president during a critical period of transition. As the board considered divesting assets linked to South Africa, Prewitt suggested that the Foundation should consider the perspectives of partners and grantees as well as the financial impacts of such a move. (Rockefeller Archive Center.)

Moving into Program-Related Investments

In the mid-1990s, the Rockefeller Foundation returned to the idea of Program-Related Investments. In collaboration with the Ford Foundation, Rockefeller invested in the National Community Development Initiative, a project that catalyzed the creation of more than 500 Community Development Corporations in central cities across the United States. Loans structured as PRIs were seen as a major tool to finance community infrastructure projects launched by these local initiatives. Rockefeller hoped to deploy this tool in other program areas.

The move required new skills within the organization and the repurposing of existing skills. Investment analysts working in the treasurer's

Protests against apartheid increased in South Africa and around the world in the 1970s. In Guguletu township near Cape Town, protestors confronted police and dogs in August 1976. (AP Images.)

office, for example, began to collaborate with their peers in the programs to analyze Program-Related Investment opportunities.

In 1996, Peter Goldmark offered the staff's proposal to the board to create what became known as the Program Venture Experiment (ProVenEx). In the words of the staff, "ProVenEx reflected the zeitgeist of the late 1990s, aiming to 'enable the Foundation to engage, in selected cases, the energies and mechanisms of the private sector in pursuit of the RF's program goals.'" The rationale was straightforward. There was far more capital available in the private sector than in either the philanthropic or government sectors. If some of that private capital could be directed toward for-profit enterprises that generated social impact, the leverage from the investment of the Foundation's money would be enormous.

The Rockefeller Foundation was regarded as a pioneer in its activities related to ProVenEx, since few other major foundations at the time were utilizing the Program-Related Investment tool at scale. In its initial concept, ProVenEx attempted different investment strategies. It functioned both as a venture capitalist, investing directly in new businesses that seemed likely to produce both investment and social returns, and as a fund of funds.

By 2002, ProVenEx had been operating for a sufficient number of years so that it was able to evaluate its performance and draw lessons to inform its investment strategy. In many cases, the Foundation was investing in businesses or organizations in highly challenging sectors of the marketplace. The Foundation also lacked a sufficient number of dedicated staff with the financial and managerial backgrounds to evaluate and monitor its direct investments. Having learned these lessons, the Foundation revised ProVenEx's investment strategy to make investments through intermediaries—financial institutions and funds—rather than directly into businesses. These intermediaries had the expertise, experience, and human resources to identify, evaluate, and invest in new businesses. In working with these intermediaries, the Foundation could leverage its greatest skills and expertise as a catalyst or convener. Additionally, the Foundation learned that not all of its programs were conducive to investment, and that it needed to be more selective regarding the sectors where it made investments. ProVenEx

1984

Combining its longtime interests in agriculture and molecular biology, the Rockefeller Foundation creates a new research program focused on bio-technology for rice and other crops. (Patrick de Noirmont. Rockefeller Foundation.)

Chapter Nine: Social Investing

invested in some of the most innovative transactions of its time and offered lessons for many subsequent social investors.

In creating ProVenEx, the Foundation had made a fundamental and important decision to fund the project with program money rather than endowment assets. This decision emphasized the focus on social impact rather than financial return. It also continued the separation between the motivations for selecting investment opportunities on the endowment side of the house (financial return on investment) and the motivations on the program side (social return on investment).

As the idea of social investing continued to evolve, it attracted a much wider range of investors, including non-philanthropists who wanted a risk-adjusted financial return on their investments but also wanted to invest in enterprises that might generate a social return. As the marketplace widened, debates emerged over the packaging and marketing of these investment opportunities. Questions were raised about definitions. How much of a social impact should an investment make to qualify as an "impact investment?"

In the context of this conversation, Foundation President Judith Rodin recognized an opportunity to help stabilize and grow this potentially significant market. In 2007 and 2008, the Foundation brought together leaders in finance, philanthropy, and development at its Bellagio conference center in Italy to explore the potential for impact investing. At these meetings, the term itself was coined and the conversation led to a decision by the Foundation's board to approve a new $38 million program to help create the infrastructure for this new industry. The Impact Investing Initiative focused on four key strategies: building networks for collective action; contributing to basic industry infrastructure, like social performance ratings; building and scaling intermediaries; and supporting basic research and policy. Key outcomes of this initiative included the creation of the Global Impact Investing Network (GIIN) and the establishment of the Global Impact Investing Rating System (GIIRS) to provide investors with a double-bottom line assessment of the performance of participating businesses.

In helping to create the GIIN, GIIRS, and other organizations, Rodin recognized that its greatest opportunities in this emerging arena were tied to its leadership role and to developing the intermediary institutions that would give investors confidence, thus growing the marketplace. It was a step that John D. Rockefeller—ever the advocate for rationalizing systems and markets—would have appreciated.

CULTURE

How do we sustain an innovative culture?

C reating an innovative organization is not easy. Sustaining one over a century is very rare. Hundreds of thousands of pages have been written by management gurus and academics offering advice to CEOs and boards of directors. Still, the path or the recipe seems obscure as organizations are shaped by the chemistries of personalities and the ways in which people in an organization are able to respond to the world around them.

One of the reasons innovation is murky is because there are different kinds. Innovation is not the same as invention. The inventor applies knowledge to make a light bulb or develop a new genetically modified seed. While it is still possible for the inventor to work alone (though they rarely do), the innovator never does. The innovator transforms the way things are done—sometimes by deploying new inventions, other times by leading people to simply do things differently. Innovation is therefore always a social process.

Adaptive innovation is incremental, a process of continuous improvement along a chosen path. It often results from monitoring and integrating the improvements in the field. Highly organized institutional cultures can be extremely effective with incremental innovation.

Fundamental or disruptive innovation is much trickier. It requires the ability and the will to abandon the world as you know it, maybe even a world in which you have been very successful, to follow a new path within a new paradigm. It requires the will to swim upstream, often for a very long time, while those around either do not see the need or the feasibility of the path you have chosen. This can be especially difficult when the human capital of the organization has been created for one paradigm, and the next paradigm demands a different set of skills. Innovators must be patient and value the lessons learned from failure.

Because innovation is a social process, it is often deeply rooted in organizations and complex social networks. Unlike bureaucratic organizations, which are primarily driven by internal rules and feedback, innovative organizations are porous, maintaining strong external networks that provide a constant source of new information. As Harvard professor Clayton Christensen has explained, organizations that aspire to fundamental innovation not only are attuned to their best customers or clients but also are scanning the outer reaches of their environment for trends and needs that may not be apparent today, but which may be critical in the future. With this feedback, innovative organizations must be able to respond to customers, clients, critics, and competitors.

In the earliest years of the Rockefeller Foundation, the trustees and staff were already attuned to the problem of sustaining innovation. But even before the Foundation reached its five-year anniversary, some feared it was already losing the battle.

CULTURE

An Early Warning

When he became president of the Rockefeller Foundation in 1917, only four years after the charter was ratified, George Vincent was warned that the culture of the board was already entrenched and isolated. He was urged to remain flexible and opportunistic. Vincent may have been the first Rockefeller Foundation president to receive this advice. He was certainly not the last.

Throughout the history of the Foundation, the culture of the organization has been deeply affected by decisions regarding program and strategy. Heavy investments in field operations during the heyday of the International Health Division, the period of the Green Revolution, or the Education for Development Program necessitated large organizations and, at times, a bureaucratic culture. Within the grantmaking entities of the Foundation, however—and into the latter decades when the Foundation's strategies focused on convening, collaborating and catalyzing change—the organization was smaller and, at times, more nimble.

Internally, the culture was shaped by the organization's values. Ideas were constantly tested. Information was gathered from around the world. A massive library catalog system included index cards for grantees as well as contacts in universities, government, laboratories, and communities in cities, towns, and villages from Montreal to Melbourne and New York to New Delhi. It was a tremendously literary culture. Officers were required to keep diaries

detailing their travels, meetings, conversations, and impressions of the people and communities they visited. Handwritten or dictated, these entries were typed by secretaries. Carbon copies were shared with other staff who had a need to know about these contacts.

Outreach programs by field staff in the early hookworm campaign in Alabama and other states in the American South set the pattern for field staff work in health and agriculture for decades. (Rockefeller Archive Center.)

These systems of information-sharing were designed to fight against the tendency for programmatic divisions to wall themselves off from the rest of the organization. From the earliest days of the Foundation, staff and trustees recognized that most of the world's problems were multifaceted and situated within complex social, environmental, political, and economic systems. Although they were sometimes criticized for strategies that failed to encompass a holistic approach to a problem, it was not because of a lack of concern. Over and over in the history of the Foundation, officers and trustees worried over how to promote interdisciplinarity.

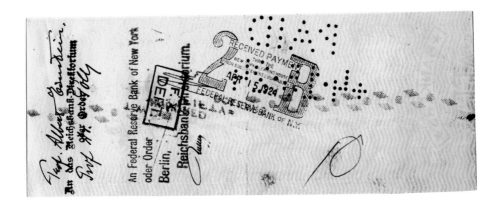

The culture was also affected by the networks in which the Foundation operated. For program officers who traveled from university to university, visiting scientists in their labs or scholars in their studies, the values and culture of academic communities shaped their perspectives as Rockefeller Foundation employees. The prevalence of guests with advanced degrees led the director of the Division of Natural Sciences to write a handbook for staff called "How Do You Do, Dr. X?" (See Chapter Seven.)

In the early years, much of the work of the Rockefeller Foundation was carried on by the International Health Board. The IHB was organized with military efficiency on the "shock troop" principle. In the fight against hookworm or yellow fever, highly trained and experienced members of the staff were used to try and contain the spread of disease. Once the disease (or its vectors) was contained, local health officials would be trained to

Grants and fellowships from the International Education Board (IEB) helped connect European and American physicists in the 1920s. With funds from the IEB, Albert Einstein hired a mathematician to help solve "the riddle of quantum theory." (Rockefeller Archive Center.)

prevent further outbreaks. The Rockefeller Foundation staffer, having worked himself or herself out of a job, was then available to be assigned elsewhere. Given this operational staff, it was essential for the Foundation to recruit dedicated professionals willing to make a career of the work. Most were medical doctors or sanitary engineers. The staff also included entomologists, biologists, statisticians, and nurses. As Foundation officer Joyce Moock pointed out, "Ironically, this precision group of technical personnel was headed by a former professor of philosophy"—Wickliffe Rose.

Former senior vice president Kenneth Prewitt once wrote that the small group of pioneers associated with Rockefeller philanthropies in these early years had "to invent what it meant to be an officer and a trustee in this new thing they called 'business-like giving.'" Although much of what they invented became a model for later foundations and generations of philanthropic leaders, the archives of the Foundation reflect abiding self-doubt and insecurity. In 1995, Prewitt summarized these fears when he told the trustees that the greatest threat facing the Foundation was "restlessness."

Wickliffe Rose directed the Rockefeller Sanitary Commission and later the International Health Board. An early member of the Rockefeller Foundation's board, Rose believed the Foundation's greatest contributions to humanity would be in the development and dissemination of knowledge. (Rockefeller Archive Center.)

CRISIS AND REORGANIZATION

John D. Rockefeller Jr. was worried. He feared that after only a dozen years in operation the Rockefeller Foundation was growing stale. "Any human institution tends to get into a rut, to confuse motion with progress, and to exalt machinery and organization above work and objectives," he wrote to Raymond Fosdick in 1925. "This is certainly true in the business world, and it is equally true in philanthropy.... It is not necessary for me to tell you that there is nothing sacred or inviolate about any type of organization. Machinery and personnel are merely the instruments by which objectives are reached, and unless we keep ourselves clear-eyed and fresh and keep the machinery elastic, we run the risk of dry-rot."

Junior went on to add: "If these Foundations are going to fulfill the high purposes that the Founder had in mind for them—indeed, if they are to escape the decay which seems eventually to attach itself to all human institutions—they must be subjected to constant, critical scrutiny, and their directors and officers must be ready at all times to redefine their aims, recognize their technique, and scrap existing machinery in favor of something that is better."

President George Vincent was also concerned. In the mid-1920s, the Foundation was like a holding company in which each executive ran his own organization, but appealed to the central administration for resources.

Economist and statistician Beardsley Ruml directed the Laura Spelman Rockefeller Memorial (LSRM), a philanthropy established by John D. Rockefeller in memory of his wife. In 1928, LSRM was absorbed by the Rockefeller Foundation. (Rockefeller Archive Center.)

Conflicts over resources abounded. At times Vincent found himself playing referee, often with uncertain authority, as other long-time Rockefeller leaders like Rose and Beardsley Ruml jousted over turf. At other times he felt totally ignored as these powerful staffers exercised their own prerogatives.

In February 1926, Vincent convinced the trustees that they should establish a committee to review the organization's structure and recommend alternatives. The committee had three members: John G. Agar, Simon Flexner, and Raymond B. Fosdick. Fosdick soon became the leader of this threesome.

As they began their work, Fosdick invited members of the board and staff to comment on the current structure. The comments ranged widely, but shed light on the culture and structure of the Foundation at the time. They also would reverberate for decades.

Executive secretary Florence Read, for example, did not see a problem with structure. Like many people, she saw the issue as one of individuals and personalities:

As executive secretary, Florence Read helped direct the far-flung operations of the International Health Division in the early 1920s. Read left the IHD in 1927 to become president of Spelman College. (Rockefeller Archive Center.)

"The right persons can work under any system and get results." Roger Greene, the head of the China Medical Board, expressed a similar sentiment: "The maintaining of such coordination and control depends much less on the form of the organization than on the attitude of the officers." Alan Gregg, who worked in the Division of Medical Education, asserted that the work of the Rockefeller philanthropies could not easily be divided into disciplines. "Rather than adjust our organization to cope with problems as they occur (and, be it noted that our field is the World and the variety very great), we cut and trim opportunities to fit the narrow and apparently inelastic limits of Divisional or Board policy."

Nevertheless, Florence Read went on to provide an interesting analysis of alternative structures. From her point of view, the trustees' and president's need for outside expertise justified the creation of separate boards or advisory committees for each program. But these boards ought to serve at the convenience of the organization and be abolished when they are no longer useful. She recommended a structure that would include an executive committee for each program made up of outside experts, with one trustee and the president of the foundation on the committee as well. Wilson G. Smillie, who worked for the International Health Board, offered a similar suggestion, a committee of technical advisors: "men of broad vision, highest attainment, and also possessing highly technical knowledge of the theory and practice of Public Health" who would work with the president and the executive committee of the Rockefeller Foundation to determine the policies of the IHB.

Others in the organization expressed frustration with the ways in which the structure impeded communication. Mary Beard, who was the IHB's associate director for nursing but reported to Edwin Embree, the director of the Division of Studies, complained that nursing education was deeply tied to medical education in general as well as public health, yet she did not have permission to communicate directly with the directors of the GEB, the IHB, or the Division

Mary Beard was associate director of the International Health Division from 1924 to 1938. She exerted a guiding influence over the development of the IHD's nursing programs around the world. (Rockefeller Archive Center.)

of Medical Education. This lack of easy communication impeded the process of bringing back from the field information that would inform strategy and policymaking.

Richard Pearce was chosen in 1919 to be the director of the newly created Division of Medical Education. (Rockefeller Archive Center.)

Roger Greene was more emphatic about the need to clarify lines of authority. He believed that in the current situation, three factors undermined the president's control: 1) his heavy public speaking schedule, which meant he was often unavailable to department heads; 2) the lack of a number two to the president (previously assigned to the "secretary" of the Foundation, Jerome Greene and later Edwin Embree); and 3) the diminished powers of the executive committee, making the president dependent on meetings of the full board to move issues forward and, at the same time, making full board meetings even more overloaded for the board.

Richard Pearce, the director of the Medical Division, wanted to strengthen the office of the president. "Perhaps the most important change of all is to give the President of the Foundation a real job. At present, with two subsidiary boards with independent groups of trustees, independent budgets and with special bylaws indicating the functions and duties of these boards, cooperation is purely a matter of personal, not official, relations. If a director wishes to cooperate it is the easiest thing in the world; if he does not wish to cooperate this again is quite as easy." He proposed abolishing the IHB and CMB boards.

Coming from almost the opposite perspective, Edwin Embree, who ran the catchall Division of Studies, suggested that rather than consolidating the Rockefeller philanthropies into one organization, they should be even further decentralized with the creation of four organizations, each with its own board and, implicitly, claims on the resources of the endowment. Under this plan, the IHB, a Medical Education Board, and a General International Education Board would carry forward the core of the foundation's ongoing work more broadly in public health, medical education, medical science, and education. Freed from having to supervise these operations, the fourth organization, the Rockefeller Foundation, would be much more focused on innovation. Thus the Foundation would be the most experimental entity in the Rockefeller pantheon. When things did not work, programs could be shut down. If they proved successful, they could be moved to one of the other organizations to manage ongoing operations and development.

As all of these voices chimed in on the discussion, many Rockefeller insiders searched among relevant institutional models. Some compared the Foundation to a university, where a president was accustomed to dealing with specialists in fields in which he had no professional expertise. Others looked nervously to government or business.

Often the debate was characterized as a conflict between centralization and decentralization. Junior suggested that a centralized structure under a visionary leader would have fewer tendencies to become rigid. Roger Greene asked whether a centralized organization would "tend to a greater rigidity in policy, and make less likely the development of original and productive ideas by the men in charge than under the present plan of separate boards.... I should think that a consolidation of all the boards might develop precisely the administrative hierarchy that Mr. Rockefeller seems to fear."

The committee established by the board to review the organization's structure had to synthesize all of these perspectives and make a decision for the long run. On November 5, 1926, the committee explained, "The Foundation originally was not, and could not have been, put together as a completely developed piece of machinery." It had inherited older entities— the Rockefeller Sanitary Commission, for example. New fields of service had been added, including the China Medical Board and the Division of Medical Education. The Foundation had experimented in a variety of

Frederick Russell (second from left), director of the International Health Division, and Edwin Embree (third from left) with Polish dignitaries in 1920. Russell expanded the administration of the IHD and introduced a more disciplined structure for research and public health administration. (Rockefeller Archive Center.)

loosely related fields gathered together under the Division of Studies. "In all this development there has been little attention given to the necessity of a centralized, coordinated administration.... The consequence of this lack of uniformity has been confusion—confusion in the field where our fine distinctions in organization and function are frankly not understood, and confusion in the home office where we have built up a complicated system of procedure and bookkeeping to match our complex situation." The committee recommended consolidation.

The committee also concluded that the president had functioned mostly as an arbitrator among the Rockefeller interests. "The idea of the President's office as an instrument by which the Foundation not only kept in touch with its present work and promoted its symmetrical growth, but also surveyed the possibilities of new work, has not been fully developed." As a result, "The function of general oversight, of general planning, of thinking in world terms from the standpoint of the Rockefeller Foundation as a whole, has been too largely neglected." The committee recommended that the president serve as the true chief executive of the foundation, "responsible to the Trustees not only for the administration of its affairs and the execution of the projects which they have approved, but for the investigation of new fields of activity and the coordination of these new fields into a united program." The board voted in 1928 to adopt the committee's recommendations in concept and directed that the details of the reorganization be worked out for the board's final approval.

Scientists and Academicians

Years of deliberation on the issue of structure and culture, however, were quickly undermined by events. The onset of the Great Depression brought new pressure on the Foundation to help relieve suffering rather than focus on "the advancement of knowledge." According to Waldemar Nielsen, a noted author on the subject of philanthropy, the staff of the Foundation seemed unable to respond, despite the urging of the board. President Max Mason's inability to lead the Foundation's response to the crisis only seemed to undermine the board's confidence in him. Moreover, although the International Health Division was moved more deliberately under the control of the president and the board of trustees, it continued to operate with a great deal of independence under its director Frederick Russell. Although this relative autonomy frustrated Mason at times, as it had George Vincent, it also allowed the IHD to sustain the culture and operations that had made it successful through the end of World War II.

The postwar era demanded that the Rockefeller Foundation adjust to a new role in the world. Large government organizations (the National Science Foundation, National Institutes of Health, Atomic Energy Commission, and others) emerged with far greater resources directed toward public health and scientific research. In addition, the Rockefeller Foundation was no longer the largest philanthropic organization in the United States, having been surpassed by the Ford Foundation. With 319 employees in New York and in the field in 1957, the trustees worried that the culture of the organization would not be able to adjust to new circumstances. "Old personnel with old patterns of thought and techniques tend to persist," a trustee report noted about organizations in general. "So do patterns of organization, for obsolete and near-obsolete purposes."

Like his father, John D. Rockefeller 3rd dedicated much of his life to philanthropy. As chairman of the Rockefeller Foundation from 1952 until 1971, he provided critical support for the Foundation's population initiatives and the Conquest of Hunger program. (Rockefeller Archive Center.)

The board's Five-Year Review Committee in 1958 looked closely at the ways in which the culture of the Foundation was adapting to changed circumstances. They noted that, given the pressures of day-to-day work, it was difficult for program officers to step back and see the forest for the trees. They discussed sabbaticals and other initiatives designed to give important time to gain perspective. The recommendation reflected a continuing tendency to see program officers as "first-rate scholars and first-rate administrators of scholarly affairs." "A Foundation officer should have done something, accomplished some things of the mind—scholarly or other—which bring him the respect of the circles in which he must operate as a Foundation officer. Otherwise, he is not up to his position of power."

It is interesting that even as the trustees expressed concern about the culture's ability to adapt, they praised the Foundation's leadership for maintaining continuity with the past. Retired officers had been asked to come back as consultants on particular projects.

Alan Gregg once suggested that three things were critical to an effective organizational culture: "From the past, shared experiences; in the present, beliefs generally agreed upon; and for the future, hopes and desires held in common."

Family planning classes in Taiwan exemplified the Rockefeller Foundation's efforts to promote balanced population growth around the world in the 1970s. (Rockefeller Archive Center.)

Concerns about the flexibility of the Rockefeller Foundation's culture and program did not go away. Congressional investigations in the 1960s seemed to confirm a sense that foundations operated in secret and were out of touch with the American people. When John Knowles became president in 1972, the zeitgeist of the age insisted that established and influential institutions like the Rockefeller Foundation were inherently staid and irrelevant. Waldemar Nielsen's influential book *The Big Foundations*, published in 1973, crystallized these critiques. Headlines on reviews of his book chastised large foundations for being passive, conservative, uncreative, and unimaginative. Yet Nielsen also insisted that the Rockefeller Foundation had accumulated an "unrivaled record. In many ways it has been the standard against which the other 'modern' foundations have measured themselves." With this kind of legacy, Knowles and the Foundation's trustees and staff faced an overwhelming challenge to sustain the pace and quality of innovation within the context of a much different world.

Institutionally, there were other factors that created an environment for change. Knowles's arrival coincided with the departure of John D. Rockefeller 3rd from the board. Like his father, Rockefeller had played a pivotal role as chairman. In his farewell address to the Foundation, he raised challenging issues that echoed from earlier eras in the Foundation's history. He expressed concern that trustees were not engaged enough with the work of the Foundation and the staff. He feared that the culture was not open to dissent. At the height of the youth rebellion of the late sixties and early seventies, he was especially concerned that senior staff failed to listen to their younger colleagues.

Knowles embraced the challenges offered by Nielsen and Rockefeller. He recognized great strengths in the Foundation's history and practice. The Foundation had been able to anticipate major issues and draw public

1988
International Clinical Epidemiological Network (INCLEN), a project launched by the Rockefeller Foundation, becomes independent. (Steve McCurry. Rockefeller Foundation.)

Chapter Ten: Culture

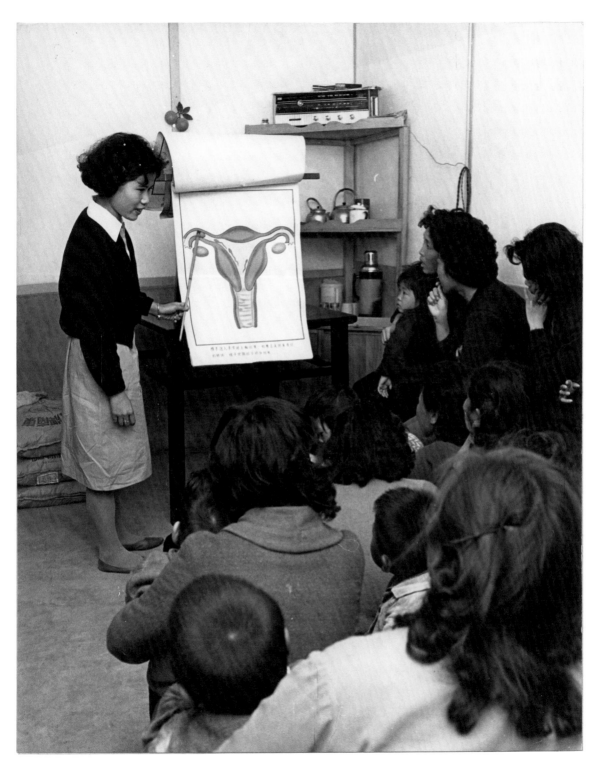

attention to these problems even as it worked on solutions. From Knowles's perspective, examples included Kinsey's studies of human sexuality, efforts to balance population growth, work in science and agriculture that made possible the Green Revolution, and the development of modern physics. Knowles noted that sustained effort had produced major victories: a vaccine for yellow fever, eradication of hookworm in the American South, the establishment of county health departments, and the expansion of universities in less developed countries. Above all, he believed that the quality of the staff, from 1913 to 1972, had been outstanding. "For all these reasons the Foundation enjoys a preeminent position both nationally and internationally, and its power for good is enormous."

Knowles testified to the strength of the culture and the staff. In the Annual Report in 1974 he described the typical program officer as "both scholar and activist, thinker and doer" whose work "can be strengthened by the scrutiny and criticism of colleagues, not only within the same discipline, but from other disciplines as well." Knowles stressed the advantages of the interdisciplinary review of grant proposals as a way to mitigate the "tunnel vision of the expert." Increasing food production, Knowles suggested, demanded technical and scientific expertise, but it also involved problems that were economic, medical, political, ethical, and behavioral. Knowles asserted that this interdisciplinary approach "has not proved excessively bureaucratic or cumbersome, and it has enhanced the spirit, coherence and quality of our work even as the individual officer remains our prime asset."

Knowles launched an intellectual rejuvenation initiative, inviting speakers to talk to the staff. In addition, recognizing that much of the innovative character of the Foundation in the past had derived from experiences in the field, a program was created to deliberately rotate staff from the New York offices to the field and vice versa. While these initiatives helped to sustain the vitality of the culture, Knowles's sometimes mercurial process of decision-making, combined with absences caused by his ultimately fatal battle with cancer, undermined morale.

The Burdens of History

By the early 1980s, the Rockefeller Foundation was "without question the preeminent large American foundation," but as Waldemar Nielsen observed, it was often burdened by its record of achievement and by struggling to live up to the stature of its former self. As the Foundation adjusted to the harsh and cumulative economic realities of the 1970s, the Foundation's new president, Richard Lyman, bore the cultural brunt of the inevitable backlash from downsizing. Survivors worried about a possible next round of layoffs, or advancement within a culture that seemed increasingly competitive, became increasingly anxious when Lyman promulgated criteria for promotion that seemed to place a heavy emphasis on academic-style achievements—publications in professional journals, for example. Lyman tried to set people at ease on the issue, saying it would be a "disservice both to the Foundation and to individual staff members to leave the impression that everyone must now find time, somehow, to publish like an aspiring Assistant Professor at Harvard or Berkeley." But Lyman wanted staff to know that these kinds of achievements would be recognized. He also noted that competition in the culture was, to some extent, unavoidable. "I don't see that as wholly undesirable," he wrote to the Foundation's Program Committee. "Among the sins often charged by the outside world against foundations in general is a tendency toward complacency."

Lyman's memo reflected his desire to both flatten the hierarchy of the organization and implement more formal performance reviews for staff. Some people in the organization felt this was destructive to the culture. According to one consultant's report from 1983, the Rockefeller Foundation was characterized by a certain degree of "rigidity and inflexibility." Some on the staff felt "that secrecy and confidentiality are overdone." There was a low esprit de corps. People were concerned that administrative costs accounted for too much of the budget. But these feelings were subtle, operating underneath an overall sense of pride and competence. Insiders and outsiders frequently said that the Rockefeller Foundation was "alert to the needs of the world around, it is capable of change, and is changing."

By the time Lyman was ready to retire, the challenges of the future were clear. In a report developed by consultants preparing for the search for a new president, the authors noted that, in many ways, the Foundation was a prisoner of its past success, and both staff and board were insistent that any future approach must preserve and build upon the Foundation's traditions. The report noted that both Knowles and Lyman had suffered from a lack of "sustained and consensual satisfaction" from the board. Knowles was seen as an "intellectual dynamo" who was too disruptive to the staff and organization. Lyman was a "proven institutional administrator" who had limited experience in the most substantive areas of Foundation activity. Most critically, after numerous interviews, the consultants recognized a fundamental difference between what the staff hoped for in a new president and what the trustees wanted.

Still, John D. Rockefeller Jr.'s fears of ossification lived on in the hearts and minds of board members through the years. Retiring from the board in 1995,

John Evans chaired the Rockefeller Foundation board from 1987 to 1995. A Canadian physician and business leader, he was also president of the University of Toronto and founding director of the Population, Health and Nutrition Department of the World Bank. (George S. Zimbel. Rockefeller Archives Center.)

John Evans confessed, "I am concerned that we may succumb to 'foundationitis,' that most disabling disease which affects so many grant makers. The symptoms are losing the humility to listen and learn rather than to teach and direct; organizing the grant-making process to suit staff convenience and efficiency ahead of grantee needs; and beginning to believe that the money is yours rather than a public trust."

Evans's concerns were those of a board member. In counterpoint, Kenneth Prewitt, the Foundation's senior vice-president at the beginning of 1995, worried that the culture was moving too fast. Foundation president Peter Goldmark was seeking to encourage risk-taking and experimentation. One of his favorite aphorisms was: "If you know exactly where you're going, you're not doing it fast enough." But Prewitt believed that the Foundation was increasingly less deliberative, marking a break from its traditions and threatening one of the Foundation's most valuable assets—its credibility.

Prewitt argued that the Rockefeller Foundation brought two main assets to the practice of philanthropy—a still-significant endowment (more than $2 billion at the time) and institutional credibility in the field. Money was able to attract and commit grantees to the processes of change. "Credibility, the second asset, gains access and attention over and beyond what the funds can buy." Credibility, in Prewitt's view, was tied to solid grantmaking. Weak grants diminished the Foundation's financial resources, but also undermined the second asset, credibility.

Prewitt believed in 1995 that the greatest danger confronting the Foundation was restlessness. "A foundation is constantly tempted to move on to the next challenge," Prewitt told the board. He urged the trustees to avoid the siren song of the next new big thing, and to follow through "year after year with the programs you earlier invented." Prewitt noted that human nature resisted patience. "Effective philanthropy is not only innovation," he said, "it is sustained implementation." Prewitt's talk with the trustees on the eve of his departure from the Foundation, encouraged by Goldmark despite the philosophical differences between the two of them, offered testimony to the abiding intellectual rigor of the Foundation's culture.

Prewitt's concerns and Evans's anxieties were shared by many of the trustees in 1997 as they worked to choose a new president to succeed Peter Goldmark. As board chair Alice Ilchman wrote, "We, of course, want to hold fast to the best practice of the past, if it is still what is called a 'usable past,' but want as well to invent and embrace the approaches and forms that suit the altered relationships of the new era."

The board chose Gordon Conway. When Conway became president, he again looked at the interrelated issues of strategy, structure, and culture. For years, staff and trustees had suggested that the Foundation's greatest strengths and successes came from an interdisciplinary or even multidisciplinary approach to the problems of development. In 1995, board member John Evans saw the diversity of talent in the Rockefeller Foundation as the organization's key source of comparative advantage.

Under Conway's leadership, the staff returned to many of the Foundation's historic strengths. There was a renewed global focus, a strengthened commitment to issues affecting the poor and vulnerable, and a return to investment in science with a focus on the root causes and initiatives that would enlist and leverage leaders and communities around the globe.

In the effort to discern the kind of president the Foundation needed in the years ahead, the conversation had inevitably returned to the character of the organization's culture; its relationships with partners, stakeholders and grantees; and the changing circumstances affecting the practice of philanthropy. As the consequences of globalization loomed even larger, staff and trustees realized that the Foundation needed a global theory of change that would ensure that programs were not working at cross purposes. Efforts to support job development in the United States, for example, ran the risk of increasing trade barriers to developing nations. The tremendous expansion of private wealth, fueled by the communications revolution, had sparked a significant

In 1995, Alice Ilchman, a development economist and political scientist, became the first woman to chair the board of the Rockefeller Foundation. (Rockefeller Archive Center.)

increase in philanthropy. The number of foundations, for example, had increased from 44,146 in 1997 to 61,810 in 2001. Meanwhile, available dollars had nearly doubled, from $15.98 billion to $30.5 billion. While the Rockefeller Foundation had dropped to fifteenth largest among private foundations, however, its grants to non-U.S. organizations ranked third behind only the Ford and Gates foundations. Growing tensions between the Western and Islamic worlds, continuing expansion of the HIV/AIDS epidemic, political instability reflected in the rise of terrorism, and increasing concern about the effects of climate change all reflected the changed landscape.

When staff assessed the Rockefeller Foundation's abiding strengths or its comparative ability to make a difference in the lives of the poor and vulnerable, a number of factors came to the fore. The Rockefeller Foundation's "brand"—developed over nearly a century and associated with so many important and successful initiatives to promote the well-being of humankind—continued to have enormous value, giving the Foundation the ability to act as a convener, to bring people together on emerging issues. Incorporated in that brand was a sense that the Foundation's long-term commitment to science, especially in fields related to health and food security, inspired confidence and trust. Generations of Rockefeller fellows, or "Rocky Docs," constituted a remarkable network of human capital that was a source of innovation in many regions of the world. The Foundation also had a reputation as an "honest broker." These strengths were not necessarily unique. The Ford Foundation, for example, after nearly a half century of international

1992

Forum for African Women Educationalists (FAWE) is born following a conference organized by the Rockefeller Foundation. FAWE seeks to promote gender equity in education. (Steve McCurry. Rockefeller Foundation.)

work, brought some of the same strengths to its work on international development, as well as a much larger endowment. But in many places in the world, history mattered.

Despite the Rockefeller Foundation's strengths, some staff worried about the organization's future. Just as earlier generations feared that then-current initiatives paled by comparison with the past, some staffers feared that "We're always trying to catch up with the reputation" and that the Foundation was "living off the works of our ancestors."

In 2005, when Judith Rodin came from the University of Pennsylvania to lead the Rockefeller Foundation, a new president once again had to face the challenge of transitioning the organization's culture to a new era and new

Chapter Ten: Culture

challenges. As Duke University professor Joel Fleishman reports, she had "clear plans for transforming the way Rockefeller did things." She wanted to realign program responsibilities, remove silo walls that separated programs from one another, and develop new multiyear strategies. Admittedly impatient to put ideas into practice, she disrupted the culture of the organization. These changes led to significant staff turnover, but also opened opportunities for new senior leadership with a fresh perspective and mentoring for junior staff.

The Foundation also had a reputation as an "honest broker."

Rodin also placed renewed emphasis on the Foundation's role as a catalyst and convener. The Bellagio Conference Center in Northern Italy, which had been an important venue for major collaborative projects in the past, became a key asset in the Foundation's programmatic portfolio. Rodin pushed the staff to pursue partnerships with other foundations and NGOs.

Like their peers in earlier eras, the staff and grantees continued to see the Rockefeller Foundation as an innovative organization. The level of employee commitment to the mission of the organization far surpassed the average among other philanthropic organizations. Undoubtedly, some of that passion and pride derived from the cultural legacy of the institution. The record of past accomplishments could be intimidating, but to those struggling to promote the well-being of humankind in the face of seemingly insurmountable problems, it could also be an inspiration.

PERPETUITY

Should the work
continue forever?

M oney enables foundations to do good. Like
families, corporations, and governments,
foundations have to manage their money
to achieve their goals. Time is a major factor. Does the
donor or the foundation's board want to see the money
spent within a specified period, or do they want the
foundation to continue to do good forever?

Whether they choose a limited life or perpetuity,
trustees must be able to manage the foundation's assets
to meet the appropriate time horizon. The tension between present and future needs is substantial, especially
during wars, disasters, or crises. But the tension can also
be felt during times of great opportunity.

Arguments have been made against the idea of perpetuity. Some believe that each generation should take
care of the philanthropic needs of its own time. Given the
uncertainty of the future, donors should favor grantmaking today. Resisting perpetuity is the only way to ensure
fidelity to the donor's intent.

The arguments in favor of perpetuity are equally com-
pelling. The long life of a perpetual foundation enables
it to mount a multigenerational attack on intransigent
problems—in science (searching for a cure for cancer, for
example) or in society (the elimination of racism or war).
Perpetual organizations are more apt to invest in the development of basic knowledge. Short-lived organizations,

anxious to see an immediate impact, may be interested only in the application of knowledge.

Regardless of the time horizon, as they seek to manage their resources, trustees have often been constrained by their founders. The assets of many American foundations in the first half of the twentieth century included stocks or bonds related to the founders' entrepreneurial initiatives. For the entrepreneur, this arrangement offered substantial advantages—shares held by the founder's charities were often used to maintain voting control in the business. Policymakers in Rockefeller's time and later, however, expressed concern that corporate goals would compromise the charitable purposes of the foundation. Moreover, legal precedent required trustees to follow the "prudent man" rule to ensure that the value of the foundation's endowment would be protected. In some circles, this meant that assets should be converted to cash or diversified. Founders who believed in their entrepreneurial offspring often did not want to see the securities they provided to their foundations liquidated, and they resisted diversification. The 1969 Tax Reform Act clarified this situation by prohibiting private foundations from owning more than a small percentage of a for-profit business.

For many board members, these issues of investing and financial management sometimes seemed a distraction from the more important work of philanthropy. But periodic financial crises have a way of reminding a foundation's board and staff that the foundation's work depends fundamentally on the assets it has available. One former Rockefeller Foundation staffer learned this lesson the hard way when the Great Depression reminded everyone that markets do not always rise to the future.

PERPETUITY

THE CONSEQUENCES OF OVERCONFIDENCE

Edwin Embree arrived with his hat in his hand. Only four years earlier, the handsome Yale graduate had quit his job at the Rockefeller Foundation to become the head of the Julius Rosenwald Fund in Chicago. With assets valued at nearly $35 million by September 1929, the Rosenwald Fund had become one of the ten richest private foundations in the United States. Most important for Embree, the founder, Julius Rosenwald, the man who made Sears, Roebuck into one of the greatest retail companies in the nation, was not afraid to take risks.

With Rosenwald's enthusiastic support, Embree had expanded the fund's massive education program for rural African Americans in the South. With board approval, he developed programs to support medical education and training of public health nurses in the African American community. The fund pledged millions to black colleges including Tuskegee, Hampton, Howard, Fisk, Atlanta, and Dillard universities. It also provided support for various Chicago institutions as well as the Urban League and the NAACP Legal Defense Fund.

Much of this work paralleled efforts by the Rockefeller philanthropies, and there were opportunities for collaboration. Julius Rosenwald served on the board of the Rockefeller Foundation. Rockefeller's General Education Board provided funding to many of the same black colleges. Embree had also invited Raymond Fosdick and Beardsley Ruml, the former head of the Laura Spelman

Rockefeller Memorial, to join the board of the Rosenwald Fund. Although Fosdick declined, Ruml agreed. In 1932, Embree hoped that this shared vision would be enough to help solve a very big problem.

Edwin Embree (left) was president of the Rosenwald Fund during the Depression. Embree had moved to the Fund in 1927 after ten years on the staff of the Rockefeller Foundation. (Rockefeller Archives Center.)

The Rosenwald Fund was essentially bankrupt. On the eve of the Great Depression, Julius Rosenwald had had such confidence in Sears that the company's stock accounted for nearly all of the Rosenwald Fund's assets. When the stock market crashed in October 1929, the value of Sears's shares—and of the fund's assets—plummeted.

At first, Embree and the trustees were not worried. They hoped the market would turn around. They had seen this kind of plunge before. In 1921, for example, the value of Sears's shares had fallen from $243 to $54.5. But the stock had recovered. In 1929, the trustees were so optimistic that this would happen again that, a month after the crash, the board committed more than $1.4 million to twenty new projects.

By June 1932, however, the optimism had faded. Sears was selling for $10 a share. On paper, the value of the Rosenwald Fund had fallen by 95 percent since September 1929. Meanwhile, the fund had made promises to all sorts of educational institutions that totaled millions of dollars. Embree hoped he could convince the Rockefeller Foundation and Carnegie Corporation to loan

COMPLETE FINAL
★ ★ ★ ★ ★ ★

The

VOL. XCVII—NO 49—DAILY

NEW YORK, TU

STOCKS OFF IN 16

the fund enough money to get by until the stock market turned around. It was a desperate move, with consequences that would affect the future of all three organizations and the field of philanthropy. It would also raise fundamental questions about whether the Rockefeller Foundation should exist in perpetuity and how it should manage its assets.

THE VIEW AT THE BEGINNING

In 1913, no one believed that the Rockefeller Foundation would last forever. With one of his earliest gifts, John D. Rockefeller Sr. had written to the trustees: "This gift is made for the general corporate purposes of the Foundation, and the principal as well as the income may be used in your discretion for any of the corporate purposes of the Foundation." In Congress, during Rockefeller's unsuccessful effort to win a federal charter, senators had insisted that the Foundation spend itself out of existence by a certain date or turn over its assets to the government, and Rockefeller and his advisors were willing to agree to these terms. Indeed, in 1910, after Senior had committed $50 million to establish the Rockefeller Foundation, John D. Rockefeller Jr. suggested to Frederick Gates that the entire sum should be spent within twenty-five years. "Why should not each generation support its own philanthropies and education to the extent that the money of philanthropic people can be wisely given away? Beyond that it would be better to be passed

MILLION SHARE DAY

on to the next generation to distribute." Gates shared this view. "It is generally held by students of civilization that endowments or charitable and religious agencies early outlive their usefulness and then tend to become hindrances rather than helps in the progress of civilization. The charities of one generation are not the proper charities of the next generation."

The charter of the General Education Board contained a provision that called for its eventual termination. Similar provisions were incorporated into the charter of the International Education Board, making this organization, in the words of Wickliffe Rose, "a bird of passage" or an entity created to deal with its own moment in history.

Yet it would be wrong to conclude that Gates and Junior were rigid on this point. As Senior once remarked, "Perpetuity is a pretty long time." The Rockefeller Foundation might exist for many generations before it finally spent its endowment. Gates, for example, believed that the broad mission of the Rockefeller Foundation gave the board the flexibility to respond to the needs of new generations. "The unique distinction and the peculiar value of the Rockefeller Foundation may prove to be in two qualities—its universality and its deathlessness. It may adapt itself from decade to decade and from century to century to the changing needs of the times." Unlike past charitable endowments, which were controlled by a dead hand from the grave, the Rockefeller Foundation would be guided by a living hand.

World War I forced the Foundation to wrestle with the idea of spending its principal. Europe was devastated. Widespread food shortages were accompanied by lethal epidemics of Spanish flu and tuberculosis. The trustees were pressured by governments and charities to provide relief. The Foundation did help with food relief and public health initiatives, and some in the Foundation wanted to do more. Edwin Embree, who in February 1920 worked for the Foundation's president, George Vincent, suggested: "Surely we shall not face in many generations a world emergency which will approach in its importance that which confronts civilization in Europe. Should we not without servitude to tradition give every possible help in our power to this situation?" With an eye to the future but feeling the burden of the immediate need, Vincent and the board agreed. They spent from principal to help.

In fact, the Rockefeller philanthropies showed little reluctance during the first half-century to spend from endowment. Some leaders believed this was the right thing to do. In 1927, for example, as members of Rockefeller's inner circle wrestled with fundamental issues of organization and program, Frederick Gates sent a series of memoranda advocating the "disendowment" of the GEB. He wanted to give the institution's remaining funds to eight major universities: Columbia, Harvard, Chicago, Yale, Johns Hopkins, Stanford, Washington University, and Princeton. Raymond Fosdick responded in a letter to Junior, asserting that "the desirability of spending from principal whenever worthy objects appear—regardless of whether any sums remain for the next generation"—was always an option. But Gates's proposal "strikes me as fantastic," Fosdick wrote, especially given the amount of money that had already been poured into the endowments and operations of these institutions and even state schools. "The amounts of money involved in college and university education are now so enormous," he said, "that the sums which we have at our disposal are relatively insignificant, and on a quantitative basis could scarcely affect the situation one way or the other."

President George Vincent also outlined a scenario for liquidating the assets of the Rockefeller Foundation within a certain period of time. He believed such a plan would allow the Foundation to avoid having to recruit and manage a large permanent staff. Under his plan, the Foundation would function as a wholesale grantmaking institution giving gifts to major entities that would carry forward the Foundation's philanthropic goals. These entities might include national research councils, the League of Nations Health Section, national health societies, or universities. The kind of

2006

The Alliance for a Green Revolution in Africa launches with lead support from the Rockefeller Foundation and the Bill and Melinda Gates Foundation. (Jonas Bendiksen. Rockefeller Foundation.)

Chapter Eleven: Perpetuity

organization Vincent imagined would need a very small staff and rely on the temporary employment of outside experts to perform due diligence on grantees.

Others on the board were ambivalent about this idea of spending from the corpus, and particularly anxious that the board seemed to have no real clear policy on the matter. In 1928, staff member Edmund Day, director for the Social Sciences, suggested to George Vincent that the important thing was for the board to make a policy. The issue should not come up on a project-by-project basis.

The debate over the issue of endowments and the larger concept of perpetuity became more focused in the spring of 1929, when Julius Rosenwald wrote an article for the *Atlantic Monthly* titled "Principles of Public Giving." Rosenwald had long opposed the idea of "the never-ending endowment." As he told members of the American Academy of Political and Social Science in 1913, "Permanent endowment tends to lessen the amount available for immediate needs; and our immediate needs are too plain and too urgent

Julius Rosenwald, the CEO of Sears, Roebuck and Company, created the Julius Rosenwald Fund and served as a trustee of the Rockefeller Foundation. When Sears' stock plunged during the Depression, the Rosenwald Fund asked the Rockefeller Foundation to help the Fund cover pledges to grantees. (Library of Congress, Prints & Photographs)

to allow us to do the work of future generations." Rosenwald stuck by his convictions when he created the Julius Rosenwald Fund, stipulating that the fund's trustees had to spend it out of existence within twenty-five years after Rosenwald's death. His argument had two main elements: the tendency among organizations to become bureaucratic rather than innovative over time, and the belief that future generations should be responsible for the needs of their own time.

An evangelist for his ideas, Rosenwald was eager for comments on his article from the Rockefeller Foundation. George Vincent agreed with Rosenwald's stance. "The case against them [permanent endowments] has been proved over and over again," he wrote. Even in cases where the trustees

Thomas Appleget (far right) was an
administrator at Brown University before
joining Junior's staff in 1925. He became
a vice president of the Rockefeller
Foundation and administered the
fellowship and grants-in-aid programs,
as well as the Refugee Scholar program.
After retiring in 1949, he returned
to Brown University.
(Rockefeller Archive Center.)

had been given the widest discretion, such as with the Rockefeller Foundation, they ought to have the power to spend principal. Vincent suggested this should apply to the growing number of community trusts [foundations] as well. Vincent hedged his thinking when it came to educational institutions, where income from permanent endowments ought to be used for ongoing operations. As long as "trustees are wise," he said, they should be trusted to decide for the future as well as the present. In any case, if the trustees are not wise, "nothing can protect it [the foundation] against decay and disaster."

Not everyone at the Rockefeller Foundation was eager to join with Rosenwald. Edward Capps, the director of the Humanities program, noted that in times of financial crisis like the Civil War, permanent endowments played a key role in keeping philanthropic organizations alive. Many colleges and universities had gone out of existence during the Civil War, Capps pointed out, because of a lack of tuition-paying students. Others, including the University of Virginia, were so severely damaged that it took decades for them to recover. Princeton had survived because of its permanent endowment. "My impression is that if boards of trustees had been allowed to encroach upon endowment funds they would not have withstood these crises as well as they did."

Capps's gentle rebuttal could hardly have been more prescient, as Embree and the trustees of the Rosenwald Fund soon discovered. As noted earlier, the stock market crash reduced the value of the Rosenwald Fund by 95 percent. This enormous drop was readily apparent to the public and to institutions that had been promised grants by the fund. For the Rockefeller Foundation, the financial hit was less apparent because the Foundation reported the book value of its assets, not the market value based on changing share prices. Nevertheless, the drop was significant, which made the Foundation's meeting with Edwin Embree all the more awkward.

By the time Embree came to the Rockefeller Foundation on June 7, 1932, the Rosenwald Fund's resources were so diminished that the fund could not make good on its pledges to a number of institutions. Embree was hoping the Rockefeller Foundation and the Carnegie Corporation would help out. Thomas Appleget, the Rockefeller Foundation's vice president, said the GEB's trustees and general counsel were convinced that another foundation could not provide temporary help to the Rosenwald Fund. Such an act "would be neither politic nor broadly legal."

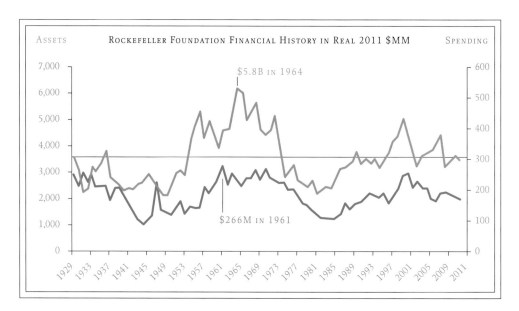

ASSETS ROCKEFELLER FOUNDATION FINANCIAL HISTORY IN REAL 2011 $MM SPENDING

$5.8B IN 1964

$266M IN 1961

The Foundation's general counsel, Thomas Debevoise, was even more emphatic in meetings with Appleget. According to Debevoise, the Foundation and the GEB "could not appropriate, underwrite or loan funds to another foundation." Either entity could, however, consider making appropriations to institutions "which might be injured in view of the Rosenwald Fund failure." Grants provided by the Rockefeller Foundation should fit the Foundation's existing programs.

By 1929 the Rockefeller Foundation had received all of the founder's gifts along with the assets of the Laura Spelman Rockefeller Memorial. Since that time, the value of the assets (shown here in millions in constant 2011 dollars) has been affected by market fluctuations and, to a lesser extent, by spending from principal. (Data provided by the Rockefeller Foundation.)

In the end, Embree did not walk away empty-handed. The GEB appropriated $200,000 for institutions that had been hurt by the collapse of the Rosenwald Fund. As agreed, these were institutions that fit within the GEB's program. The grants were made for one year only, with no commitment for future funding. They were also made with the understanding that if the Rosenwald Fund's fortunes turned, and it was able to meet its obligations, funds provided by the GEB would be repaid.

Although the GEB made these grants, Debevoise asserted that the trustees of the Rosenwald Fund bore "considerable responsibility" for failing to sell Sears stock before the price collapsed. If he knew the details of the Rockefeller Foundation's investment program, Embree may have taken offense at Debevoise's comments. The Rockefeller Foundation's trustees had not been any more prudent in their management of the Foundation's assets. They too had done little to diversify the assets given to the Foundation by the founder. In some sense they were simply luckier. Moreover, the Foundation's investment management practices illustrated how important the offices of the Rockefeller family remained to the basic operations of the Foundation and to the other Rockefeller philanthropies.

INVESTMENT POLICY

J ohn D. Rockefeller gave the trustees remarkable freedom when it came to investment management, although for decades they did little with this freedom. With one of his earliest gifts to the Foundation, Rockefeller wrote to the trustees:

> It is more convenient for me to provide funds for the Foundation by a gift of these specific securities rather than by a gift of cash, and I believe the securities have intrinsic and permanent value which would justify you in retaining them as investments, but in order to relieve you from any uncertainty or embarrassment with regard to them, I desire to state specifically that you are under no obligation to retain any of these investments, but are at liberty to dispose of them and change the form of investment whenever in your judgment it seems wise to do so.

The idea of investment diversification was an accepted practice even in 1910. The *Washington Post*, for example, reported speculation, soon after the Rockefeller Foundation charter bill was submitted to Congress, that the soon-to-be-created Foundation would gradually liquidate its shares in Standard Oil in favor of more conservative securities as was "proper" for trust funds, savings banks, and insurance companies. This assumption sparked concerns on Wall Street that the Foundation would flood the market with Standard Oil stock.

There were political pressures for diversification as well. During the Senate hearings, some members expressed concern that the Foundation's assets would include a large share of Standard Oil stock and that the Foundation might be a subterfuge for Rockefeller's business interests. Echoing these concerns, the Department of Justice asked the Foundation in April 1915 to provide a statement explaining who actually voted proxies on the Foundation's stock.

Surprisingly, the board did little to diversify the Foundation's assets during the first half-century of its existence or to shift control away from the Rockefeller family offices. The board established a finance committee to

Louis Guerineau Myers

From his office at 26 Broadway, Louis G. Myers managed the assets of various Rockefeller philanthropies including the Rockefeller Institute for Medical Research, the General Education Board, and the Rockefeller Foundation. (Rockefeller Archive Center.)

manage its investments, but in reality the Foundation's assets were managed by staff in the family's offices at 26 Broadway who operated a single treasurer's office that oversaw finances for all of the Rockefeller philanthropies. Expenses for running the treasurer's office were apportioned among the several boards.

In the early years, the day-to-day responsibility for managing the Foundation's assets fell to Louis Guerineau Myers, who served as the treasurer of the General Education Board, the Rockefeller Institute for Medical Research, and the Rockefeller Foundation. After the Laura Spelman Rockefeller Memorial was created, Myers became the treasurer for that institution as well. A lean, silver-haired native of Bayonne, New Jersey, and a connoisseur of antique furniture and pewter, Myers had been associated with businessman and philanthropist George Foster Peabody, who served on the board and as treasurer of the General Education Board in 1905. Myers became assistant treasurer of the GEB in 1909. He took direction from the finance committee, which in 1922 consisted of three men: John D. Rockefeller Jr., Raymond Fosdick, and Frederick Strauss. Myers was also guided by Bertram Cutler, who managed much of the work in Junior's office.

For the most part, Myers's management of the portfolio was reactive. About 80 percent of the original portfolio had been invested in stocks, with the remaining 20 percent invested in corporate bonds. During World War I, the Foundation bought government war bonds and increased its share of government securities to almost a third of the portfolio. After the war, these issues were sold and government bonds again accounted for less than ten percent.

The effects of the crash of the stock market and the onset of the Depression on the Rockefeller Foundation were not immediately apparent to the public or even to insiders at the Foundation, because the Foundation's annual report failed to present a transparent view of the status of the endowment. In December 1931, Roger Greene, the head of the China Medical Board, wrote to suggest that there should be more information on investments in the report. The treasurer's statement should show how the portfolio was diversified, and give information on the return on investment from various forms of investment. Rather than report only the book value of its holdings, Greene thought it should report their market value. Greene also thought the Foundation should disclose the purchase and sale of various assets and equities.

Max Mason, the president of the Rockefeller Foundation, wrote back to say that the day-to-day investments were made by the finance committee, which included men who were experts in investing. Sharing information about their transactions would likely lead to second-guessing by those who were less competent and to distortions in the mind of the public. Mason also recognized that the Foundation's assets did not reflect a theoretical strategy for prudent investing. "As you know, most theories as to investment include the recommendation of a thoroughly diversified list. In our case we cannot say that our list is thoroughly diversified." In fact, the portfolio had changed little since the assets had been given by Rockefeller.

In 1932, about sixty percent of the Foundation's total assets was in stocks. Stocks and bonds associated with the pre-breakup assets of Standard Oil made up more than 70 percent of the total. The rest of the Rockefeller money—some $72.3 million—was invested in bonds, about 15 percent of which could be traced to the pre-breakup assets of Standard Oil. Explaining the Foundation's investment policy, Mason wrote: "What we have done still seems to have been the only thing to have done. We have bought or sold when it seemed opportune. Not having had, therefore, the chance to pursue a theoretical policy we can naturally have none to state."

The Rockefeller Foundation's investment management policies also showed how interwoven the Rockefeller Foundation's philanthropies remained, even after the 1929 reorganization. In May 1932, "the Finance Committee of the Foundation, Board and Institute" met and decided to instruct the treasurer not to lend money to highly

In 1928 Jerome Greene returned to the Rockefeller Foundation as a member of the board of trustees. He urged the board to take greater responsibility for the management of the Foundation's assets. (Rockefeller Archive Center.)

leveraged stock market speculators (using call loans) and instead to invest available cash in government securities. In the spring of 1933, with inflation on the horizon and significant cash balances in the accounts of the Rockefeller Foundation, the GEB, the Rockefeller Institute, the Spelman Fund, the IEB, and the CMB, Fosdick expressed concern to Junior that something needed to be done. The two agreed to a meeting of the members of the finance committees of each organization, some of whom served on several of the Rockefeller boards.

Jerome Greene, who was now a member of the Rockefeller Foundation board, was frustrated by the situation. After Louis Myers died in 1932, Greene suggested that the Foundation rethink the role of the treasurer. In the past, he said, the treasurer's role had been regarded as "substantially like that of the cashier of a bank who is responsible for the integrity of the accounts." With Myers's death, and with all Rockefeller-funded philanthropies looking to disassociate from the family offices at 26 Broadway, Greene believed the time had come to appoint "a prominent member of the financial community who would have more to do with finance than the late Treasurer."

"It is true that the various Boards get a high-class investment service from Mr. Rockefeller's office," Greene later wrote to Raymond Fosdick, "but there is something about that relationship which in the long run seems to me to be neither in the best interest of the Boards or of Mr. Rockefeller himself. I say this although I appreciate the wholly unselfish purpose which has actuated Mr. Rockefeller and also the fact that the portfolios of the various boards, having been so largely predetermined by Mr. Rockefeller's gifts of securities, could doubtless be managed more easily and efficiently by persons previously familiar with them."

Greene's advice went unheeded. Myers's assistant and Junior's college friend, Lefferts Dashiell, was promoted to the position. But Greene did not give up. In 1935, in a confidential memo challenging the autonomy of the board (see chapter IV), he again highlighted the need for a finance committee and treasurer independent of the Rockefeller family offices. The Davis Committee, created in response to Greene's memo, agreed with his concerns and recommended changes to strengthen the Foundation's board and bring independence to the office of its treasurer. But in practice, little changed.

When Dashiell died in office in 1938, Greene urged Fosdick, who was now president of the Foundation, to recruit a major figure from Wall Street. But again the treasurer's assistant—Edward Robinson—was promoted. The treasurer's office continued to manage the portfolios of multiple Rockefeller philanthropies.

The debate over how the Rockefeller Foundation and other private philanthropies managed their assets was renewed in the fall of 1938 when reporter Horace Coon published *Money to Burn*, the first serious investigative look at private foundations. Among other things, Coon charged that the Foundation had never been subjected to an "independent outside audit." Treasurer Robinson dismissed this claim. The Foundation's books were audited every year, he said, and a statement to that effect was published in each annual report. "If the meaning is that there is no audit of the policy of appropriations," Robinson wrote to Foundation president Fosdick, "that is an entirely different matter and not one for me to discuss."

Coon also criticized the Foundation for reporting only the book or ledger values of the Foundation's assets, which considerably understated the value of the Foundation's resources. Robinson confessed that he did not know why the Foundation followed this practice, especially since prices for nearly all of the stocks and bonds listed in the portfolio were listed on public exchanges. Robinson would later make several recommendations for policy changes based on the criticism in Coon's book: the Foundation should provide market values for assets, keep records of all security transactions, including write-downs, and explain why it carried a large uninvested cash balance.

In an era with few large mutual funds or pension funds Rockefeller and Carnegie drew attention from investors eager to survey their investment strategies. In 1942, the American Investors Union looked at the Foundation's portfolio and noted that it continued to be "heavily over-balanced on the side of oil stocks and bonds" and characterized by a "lack of diversification." In contrast to the Carnegie Corporation, which had more than 60 percent of its assets invested in government bonds, the Rockefeller Foundation had suffered from its investments in stocks and bonds (especially in non-petroleum related industries). As a result, the Foundation had taken a "shellacking" in the market. Readers could draw a clear conclusion that the Foundation's investment managers had been unwilling to take losses and get out when they should have, and had otherwise failed to exercise appropriate oversight. Internally, the Foundation's treasury officials found no fault with the American Investors Union's presentation of the facts, although it is not clear what immediate impact the American Investors Union critique had on investment management.

A year later Chairman Walter Stewart was worried. An economist and head of the Institute of Advanced Study at Princeton, Stewart was "shocked at the casual way in which trustees undertake to manage the investment of money." The Foundation had not been greatly harmed in the past, but

Walter Stewart, a renowned economist and director of the Institute for Advanced Study at Princeton, succeeded John D. Rockefeller Jr. as chairman of the Foundation in 1943. (Alfred Eisenstaedt, Rockefeller Archives Center.)

he worried about the future. In a handwritten note to Fosdick, he conceded that two of the most active members of the finance committee "are men of such prestige in the financial world and manage such large institutions as to establish a presumption in favor of their knowledge and wisdom." But Stewart was not impressed. He felt the Foundation needed more focused expert advice. "Our present arrangement is distinctly third rate." Stewart also noted that unlike other officers, the Foundation's treasurer had to contend with board expertise and, understandably, found it hard to challenge the advice of the committee members.

Fosdick concurred with Stewart. He confessed: "In the days when I served as a regular member of the Finance Committee the same air of casualness prevailed. Thus far, I think the success of our finances is due more to sheer luck than anything else, i.e., the fact that oils have always been good. But at a time of crisis like this, I am not at all convinced that this type of policy is going to see us through."

But no transformation of the Foundation's investment strategy resulted from this exchange. In March 1945, Stewart was unhappy that the finance committee did not meet on a regular schedule and that, when it did meet, there was usually no agenda. "We meet at luncheon and after pleasant general conversation," he wrote, "we spend some time reviewing the list [of securities] and deciding whether particular securities should be sold." The meetings left little time for discussions of strategy. "Giving money away wisely may be a more difficult art than the preservation of capital," he conceded, "but in present circumstance I believe our investment position also requires orderly and deliberate consideration."

Part of the problem with investment management was structural. In 1945, Fosdick noted that the treasurer reported to the board and not to the president. When Chester Barnard succeeded Fosdick as president, he made it clear that as a personnel matter he would supervise both the comptroller and the treasurer. Barnard also set out to strengthen the board's role in investment management. In a letter to John Dickey, a board member and the president of Dartmouth College, he wrote that the finance committee "does not function satisfactorily." It no longer included any member who was "personally authoritatively informed about securities in detail" and had only one financier—Winthrop Aldrich, who was the head of Chase National Bank.

Chapter Eleven: Perpetuity

Barnard made it a priority to recruit someone to the board who would have this expertise.

Still, the Foundation's investment management remained very passive. When the board finally agreed to hire an outside investment counselor in 1948, the man picked for the job, John Bridgwood, a vice president at Chase, noted that "in spite of its size the composition of the present portfolio is such that the number of items to be followed is relatively small." But Bridgwood made few changes. In 1954, *Business Week* reported that shares of Standard Oil of New Jersey still accounted for half of the Foundation's assets. In 1963, when assistant treasurer Theodore R. Frye wrote a short history of the Foundation's investment policy, he reported that except to appoint a finance committee and empower it with the ability "to make and change investments," the board had no policy or overall investment strategy. "The Finance Committee's judgment in exercising these powers has never been restricted by any formalized statement of policy in charter, by-laws, board minutes, or elsewhere." He claimed that the Foundation had pursued a policy of diversification over the years, but this claim was exaggerated. In fact, the Foundation had shifted to an even greater reliance on a small group of equities, which made up 85.99 percent of the portfolio in 1963. In the early 1930s, for example, corporate bonds accounted for up to 40 percent of the portfolio. By 1963, they accounted for only 2 percent. Preferred stocks, which made up more than 10 percent of the total at one time, had been completely eliminated. Government securities accounted for less than ten percent of the portfolio (except during World War II). At the beginning of 1962, the Foundation owned stock in just thirty-eight companies, including 5.932 million shares of Standard Oil, which accounted for a huge percentage of the total portfolio.

The Rockefeller Foundation was not the only private foundation whose portfolio was still structured around the founder's gifts. Until 1956, the Ford Foundation owned 88 percent of Ford Motor Company's stock. The Foundation's income derived almost exclusively from the company's dividends. That year, the Foundation sold 22 percent of its Ford stock in the first public offering of Ford shares. To further diversify their assets, the Ford Foundation and the Rockefeller Foundation agreed in 1962 and 1963 to exchange a total of $14,362,000 in securities—Standard Oil of New Jersey for Ford Motor

Management guru Chester Barnard became president of the Rockefeller Foundation in 1948. At the time, the Rockefeller Foundation had 244 employees in New York and in field offices around the world. (Puigney. Rockefeller Archive Center.)

Company—to allow both entities to restructure their portfolios. These transactions helped make Ford Motor Company the largest single non-oil corporate equity in the Foundation's portfolio by 1966 (worth $25.9 million). Nevertheless, as late as 1966, oil stocks still accounted for $486 million of a nearly $815 million portfolio.

A Strategy for the Long Haul

For years, the lack of definition in the investment program reflected continuing uncertainty over the future of the Foundation. There was a trend toward investing for permanence, but no definite policy. After debating the issue on one occasion in 1936, board member James Angell, the president of Yale University, wrote to Junior to say that it was "extremely important that [the Foundation] should husband its resources, so far as concerns capital, that it may be in the strongest position to assist at least in the salvaging of the most important human undertakings which may be threatened with destruction." Angell noted that he had never agreed with Rosenwald that endowments were wrong. But he may have been most interested in having the Foundation and the GEB help build the endowments of institutions such as Yale.

Responding to Angell in 1936, Junior equivocated on the issue of perpetuity. By 1939, however, he was much less inclined to see the Foundation dip into principal to finance current operations. He suggested that current operations and grants be limited to the Foundation's cash and cash-equivalent investments, plus an amount equal to 10 percent of the market value of the balance of the portfolio. Raymond Fosdick reluctantly agreed. Yet at the December 1939 trustees meeting in Williamsburg, the board passed three resolutions on financial policy, including one that suggested that the principal fund should be exhausted within a period that might be as short as forty years.

Ambivalence on the issue continued during the war. Trustee Owen D. Young, the broadcasting executive who founded Radio Corporation of America (RCA), wrote to Raymond Fosdick in 1943: "When I sat on your Board, I was inclined to be liberal with the expenditure of capital funds, even though it brought the Foundation to an end in a relatively short period. Now, with the changed condition of the world and the great need during the years ahead for relatively small grants [for penicillin and Chinese mass education] which may bring extraordinary results, I am inclined to feel that the maintenance of this pool of aid and its experienced personnel should be jealously safeguarded to insure perpetuation."

A majority of board members in 1946, however, did not agree with Young. Polled by a special committee of the board, the majority believed that the board should adopt a plan to terminate the Foundation within twenty-five years. All the trustees were willing to dip into the Foundation's principal fund "if opportunities develop for meeting needs and wants of importance and urgency." With the end of World War II, those opportunities seemed readily apparent. Accordingly, at the December meeting in 1946, the board authorized the treasurer to draw from principal "whenever and as often as there shall not be sufficient funds" in the Foundation's appropriations accounts.

John D. Rockefeller Jr. personally financed much of the restoration of Colonial Williamsburg. While he was chairman, the Rockefeller Foundation's board frequently held its annual meeting in the Council Chamber of the Capitol building. (F.S. Lincoln. Colonial Williamsburg Foundation.)

Very quickly, however, it became clear that this kind of policy imposed little or no discipline on the organization. Barnard characterized it as "pretty wide open" or, as he wrote to the officers, "so wide open as to encourage all the extravagance and carelessness that man could dream of." Barnard announced that he would generally disapprove of expenditures from principal unless "they are very clearly justified as of more than ordinary promise or except as they represent important opportunities not often afforded."

But eight years later a new president, Dean Rusk, announced that the Foundation would spend up to $5 million a year for five years from its corpus to finance increased activity in underdeveloped nations in the third world, so that it would not have to reduce spending for research and training in advanced countries to afford this initiative. Rusk asserted that the opportunities were great and that "the impressive increase in the market value of the Foundation's holdings" provided an unusual opportunity to dip into principal. Indeed, between 1940 and 1955 the market value of securities in the Foundation's portfolio rose from $141 million to $557 million, erasing the losses incurred after the stock market crash of 1929—even accounting for inflation. Rusk suggested that the "welfare of mankind" would be far more dependent in the future on "what happens now in the countries of Asia, Africa, the Middle east, and Latin America."

As late as 1963, the board still had no restriction on spending capital. A report created by the treasurer's office noted that, since the creation of the Foundation, the board had spent just over $82 million from principal, on the way to overall spending of $763.6 million. Although the board engaged in an extended discussion of the issue of spending from capital in April, 1964, the board concluded that "while liquidation of the Foundation at any definite date was not contemplated, the Trustees should feel free to use principal from time to time in any amount necessary to respond to opportunities of major importance for the well-being of mankind." While the Foundation's endowment was benefiting from healthy returns, the trustees could afford to dip into capital, but they noted that "the matter should be reviewed frequently in the light of changing financial conditions and world needs."

Passage of the Tax Reform Act of 1969, the financial crisis of the 1970s, new accounting

2005

In the wake of Hurricane Katrina, the Rockefeller Foundation commits more than $7 million to recovery efforts and long-range planning focused on building resilience. (Jonas Bendiksen. Rockefeller Foundation.)

Chapter Eleven: Perpetuity

rules, and changes taking place in the investment world—along with a retrospective look at the success of Chase's investment advisors—finally led the Rockefeller Foundation to adopt a fundamentally new investment management strategy in the mid-1970s. Implementing new recommendations from the accounting profession, the Foundation abandoned the use of ledger or book values for its securities in 1973, reporting market value instead. The change was significant. It raised the reported value of the Foundation's Principal Fund from just under $300 million in January 1972 to nearly $778.7 million.

The apparent good news on the balance sheet, however, would not be matched by the reality of market performance in the 1970s. Like most other investors in the era, the Foundation experienced a major drop in the value of its investments. By the end of 1974, the value of the Principal Fund had fallen to $574 million. Although the markets began to recover, the nominal value of the fund did not reach the January 1, 1972, level until the end of 1979. In the meantime, with inflation rampant, the purchasing power of those assets declined significantly.

Disappointments in the stock market were exacerbated by transitions in the management of the Foundation's assets. A study by the treasurer's office in 1971 had produced an unsettling insight. Although the Foundation was still heavily invested in oil stocks, its efforts at diversification had not produced better long-term growth for the endowment. In fact, cash reinvested from the sale of oil stocks had not produced returns equal to what the oil stocks would have produced.

The finance committee's answer was to broaden its sources for investment advice and management. The committee assigned assets worth approximately $200 million to four equity fund managers. At this time, the Foundation's endowment was worth about $840 million. Almost all of it—96 percent—was allocated to the stocks of just forty-four companies. The remaining 4 percent was in fixed-income investments. With this shift in investment strategy, the Foundation also reconfigured the role of the treasurer's office in a way that finally reflected Jerome Greene's vision. The treasurer's office now became responsible for monitoring the outside fund managers. It also took over the short-term management of the portfolio, relieving the finance committee from this responsibility. And it initiated a stock-lending program.

Gradually, the outsourcing of fund management continued. In October 1973, another $75 million was placed with two bond fund managers, In 1976, for the first time, the finance committee contracted with outside investment managers to handle portions of the Foundation's portfolio. Meanwhile, it continued to retain Chase to handle "the remainder of the account." According to the minutes of the board, "This dual system provides the advantage of a comparison between portfolio management by advance approval on the one hand, and by ratification of transactions effected by investment managers on the other."

Unfortunately, these changes occurred under abysmal market conditions. In 1977, "alarmed by the decline in the real value of the portfolio and the implications of this for the Foundation's future," the finance committee commissioned a study by Wells Fargo Bank. The study highlighted the need for the Foundation to rationalize the investment process and reduce its role in active management of the endowment even further. In 1980, this system was expanded from two fully discretionary equity managers to four, while the number of outside bond managers remained the same at two. By this time the Foundation had also established investment guidelines for diversification and levels of risk.

"...when former Stanford University president Richard Lyman came to New York to lead the Rockefeller Foundation in 1980, he ex-pressed his concern that the Foundation was 'spending itself out of existence.'"

Despite all these initiatives, when former Stanford University president Richard Lyman came to New York to lead the Rockefeller Foundation in 1980, he expressed his concern that the Foundation was "spending itself out of existence." As asset values declined significantly in the mid-1970s, the Foundation had generally maintained its level of appropriations by spending out of principal. Lyman slashed spending for operations by $3.5 million a year and, after Congress reduced the minimum payout required of private foundations, Lyman cut the grantmaking budget as well.

Fortunately for Lyman and the Foundation, the stock market boomed in the mid-1980s. Under the leadership of trustee James Wolfensohn, who headed the investment committee, the Foundation continued its move toward outside investment management. By April 1982, virtually the entire portfolio had been given over to outside managers. Over the next five to six years, the endowment was diversified from three asset classes to six. For the first time in the Foundation's history, it was not managed by the Foundation's own treasury office or Rockefeller office insiders. Instead, the treasurer's office focused on establishing investment policies, identifying investment advisors, monitoring the performance of those advisors, and controlling the risks associated with the portfolio. The role of the treasurer's office was transformed "from one limited to the passive execution of decisions originating in the Committee to that of prime mover in originating strategies and setting the investment agenda." Meanwhile, according to the Treasurer's Office, the role of the finance committee shifted from "direct responsibility for managing the endowment to that of policy setting and oversight." In effect, by the late 1980s, Jerome Greene's vision had been realized—albeit half a century later.

The changes, combined with a burst of good years in the stock market, led to a tremendous rise in the value of Foundation assets. Between 1982 and 1989, they increased from roughly $850 million to nearly $1.5 billion (in constant 1994 dollars). By the mid-1990s, the portfolio was managed by seventy external investment advisors handling marketable and non-marketable securities.

The professionalization of the treasury function (which was paralleled in other parts of the nonprofit world), led to a more disciplined process of forecasting and budgeting. By the mid-1990s, the finance committee regularly established asset allocation guidelines and performance targets. Investment objectives were driven by two clear goals: "to provide resources for the Foundation to continue spending at current program levels and to maintain the purchasing power of the assets into the foreseeable future."

For the moment, the question of perpetuity had been put aside, replaced with the concept of a "foreseeable future." When a new financial crisis hit in 2008, eroding the value of the Foundation's endowment, a new generation of trustees was forced to confront the question of perpetuity and consider spending and investment management in light of the future. This time, however, the investment strategies and the commitment to the foreseeable future were in place.

Philanthropy and the Financial Crisis of 2008

When the financial crisis hammered the world's financial markets in 2008, the Rockefeller Foundation and many philanthropic organizations once again faced a dilemma. With major declines in the value of their endowments, they could cut spending and grants to preserve the value of their endowments. Or they could maintain their spending to meet the increasing needs of their grantees during the financial crisis, knowing they would erode the long-term value of their assets.

In June, 2009 President Rodin and her staff organized a special board study session to confront this question of stewardship. Reading from John D. Rockefeller's gift document, General Counsel Shari Patrick shed light on the founder's intent in establishing the Foundation, including an analysis of his attitude toward perpetuity. Chief Investment Officer Donna Dean outlined the factors that influenced the Foundation's annual projections for charitable expenditures.

After the presentation, many board members, like their predecessors, were awed by the extraordinary flexibility that the founder had given to the trustees. But if some in the room were hoping, after nearly a hundred years, for some resolution of the question of perpetuity, they were disappointed. Like earlier trustees, the members expressed general support for the concept of perpetuity, but they retained for themselves and their successors the right and the responsibility to decide in the moment whether the needs and opportunities of the present outweighed the prospects for the future.

With Rockefeller Foundation support, John Grant, Jimmy Yen and C.C. Chen launch community based health programs in China.

Warren Weaver becomes director of the Division of Natural Sciences. Under his guidance, the Rockefeller Foundation incubates and develops the emerging field of molecular biology.

Dr. H. W. Florey, a professor of pathology at Oxford University, receives the first of a series of small grants to study the potential for penicillin to combat infection.

1917 **1920s** **1928** **1932** **1935** **1936**

Rockefeller Foundation President George Vincent outlines a plan to promote scientific medical education around the world.

Scientists begin work in the Rockefeller Foundation's yellow fever laboratory in New York (later the Virus Laboratory) under the auspices of the International Health Division.

Rural reconstruction grants offered for the first time to promote agricultural science and veterinary medicine.

John D. Rockefeller creates the Rockefeller Institute for Medical Research (Rockefeller University).

Following the incorporation of the Rockefeller Foundation, the trustees establish the International Health Commission to carry the battle against hookworm to other countries.

With funding from the Rockefeller Foundation, Johns Hopkins University creates the first graduate school for public health.

1897   1901   1909   1913   1914   1916

On vacation, Frederick Gates reads William Osler's *Principles and Practice of Medicine*. The book inspires him to urge John D. Rockefeller to fund medical research.

Rockefeller Sanitary Commission is established to fight hookworm disease in the American South.

China Medical Board (CMB) is created to promote scientific medical education in China. The CMB's major work is the development of Peking Union Medical College.

FROM ONE INSPIRED IDEA TO THE NEXT

W orking alone late at night in a laboratory or collectively in the fields of a demonstration farm, Rockefeller Foundation grantees have been engaged in a massive effort to improve the well-being of humanity by developing new knowledge or new ways to address human needs. Over the course of a century, hundreds of thousands of individuals around the globe have shared in this innovative work. The Rockefeller Foundation's contribution has been to provide resources to further this collective effort and to help make the connections that lead from one inspired idea to the next.

This graphic timeline captures the spirit of that innovative process, but reflects only a microcosm of the achievements of the Foundation's grantees and staff across many disciplines.

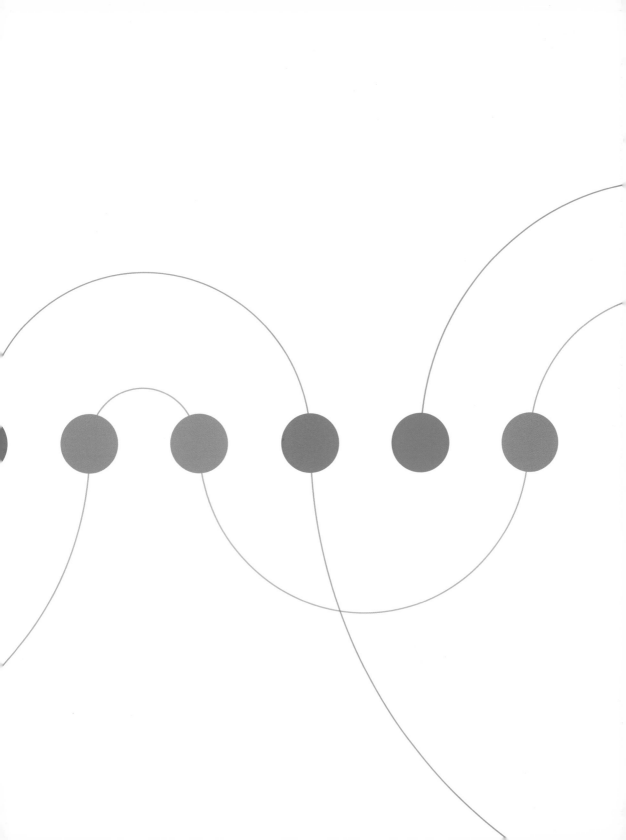

Asian Clinical Epidemiological Network meets for the first time. This initiative is the forerunner of INCLEN.

The Working Group on Female Participation in Education is convened by the Rockefeller Foundation to increase female participation in primary and secondary education in Africa.

Launch of Transforming Health Systems initiative aims to help governments achieve universal health care coverage.

1978

1983

1984

1990

2006

2008

Rockefeller Foundation helps to convene the first meeting of the Great Neglected Diseases Network.

Combining its longtime interests in agriculture and molecular biology, the Rockefeller Foundation creates a new research program focused on biotechnology.

Rockefeller and Gates Foundations combine to launch the Alliance for a Green Revolution in Africa (AGRA).

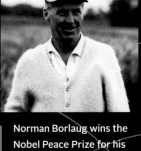

Mexican agriculture program launched to increase yields and meet the needs of the country's growing population.

The International Rice Research Institute (IRRI) is created with funding from the Rockefeller and Ford Foundations. IRRI becomes a model for a host of international collaborative agricultural research projects established over the next several decades.

Norman Borlaug wins the Nobel Peace Prize for his successful efforts to promote the Green Revolution through the Rockefeller Foundation's Conquest of Hunger program.

1937   **1943**   **1951**   **1960**   **1963**   **1970**

Max Theiler and his co-workers develop the vaccine known as 17D to prevent yellow fever.

International Health Division is closed as new international agencies including the United Nations and the World Health Organization emerge to carry the IHD's work forward.

Conquest of Hunger program is launched. Building on lessons learned in agriculture programs in Mexico, Colombia and other countries, the program seeks to help developing countries feed their people.

University Development program begins. The effort seeks to promote economic and social well-being by enhancing higher education and research in African, Asian and Latin American nations.

"Long before the advent of the personal
computer or social networks, Foundation
staff used these cards to keep track of
the connections the Foundation had
made with people who had ideas and
problems to be solved."

CONCLUSION

A few years before he established the Rockefeller Foundation, John D. Rockefeller Sr. observed: "Today the whole machinery of benevolence is conducted upon more or less haphazard principles." He and his son and Frederick Gates believed that the business of philanthropy could be organized far more effectively. Just as his most profound innovations in the business of petroleum had been in the organization of its work, Rockefeller proposed to further the transformation of the practice of philanthropy by creating a new kind of institution. In the language of his day, he called it a "benevolent trust." Today we call it a private foundation.

Rockefeller was clear that the process of creating this new institution belonged to many people. Other donors were already stepping forward. With these new institutions, he hoped, philanthropists would "look the facts in the face; they will applaud and sustain the effective workers and institutions; and they will uplift the intelligent standard of good work in helping all the people chiefly to help themselves."

Rockefeller was humble enough to know that he could not forecast the future of this new institution. "When it is eventually worked out, as it will be in some form, and probably in a better one than we can now forecast," he said, "how worthy it will be of the best efforts of our ablest men!"

Over the next century, as Rockefeller predicted, there was indeed a revolution in the practice of philanthropy. Moving beyond charity, the new institutions devoted resources to understanding the root causes of problems ranging from disease to malnutrition and illiteracy. Using science and the scientific method, practitioners at the Rockefeller Foundation and elsewhere developed new technologies—from medicines to hybridized seeds—to promote the well-being of humankind. Long before the field developed the concept of a "portfolio approach" to philanthropy, the Foundation addressed problems in health, agriculture, and education simultaneously to increase the odds of achieving a breakthrough. The Rockefeller Foundation learned by doing, sending staff into the field to work with local officials and indigenous communities to tackle overwhelming problems. Often their accomplishments fell far short of their aspirations.

As with all innovative organizations, the strengths of the Rockefeller Foundation as it has evolved over a century are anchored in paradox. Focused on developing systems for grant management and avoiding "scatteration," the Foundation remained remarkably flexible and opportunistic. Committed to a practice of wholesale philanthropy that sought to impact systems of benevolence ranging from the American Red Cross to national scientific research councils, the Foundation often enabled profound innovation by distributing small but timely grants. Endowed with resources that allowed it to pursue its mission single-handedly in its earliest days, the Foundation recognized that success was dependent on collaboration with governments, other philanthropists, and, above all, the recipients of the Foundation's grants.

The process of innovation depended on the evolution of practice. The board of trustees had to come to understand its role as well as its duty to represent the broad public that the Foundation sought to serve. They also had to come to terms with the future, recognizing a responsibility to pass on to the next generation the resources to continue the organization's work. Foundation presidents had to nurture the intellectual curiosity and idealism that attracted staff to the mission while keeping the organization focused on pragmatic solutions to the most intractable problems. Staff, like Rockefeller, often besieged by grant seekers, had to constantly listen and absorb as they traveled the world visiting individuals and institutions, each convinced that they were on the threshold of making a real and permanent difference in the world.

This process of listening and of building networks has been the cornerstone of the innovative framework that the Rockefeller Foundation developed. On the 19th floor of the Foundation's offices on Fifth Avenue in New York, an artifact of a bygone era provides silent testimony to this practice. Tens of thousands of index cards fill the drawers of an old oak library catalog. Each card records the name of a grantee or a contact. Long before the advent of the personal computer or social networks, Foundation staff used these cards to keep track of the connections the Foundation had made with people who had ideas and problems to be solved.

Today, as Foundation staff work on smartphones, tablets, and laptops, they continue to update the paper cards in the catalog, as if to demonstrate that not everything in the Foundation's history or practice can be digitized. In the sweep of a century, the relationships represented by the cards reflect the enduring legacy and the ongoing strength of the Foundation's practice. As the pace of global collaboration continues to accelerate, those relationships drive the continuing process of philanthropic innovation in Africa, Asia and the rest of the world. Like the founder, Rockefeller Foundation staff and partners understand that the future of philanthropy lies beyond the imagination, but it is and will be worthy of the best efforts of all of humankind.

Beyond Charity is part of the Rockefeller Foundation's Centennial initiative. Members of the Rockefeller Foundation's staff were deeply involved with the development of this book. Dr. Judith Rodin helped to inspire the concept. Michael Myers, with the close and capable assistance of Carolyn Bancroft, provided critical guidance and encouragement. Robert Bykofsky, Elizabeth Pena and the staff in Records Management helped identify and access current and historical materials that tell the story. Kathy Gomez collected spectacular photographs highlighting the Foundation's recent work. In the General Counsel's office, Shari Patrick and Erica Guyer provided legal guidance and feedback. Meanwhile, a number of individuals read and provided helpful comments on some or all of the manuscript including Margot Brandenburg, Charlanne Burke, Neill Coleman, Donna Dean, Brinda Ganguly, Heather Grady, Erica Guyer, Justina Lai and Gary Toenniessen.

At the Rockefeller Archives Center (RAC) in Tarrytown, New York, President Jack Meyers and Vice President James Allen Smith went out of their way to make our team feel welcome. Historians Teresa Iacobelli and Barbara Shubinski shared much of the research they have done for RAC's own centennial project. Michele Hiltzik, Tom Rosenbaum and the other archivists on staff helped find materials and were infinitely patient as we struggled with 100 years of acronyms and filing systems. Meyers, Smith and Shubinski all read early versions of this work. I am especially grateful to Rosenbaum for his careful reading of the penultimate draft.

Members of the team from Teneo Strategy, the Foundation's strategic partner on the Centennial, were intimately involved with this book from day one. Andy Maas drove the bus, Max Dworin kept us on the road and Michael Coakley made sure we had fuel in the tank. Tom Shea provided commentary. Working with this team has been a pleasure.

Researching and writing this book was a team effort. Rebecca Rodriguez helped assemble bibliographies and research. Amanda Waterhouse tracked down documents, found journal articles, discovered photographs and read chapters. Zachary Abrahamson helped draft a critical section. Regina Jahr provided the perspective of a community foundation director. Sam Hurst read and helped improve several drafts. Madeleine Adams was an excellent editor. Ernie Grafe copyedited the entire work. Eric Zimmer and Mike Kaiser compiled the index. Mindy Johnston and Leigh Armstrong tracked down photographers and copyright holders to make sure we recognized the creators of works that have been buried in the archives for many years. At Pentagram, Michael Gericke and Matt McInerney turned dull prose into a gorgeous book. Meanwhile, Lois Facer was involved every step of the way as counselor, researcher, photo manager and partner.

Everyone named above did their part to make this a better book. Any errors or omissions that remain after all this help are mine alone.

Eric John Abrahamson